PEDAGOGY AND THE UNIVERSITY Libraries

Also available from Continuum

Teaching and Learning in Higher Education – Linda Evans
Lifelong Learning – Jim Smith and Andrea Spurling
Widening Participation in Post-Compulsory Education – Liz Thomas
Universities and the Global Knowledge Economy – Henry Etzkowitz and
    Loet Leydesdorff
Understanding Habermas – Erik Oddvar Eriksen and Jarle Weigard
Essential Frankfurt School Reader – Andrew Arato and Eike Gephardt
Society and Its Metaphors – Jose Lopez

PEDAGOGY AND THE UNIVERSITY

Critical Theory and Practice

Monica McLean

continuum
LONDON • NEW YORK

Continuum International Publishing Group

The Tower Building	80 Maiden Lane
11 York Road	Suite 704
London	New York
SE1 7NX	NY 10038

British Library Cataloguing-in-Publication Data
A catalogue record for this book is available from the British Library.

ISBN: 0–8264–8471–9 (hardback)
ISBN: 9781847061249 (paperback)

Library of Congress Cataloging-in-Publication Data
A catalog record for this book is available from the Library of Congress.

Typeset by YHT Ltd, London
Printed in the United Kingdom by Biddles, Norfolk

For my children and grandchildren

Contents

Acknowledgements

A book like this, which pulls together a way of thinking in which personal passions and professional interests intertwine, and which has probably been gestating for my adult lifetime, is an acknowledgement to many people, many of whom I no longer know and whose names I have forgotten. For example, at Homerton College, Cambridge I was profoundly influenced by the combination of progressive teacher educators and the student movement; and later, in the Inner London Education Authority my work for an adult literacy scheme was informed by reading groups (where I first read Freire) and activism. More recently, I have been helped to think by colleagues at Keele University and at the University of Oxford; Jenny Ozga, Ken Jones and Keith Trigwell have provided inspiration. I am particularly indebted to Andrea Abbas and Paul Ashwin: their ideas, our conversations and the many hours of work that we have done together are woven throughout the book. I would not have been able to write this book without the highly enjoyable and rewarding contact with many university teachers who have joined the courses I have taught at Keele and Oxford. I am especially grateful to those of this group with whom I have researched and published about university teaching – Hannah Barker, Jo Bullard (and the eight geographers who contributed to our study) and John MacMillan; and also to Lief Jerram, Mat Paterson and Kara Shaw who have contributed their accounts to this book.

More generally, my extended family and my friends have encouraged me greatly by taking an interest and cheering me on. Iraj has been a rock and helped me the most. I mention three others because they also write and have given me invaluable hints: many thanks to Richard Godden, Sarah LeFanu and Charles Swann. I am very grateful to Anthony Haynes at Continuum who has kept me going with a judicious mix of approval and advice.

1

University pedagogy for a better world

Teaching is not only a job of work. A teacher is charged with waking students to the nature of reality, providing rigorous introduction to a certain discipline, and creating an awareness of their responsibility as citizens trained in the art of critical thinking. Of course most young people in the history of the world, even the brightest among them, have not been nurtured in this way. Education is expensive, and – unfortunately – this expense has been largely supported by states that want certain things taught and many things avoided. But education is never as much about the past as about the future. Indeed Paolo Freire, a theorist of education, once reminded us 'that to think of history as possibility is to recognize education as possibility. It is to recognize that if education cannot do everything, it can achieve some things.' (Jay Parini, *The Art of Teaching*, p. ix)

Education is political, cultural and social action. It is bound up in the interplay between state and civil society shaping who we are, what we do, how we think and speak; and, what we receive from and give to society. The business of education is the creation and recreation of culture, society and personal identity. Systems of education comprise networks of workers, practices and policies for nurturing learning capacity for the benefit of individuals and for the benefit of society. Education is seen both as a force for social change and as the vehicle for reproducing existing social hierarchies. This book takes the first view and focuses on university education. The main question that it addresses is: How can university teachers practise pedagogy which is attentive to how their students might as citizens of the future influence politics, culture and society in the direction of justice and reason? I use the expression 'critical pedagogy' throughout to convey this focus of attention.[1]

The term as I use it requires some elaboration for it to be understood as shorthand for a conglomeration of ideas that are discussed as the book progresses. Put simply, critical pedagogy has as its final aim changes in society in the direction of social justice. It has a respectable lineage. It is associated with the internationally renowned Brazilian educator Paulo Freire (1921–1997) who is one of the most important and influential writers on critical education. Of the many books he wrote about the theory and practice of critical pedagogy,[2] the most well known and influential is *Pedagogy of the Oppressed* (1972a, 1996) which sets out pedagogic theory and methods for a national adult literacy programme for peasants and workers in Brazil (he was exiled by the military dictatorship in 1964 but returned in 1979 and became Secretary of Education in 1989). *Pedagogy of the Oppressed* is about education for people suffering every day from huge economic and social inequities, nonetheless, Freire's ideas are applicable to other contexts. He insisted that education is always political; and – because all educational policies and practices either enable or constrain injustices – that every educator should be asking such questions as What am I teaching and why am I teaching it? and, How am I teaching and why this way? In whose interests am I teaching?

Other significant scholars of critical pedagogy – mainly in relation to schooling in the US – are Michael Apple and Henry Giroux who both see education through political, historical, cultural and socio-economic lenses. The analyses of both integrate local problems and global trends, and both have written extensively. Briefly, Apple[3] reveals how curriculum is never neutral, how some groups' knowledge is legitimized, while other groups' knowledge is marginalized and how, in our times, business ethics drive what counts as official knowledge producing students who are passive consumers. He promotes the idea that educational institutions can contribute to the transformation of society by establishing practices which exemplify democratic ideals. For Giroux,[4] education is a part of the public sphere in which the struggles of cultural production occur, so for him, too, education is ineluctably political. He, too, thinks that schools could resist inequality and instrumentalism and be sites where justice is pursued through the education of students as emancipated citizens by teachers who are transforming intellectuals. The debt that I owe all these critical educators will be evident in the chapters that follow. The big ideas about resistance to inequities and the political and social potential of education to transform individuals and society are ever present. Their legacy also allows me to use the concept of pedagogy to encompass the interrelationship between teaching and learning, as well as the principles, policies and practices that shape pedagogic encounters. Sometime I draw on their work directly, but more often it is an indirect and pervasive influence.

In the main, though, the framework for my particular interpretation of critical pedagogy is provided by the critical theorist Jürgen Habermas whose concepts assist me to make the following optimistic argument which will be unpacked throughout the book: we cannot deny that much is awry with university education these days, and that traditional and sound practices are under attack; nevertheless, if we can be reasonable, critically examine our own practices and come to agreements with each other about what is right, the turbulent environment of university education contains grounds for hope for constructing university pedagogy which might contribute to solving current and looming social problems. Even though I am cautious, telling a tentative tale by interlacing optimism with many caveats, my aim is to persuade (and my hope to inspire some readers).

While I am aware that critical theory and pedagogy do not appeal to mainstream interests, I have tried to make the theory accessible to non-specialists and also – though it is by no means a 'how-to' book – I want to show the practical relevance of social theory: it need not be remote and abstracted from everyday concerns and practice. I hope to persuade academics, university managers and government agencies responsible for university teaching that it might be worth seriously considering the political, social and ethical aspects of university pedagogy. For the same reason, while critique is an essential element of critical theory, I have organized the book to place a heavier emphasis on possibilities. For nearly fifteen years I have directed, taught and examined courses about university teaching. In this capacity, I have heard and read a great deal about the struggle to teach: my strong impression is that the urge to teach well is insistent and that this motivation can be encouraged or discouraged by policies and systems. Moreover, most academic teachers who I have met want their students to understand the discipline they are studying as an important lens for understanding the world and for guiding action; above all, they want their students to be critical thinkers. So there are grounds for thinking that university pedagogy can be yoked to contemporary society in the manner suggested by Freire, Apple and Giroux.

The book is a challenge and counter-argument to contemporary constructions of what is good university teaching and learning. Running through are the contentions that there is a dynamic relation between the university education of a country and its democratic ambitions; and that, while at present the relationship is weakened, it still exists and can be strengthened. Current policy interventions construct university education as a technical-rational pursuit and overemphasize its economic purposes. Higher education teaching and learning should rather be constructed as intellectually challenging and for emancipatory as well as economic purposes. Habermas's theories are resources both for critique and for thinking about alternative, principled approaches to developing university pedagogy in the conditions of the twenty-first century. The angle that I take on the problem of harnessing the higher commitments and interests of academic university teachers – pace Habermas – stresses the central role of solidarity in order to influence structures and systems. The device used to persuade readers that this is possible is to show how Habermas's theories play out in the everyday lives and experiences of university teachers and students. Empirical examples will be drawn from research undertaken in higher education settings, many are from the UK higher education with which I am familiar – but many are operating abroad and I keep in mind international comparisons.

My broad approach is sociological. The significance of this is elegantly put by C. Wright Mills in *The Sociological Imagination* (1959): 'the task [and] promise [of sociology is] to grasp history and biography and the relations between the two within society' (2000, p. 6). Much of what I deal with is an iteration of the classic sociological problem of structure and agency, that is, the problem of who makes history and society, the problem of the extent to which (if at all) humans act freely within an overarching system of social forces. With respect to education, the historian, Brian Simon, explains the structure/agency problem by saying that since people constantly change their world, and by changing it change themselves 'the whole historical process must be accounted essentially educative – and indeed this is why it is illuminating to refer to education as the mode of development of human beings in society.' (2005, p. 145). Specifically, I handle the subject of critical theory and university pedagogy by:

- exploring the socio-historical role of universities;
- examining the notion of Enlightenment modernity as an unfinished project;
- using Habermas's theory of the colonization of the lifeworld to explain how the imperatives of money and power distort university teaching and learning which is an area of human activity that relies on human relationships and communication;
- using Habermas's theory of communicative action to propose goals for university education in contemporary society;
- using the concept of communicative reason to suggest what attributes of mind and character university teachers might aim for in their students as future citizens; and, to suggest how university teachers might develop their capacity to work collectively and creatively for pedagogic improvement and equity;
- selectively using other theoretical perspectives, either consonant or dissonant with Habermas's, to inform arguments and analysis as the book proceeds;
- attempting to inter-relate the concrete details of everyday university learning and teaching with abstract theory about the social and political world by using empirical examples throughout; and,
- articulating how alternative, better futures for university pedagogy might be constructed.

The book is structured as follows. The next two chapters provide an orientation and context. Chapter 2 explains Habermas's position as a critical theorist and elaborates my conceptual framework, and Chapter 3 depicts the socio-historical circumstances in which academic teachers work and identifies cultural and social resources which could be mobilized in the service of critical pedagogy. Then two chapters lean towards critique by examining colonizing tendencies in the socio-cultural world of university learning and teaching. Chapter 4 examines the detrimental effects on university teaching of managerial practices and of audit cultures, it also draws attention to the complicity of academics; while Chapter 5 reveals the severe inadequacies of simple, mechanistic constructions of teaching. The last four chapters comprise the bulk of the book and sketch out the grounds for hope for critical university pedagogy that can be found in Habermas's theory of communicative reason and action. Chapter 6 proposes student subjects who are highly competent analytic and critical thinkers oriented towards solving problems in society and it explores the type of university pedagogic experiences – founded on general principles of practice – that might produce such students. The main concern of Chapter 7 is to delineate a critical pedagogy that is acceptable to academic teachers themselves but also to government and the public. The route it takes is to employ the concept of public intellectual to explore both the idea of students being educated to act as critical intellectuals in society and also the idea that university teaching must be viewed as an intellectual pursuit to achieve the intellectualizing of students. Chapter 8 proposes a number of ways of looking at how to create the institutional conditions in which critical pedagogy might flourish. The final chapter draws together the main themes of the book and argues for the desirability and feasibility of critical pedagogy.

As a final note that refers to the book as a whole, I have had some difficulty deciding on nomenclature for those who teach in universities. I have decided to use interchangeably 'university teachers', which refers to the location of teaching, and 'academic teachers', which refers to what is being taught because I want readers to have in mind both location and content. I want, too, to include all those who teach in universities: tenured academics as well as all the others who teach by way of a range of part-time and short-term arrangements and research students who teach. Although my focus is teaching, I argue against splitting this aspect of academic work off from research and administration or service, so when I am thinking of the academic role in its entirety I tend to use the term 'academic-as-teachers'.

Notes

1 Language is loaded with significance. Pedagogy is a term not to everyone's taste, but all terms annoy someone and all terms can become contaminated. I also use the currently orthodox phrase 'learning and teaching' throughout the book because I want to connect to current debates which are couched in these terms. 'Education' is a term that is little used these days to express what happens to students in universities, it could do with reinstatement, and I use it from time to time.

2 For example, *Cultural Action for Freedom* (1972b), *Education: The Practice of Freedom* (1973), *Pedagogy in Progress* (1978) and *Pedagogy of Freedom* (1998).

3 See, for example, 1993,1995, 2004.

4 See, for example, 1981, 1983, 1988, 1989, 1992, 2001.

2
Critical theory and the transformation of university pedagogy

What is currently taken for granted is at any given moment practically impenetrable. It demands an extraordinary force of effort to realize that a thousand other 'nows' were once taken just as much for granted, and that yet another thousand 'nows' that never were could be. (Sven Lindqvist, *A History of Bombing*, Section 169)

Introduction

This chapter provides background for the rest of the book. I explain why critical theory is an important resource for thinking about what is currently wrong with university pedagogy and what can be done to improve it. Next I justify why, of all critical theorists, my choice is to focus on Jürgen Habermas and I sketch the conceptual framework drawn from his work which informs the book. Following on, I explain that a commitment to Habermas's critical theory leads me to propose a university pedagogy that aims to contribute to the solution of current social problems. The chapter ends with an exegesis on the method of my explorations, explaining how the methodology is bound to my commitment to critical theory.

What does critical theory offer?

In general, I am interested in enlisting both abstract theory and concrete evidence about everyday lives to deepen my understanding of the field of education. Investigation of aspects of the social world always involves theories: acknowledged or not, they are at work guiding researchers' selection and interpretation of empirical evidence. Making theories explicit allows interrogation, testing, modification and development of beliefs, values and arguments in the research process. My interest in the improvement of university pedagogy has led me to seek a theory that provides a framework for critiquing current university pedagogic goals, practices and policies in a manner that will also generate ideas for the future. I have sought a legitimate theoretical framework that endorses my beliefs about the nature and purpose of university education in contemporary society. Further, I want to articulate relationships between shifts and movements at the levels of the state and society in rich countries (macro level); at the level of higher education in England (meso level); and, at the level of the experience of individual and groups of students and academic teachers (micro level). Critical theory provides me with the macro-level lens that can guide my project at all levels.

The name 'critical theory' is associated with the 'Frankfurt School' of neo-Marxist social theorists – among them Theodor W. Adorno, Herbert Marcuse and Max Horkheimer – from the Institute for Social Research set up in 1923 in Frankfurt-am-Main in Germany. When the Nazis came to power during the 1930s they were forced into exile in the United States and the Institute was not reopened until after World War II in 1950. Despite identifiable origins, critical theory is not *a* theory of society or a homogeneous school of thinkers or a method, yet it is generally seen as building on Marxist theories by revealing hidden oppressions and by being openly directed towards political action. It is also characterized by being against positivism. The term 'critical theory' was first used by Horkheimer in 1937. He rejected the assumption underpinning prevailing research methodologies that techniques will uncover objective truths about the social and political world. As an oppositional alternative, he proposed critical theory which attempts to generate knowledge from speculative attempts to understand the interwoven, interdependent nature of the human subject and the objective world. Such knowledge, Horkheimer argued, would lead to a critical understanding of society and also be practical by guiding political and social action.

Whatever the differences between critical theorists, there is a common dual commitment to critiquing current conditions and to propelling action towards future emancipation and social justice. The commitment is motivated by a belief – common to both critical theory and Marxism – in the ambiguity of modernity that Goran Therborn sums up well:

> On the one hand affirming the positive, progressive features of capitalism, industrialisation, urbanisation, mass literacy, of looking to the future instead of the past or of keeping one's eyes down on the earth of the present – and, on the other, denouncing the exploitation, the human alienation, the commodification, and the instrumentalisation of the social, the false ideology, and the imperialism inherent in the modernisation process. (1996, p. 53)

This dual commitment to 'grasping the two horns of modernity, the emancipatory and the exploitative' (Habermas, 1997, p. 55) is the key to my project.

Critical theory is normative: the purpose of critique is to delineate a more just and free future. 'Critical' refers not only to a critique of social conditions, but also to Kant's idea of self-reflective examination of the limits and validity of our own knowledge and understandings. Critique involves reflection on what we take for granted, identifying the constraints of injustice, and, freeing ourselves to consider fairer alternatives. Yet, it is important to be quite clear that critical theory does not aim to produce definitive knowledge, nor does it posit straightforward, inevitable progress. Critical theory constructs arguments, which should always be kept open, about how we are doing and what it would be wise to do; it aims, in particular, to put brakes on moves by the powerful and inhumane to distort human life. Tim Dant (2003) suggests that the horrors of Nazism motivated the Frankfurt critical theorists when he says that for critical theory: '... the argument is never resolved, there is no *quad erat demonstrandum*, no closing down of the debate. It is an argument against the possibility of a final solution' (p. 17).

Why Habermas?

The particular critical theory that I have chosen to provide the scaffold for thinking about university pedagogy is that of Jürgen Habermas who was Adorno's assistant and in 1964 succeeded Horkheimer as professor of sociology and philosophy at the University of Frankfurt. I have used Habermas's work because he opens up the possibility of being simultaneously hopeful and radical about the future. I consider him to be a critical theorist, even though he has often denied that he is a critical theorist of the Frankfurt School partly because he distanced himself from the cultural pessimism of the older generation who were working and writing about the 'self-destruction of the enlightenment [in] the shadows cast by the ovens of Auschwitz' (Therborn, 1996, p. 55). Habermas's reconstruction of critical theory is an insistence that we have not yet done with the ideals of the eighteenth-century philosophers of Enlightenment; rationality and progress might yet go hand in hand, though it cannot be taken for granted. There are many obstacles: the interests of money and power, as well as living in times, in which, on the one hand, people are suspicious of hope and contemptuous of idealism;[1] and, on the other, are attracted to many varieties of irrationalities.[2]

Habermas's Enlightenment is an 'unfinished project' which 'would not merely promote the control of the forces of nature, but also further understanding of self and world, the progress of morality, justice in social institutions, and even human happiness' (1997, p. 45). To this end his theory is bold and comprehensive. He provides the broadest of canvasses, a theoretical frame founded on a clearly stated political agenda: society based on equality, freedom, democracy, autonomy and collective empowerment. More specifically, he identifies:

> The greatest moral-political liabilities of our time – hunger and poverty in the third world, torture and continuous violations of human dignity in autocratic regimes, increasing unemployment and disparities of social wealth in Western industrial nations and finally the self-destructive risks of the arms race. (Habermas, 1990, p. 211)

I choose Habermas to explore university teaching and learning because he gives me some purchase on the intellectual, moral and practical problems that it poses. Education is seen as a solution to human problems and as a field of study, its knowledge has traditionally been broad and inter-disciplinary and so it fits well with Habermas's work which fuses epistemology, psychology, sociology, ethics, philosophy and political science to establish a basis for an optimistic view of human development.

The encyclopaedic range of Habermas's work has been undertaken over thirty-five years, with ideas and arguments developing over time.[3] From this opus I have drawn three major ideas, and a number of subsidiary ones to inform my thinking about university pedagogy at this moment in history. For the present, I introduce the three major ideas briefly and they will be unpacked further as the book proceeds. The first, already introduced, is overarching and is Habermas's notion of modernity as an unfinished project 'offering a highly conditional promise of autonomy, justice, democracy and solidarity' (Outhwaite, 1996, p. i) that we can continue to pursue by mobilizing the resource of reason. The 'promise' resides in the current conditions created by modernity for increasing capacities for self-interpretation and self-conscious action. The other two ideas, which function as the organizing themes for the book, are the 'colonization of the lifeworld' and 'the mobilization of communicative reason'[4] which together express the two horns of modernity.

Habermas's optimism about the human capacity to pursue Enlightenment ideals is based on the potential of language. He makes two major interrelated assumptions: first, that the purpose of language is to make meaning and reach understandings with others about these meanings; and, secondly, that every user of language is capable of meaningful speech oriented to reaching agreements. The universal ability to make meaning and the human motivation to come to agreements with others about how to act is the capacity for communicative reason. For Habermas the potential for emancipatory change is in the creation of 'ideal speech situations' in which people, free from constraints and power relations, rationally discuss and reach agreements about social matters. Intersubjectivity rather than the individual subject becomes the prime focus: 'Participants in interaction .... coordinate their plans for action by coming to an understanding about something in the world' (1987, p. 296). This is the theory of communicative action.

But communication is distorted when 'lifeworlds' are 'colonized'. These two concepts are keys to understanding the argument that I unravel in this book. For Habermas the 'lifeworld' is a broad, complex world made up of the practices, customs and ideas of individuals or groups. More precisely, the lifeworld is a human resource made up of culture, society and personality. 'Colonization' refers to the inappropriate invasion of the individual or collective lifeworld by money and power (often simply called 'system' by Habermas). When the lifeworld is unthreatened it tends to be taken for granted; in a colonized lifeworld background consensus is lacking and attempts at communication are distorted and the result is a range of problems associated with loss of meaning and motivation. But the difficulties of colonization also invite resistance. The mobilization of communicative reason and action, explained above, is the counter to colonization and strategic action. The concept of communicative reason contains Habermas's ideas and arguments about the potential for self-aware and emancipated groups of individuals, dislocated from their previous lifeworld, coming to reasoned, uncoerced agreements through competent use of everyday language. In such reasoned communication, participants agree to allow the 'better argument' to guide action oriented towards improving social conditions.

Between them, the ideas of modernity as an unfinished project, the colonization of the life world and the mobilization of communicative reason and action provide the lenses for my analysis of the contemporary crisis for university education, and the basis of some ideas about a possible future reconfiguring of university pedagogic practice and policy. I hope that the subtleties and usefulness of these concepts will be clarified as the book proceeds.

Critiques of Habermas

Since I make extensive use of Habermas's ideas, and I know that his work attracts censure as well as approbation, I must spend some time justifying my preference for his theory in the light of critiques that have been made. Anthony Giddens (1985) points out that, because Habermas's writing is not easily placed intellectually or politically, he has drawn criticism from all sides: he has revised Marx too much for Marxists, and is too Marxist for postmodernists. But the sheer volume and length of his work written over a long period of time during which he changes and develops ideas can make it difficult to discern the major thrusts of his arguments; added to this is his notoriously abstruse style of writing, which is rather distressing in one so committed to communication. It might be that one of the reasons that Habermas is so often in the position of engaging with his critics is that it is difficult to be certain that one has grasped his meaning.[5]

Here, though, I will deal with the strong criticisms that relate to the larger and clearer of his ideas, in particular the theory of communicative reason and action. Perhaps the most important criticism comes from his antecedent critical theorists in the Frankfurt School. Alvesson and Skoldberg (2000) explain why:

> Adorno and Horkheimer are critical of the ideal of the Enlightenment as such, based on the capacity of scientific and technological knowledge to control nature and on the development of a calculative, impersonal kind of reasoning. They claim that a privileging of this ideal leads to a form of rationality that pushes instrumental thinking so far as to produce its own opposite (irrationality), turning also the social into an object of rational, means-oriented action, permitting mass murder as in Auschwitz as well as the objectification and streamlining of human needs and desires. Thus the dominance of a technological rationality ultimately means that everything becomes subject to calculation and prediction; that man [sic], nature and production are all transformed into objects of manipulation, vulnerable to unlimited control and adjustment. (p. 113)

Habermas makes the analysis of the older generation of critical theorists his starting point: he believes, like them, that a one-sided modernity which emphasizes technical-rational solutions places considerable obstacles in the way of both political and ethical debates and serious cooperative action to solve social problems. But he argues that, simultaneously, it has become more possible to question received ideas and norms so that we have the option to take up and develop our potential to become politically and ethically – as well as technically – rational. Perhaps, as Habermas himself might put it, it is an empirical question, as yet unanswered, whether it is rational and right to believe that reason still has the potential to be a major force for good in the world.

Certainly, his claim to the universal presupposition that human language users are oriented to reaching rational understandings with others is not accepted by relativists who believe all reason is local and contingent. This type of criticism comes from a postmodernist perspective which radically questions the concept of 'modernity'. Habermas himself responds by identifying two distinct forms of postmodernist theory. The first is 'neoconservativism' whose adherents do not believe that the 'functional laws of economy and state, technology and science' are open to influence in a modern state; and, the second is that of the 'anarchist' who has 'unmasked' reason as 'the sheer will to power' (1990, p. 3) which is close to the older critical theorists' view that reasonable possibilities are remote because reason itself has been coopted by 'the system'. From Habermas's point of view, both versions reject an internal and exploitable relationship between modernity and rationality. Furthermore, he exposes the contradictions in postmodernists' thinking: that is, while denouncing 'grand narratives' they are, nevertheless, 'inspired by a special sensitivity for complex injuries and subtle variations' – especially evident in Foucault's work – and 'tacitly envision' a moral change in society (*ibid.* p. 337).

While I am easily convinced that we do not need to reject Enlightenment ideals because they have not been realized, a criticism of Habermas's work that I have been more cautious about rejecting is that he underestimates the difficulties of undistorted communication in conditions of material inequality in which asymmetrical power relations exist in terms of race, gender and class; and in which the Western Enlightenment tradition is privileged over other culturally different traditions. Here is Edward Said (1994a):

> Frankfurt School critical theory, despite its seminal insights ... is stunningly silent on racist theory, anti-imperialist resistance and oppositional practice in the empire. And lest that silence be interpreted as an oversight, we have today's leading Frankfurt theorist, Jürgen Habermas, explaining in an interview (originally published in the *New Left Review*) that the silence is deliberate abstention: no, he says, we have nothing to say to 'anti-imperialist and anti-capitalist struggles in the Third World', even if he adds 'I am aware of the fact that this is a euro-centrically limited view'.[6]

With this attitude, it is argued, the search for consensus merely reproduces existing forms of domination. In similar vein, Anthony Giddens (1985) raises the question of how the lifeworld can be defended other than by transforming the very political and economic systems which are threatening.

These criticisms are substantial and not easily addressed. A partial answer is that Habermas's theories deliberately focus on what he calls the 'psychic' effects of distortions by power and money in any particular circumstances:

> The deformations of a lifeworld that is regulated, fragmented, monitored, and looked after are surely more subtle than the palpable forms of material exploitation and impoverishment; but internalized social conflicts that have shifted from the corporeal to the psychic are not therefore less destructive. (Habermas, 1990, p. 355)

His interest is in the human capacity and motivation to defend against psychic deformations caused by inappropriate incursions on the part of the 'system'. It is possible to argue that this stance parallels Gidden's own 'structuration theory' whereby 'there is always an agent involved in the reconstitution and reproduction of structure' (Giddens and Pierson, 1998, p. 78). For both Giddens and Habermas social structures can constrain powerfully, but social actors are agents who can resist structural constraints. Certainly, 'psychic' deformation expresses my concerns about university pedagogy more precisely than material effects.

Related criticisms are that Habermas's prescriptions of *ideal* discourse have small purchase on *real* political issues; that it is difficult to examine and demonstrate consensus around the 'better argument'; and, that dissensus should be valued as much as, if not more than, consensus (Newby, 1997; Giddens, 1985). With all these criticisms in mind, I think that the *principles* that Habermas outlines are a foundation for thinking about action based on people coming together to examine social conditions and to agree about how to improve them. This is particularly so for education. In Habermas's terms, education is a 'public sphere' – an area of social and political life – that depends, at some level and to some degree, on society coming to agreements about what it is for and how this should be achieved. It seems to me that whether or not it is explicit, 'an argument', with which we can choose to engage, is implied in the arrangements made for education. Attempts at agreements are, in any case, constantly made, for example between students and academics, between managers and academics, and between vice-chancellors and organs of the state. This does not mean that education should not accommodate, indeed encourage, a good deal of 'dissensus'. In *The University in Ruins* Bill Readings (1996) proposes a new but more modest role of the modern university: it should become, simply, a place where people 'think together' and 'keep questions open'. Playfully, Readings calls for us to agree that it would be a 'good thing' to institutionalize disagreement in universities, adding that this would be something 'with which Habermas would be in accord' (p. 167).

For all the many criticisms of Habermas's work, for me it has the power and scope to be an extremely useful resource for seeking insights and making arguments about critical university pedagogy. I am not seeking a monolithic social theory. As Rowland (1993) reminds us: '[theories] should be treated with caution. They are all narratives. They each tell a story, but only one story. They may shed light on an aspect ... but, in the process, cast others into the shadows' (p. 16). All the same, I place myself in a precarious position by choosing a theorist who is not at all cautious, who attempts to shed light on all aspects of contemporary social, psychological and political life. Yet, despite his own unflagging efforts to establish universal presuppositions, Habermas (1994) himself wrote tentatively:

All social theories are highly abstract today. At best, they can make us more sensitive to the ambivalences of development: they can contribute to our ability to understand the coming uncertainties as so many calls for increasing responsibility within a shrinking field of action. They can open our eyes to dilemmas that we can't avoid and for which we have to prepare ourselves. (1994, pp. 116–117)

Many of the criticisms I have outlined in this section seem to me to arise from the high level of abstraction of Habermas's 'macro' categories and theories. In the pages that follow I attempt to increase their explanatory power by interlacing them with congruent 'meso' theories about the particular social world of university education. My task then is to bind the 'macro' theories to 'micro' accounts of the everyday lives of students and academic teachers often by way of 'meso' theories. I attempt to be both critical and pragmatic.

University education for transformation

Critical theorists tend to use the term 'emancipation' to refer to gaining freedom from the pre-Enlightenment shackles of religion and tradition. But, in terms of education, we can also usefully employ the more modest, neutral term 'transformation': individuals and institutions can be transformed for better or worse whether or not we are seeking radical change. Habermas's critical theory, however, suggests 'transformation' in a particular direction and guides the formulation of questions about pedagogy and the university. Examples are:

- What kind of university education counts as 'emancipatory' or 'transforming'?
- What would university pedagogy which is reaching for the goals of social justice look like?
- What kinds of institutions, curricula, pedagogies and academic behaviours would be congruent with these goals?
- Does the concept of the 'colonization of the lifeworld' explain what constrains achieving emancipation or transformation through university pedagogy?
- Does the notion of communicative reason give us grounds for hope for a pedagogy informed by critical theory?
- Does the idea of modernity as an 'unfinished project' help us draw the contours of an emancipatory/transforming university pedagogy?

While I shall not be addressing these questions algorithmically, they are the backdrop to the discussions in this book.

I need now to set the scene for answering the questions above by outlining how Habermas configures university education. In Habermas's terms all education produces and reproduces the lifeworld, mediating the individual and society (including the economy and polity). And he locates the university between the social and cultural structure of the lifeworld and the instrumentalized imperatives of the 'system'. The historical debate about the 'idea of the university' will be elaborated in the next chapter, but, for the time being, I will sketch out the main threads of Habermas's contribution. He theorizes the modern university in an essay called 'The idea of the university: learning processes' (1989) and in the book *Towards a Rational Society: Student Protest, Science and Politics* (1971).

Habermas believes that we must critically reappraise the traditional idea of the university as autonomous of state and public, and united in the pursuit of truth and knowledge. The reappraisal he suggests centres on a new unity for universities which he derives from a 'structural connection' between the 'learning processes' of universities and the processes of democratic decision-making. The new unity is based on critical argumentation and communication which are shared by 'scientific and scholarly activity [and by] societies which are not fixed once and for all and which ... must reach an understanding about themselves.' (1989, p. 125).

Drawing on Talcott Parsons' seminal work, *The American University* (1973, written with Gerald Platt), Habermas identifies four functions of universities:

- the first concerns technical knowledge or the generation of technically exploitable knowledge for producing wealth and services;
- the second is the academic preparation of public service professionals – professional and vocational knowledge;
- the third is the transmission, interpretation and development of cultural knowledge (which he also refers to as the 'tasks of general education', 1989, p. 121); and,
- the fourth concerns critical knowledge or what he refers to as 'the enlightenment of the political public sphere' (1989, p. 118).

He also discusses forming 'the political consciousness of students' (1971, p. 3). By this he means 'reproducing a mentality' (1971, p. 3) which straddles cultural and critical knowledge and takes different forms in different sociohistorical conditions. He points out that in Germany prior to the 1960s forming the political consciousness of students had, in fact, been unconscious and apolitical 'deriving from the culture of humanism, and of loyalty to state authority' (*ibid.*).

At the heart of Habermas's argument that universities are essential to the lifeworld of society is that the four functions are 'bundled' within them, that is, quite uniquely, different functions are fulfilled simultaneously in the same institutions (1989). It is precisely this 'bundle' of technical, professional, cultural and critical functions that implicates universities in the production and reproduction of the lifeworld (culture, personality and integration into society). Nevertheless, functions and values are fused and at different historical junctures different functions are emphasized, expressing different values; and, functions become split off from one another. The argument that underpins my discussion about university pedagogy is that currently education reflects 'one-sided modernity' which is portrayed by state policy and is enacted in many practices as 'technical-rational' at the expense of other functions and values. At the same time, I believe that Habermas offers grounds for hope in his claim that the university's four functions necessarily bind them at least as strongly to the lifeworld as to bureaucratic spheres. He asserts that the university cannot dispense with any of its functions and that 'it cannot define itself with regard to society exclusively in relation to technology' (1971, p. 3).

Social and individual interests shift over time (Habermas, for example, wrote about universities in the 1960s and 1980s), so in relating critical theory and university pedagogy in the early twenty-first century I need to be more explicit. Jerome Bruner (1974) argued that the pedagogy of any era should concern itself with the historically situated 'urgencies of our society', what Habermas refers to as the 'moral–political liabilities' of our age. The questions, then, are what are these urgent liabilities and what educational purposes would reflect them? My commitment to the purposes and values of critical theory and my understandings of the current higher education system globally lead me to propose, tentatively, the following three purposes for a contemporary university education:

- to re-balance the emphasis in university education on economic wealth and individual prosperity to take in, as equal partners, the other traditional aims of education: individual fulfilment and transformation, and citizenship in a democracy;
- to address the inequities of the connections between origins and destinies in terms of class, ethnicity, gender and disability;
- to address complex and serious global problems, in particular, poverty, the environment and conflict.

Taken together, these purposes are what Jürgen Habermas and other critical theorists refer to as 'emancipatory' or 'transformative'. If university education was focused on such purposes quite different questions than those prevailing at present might be raised. For example: 'Are universities reproducing inequalities in society or challenging them?' or 'What forms of interpersonal behaviour are capable of resolving social problems?' or 'Is self-interest encouraged by the values of individual performance, differentiation and competition now so evident in education?; and, 'If so, is this having deleterious effects on our society?'

From the beginning I want to make it clear that there are a number of stances from which, despite discussing colonization, I want to distance myself. I do not subscribe to 'narratives of decline' or any form of 'golden ageism' (I will discuss this in more detail in the next chapter), rather I regard the current circumstances as complicated and contradictory, containing both options and constraints. My position is with those interested in the options presented by educational endeavour in all sectors and guises to envision and enact alternative, possible, better futures without falling prey to what Claus Offe (1996) calls 'heroic idealism' (p. 43).

It is important, in this respect, to hold on to the part of the history of universities when they were central institutions in the transformative project of modernity. Gerald Delanty's book *Challenging Knowledge: The University in the Knowledge Society* provides us with a configuration of possibilities for universities in contemporary society which enhances Habermas's broad-brush analyses by clarifying what 're-appraisal' of the university might look like. He argues that universities should focus on a new kind of citizenship that is responsive to the changing nature of knowledge production and reproduction by recovering the 'cosmopolitanism' – a term he prefers to the more pessimistic 'globalization' – of the pre-modern universities. 'Cosmopolitanism' is defined as 'promoting the self-transformation of cultures through a critical self-engagement with each other' (p. 128) and Delanty believes that universities are particularly well placed for this enterprise: universities could take up the challenge of cosmopolitanism, making their own goals focused on what he calls 'cultural and technological citizenship'. Delanty explains that democracy consists of three central spheres of democracy: the first is 'constitutionalism' which he defines as the rule of law which restrains the state; the second is 'pluralism' or the representation of the interests of all groups in society; and, the third is 'citizenship', the participation of the public in the polity. Citizenship is about rights, duties, participation and identity, and it can be antagonistic. For Delanty, the heart of a university pedagogy that addresses the problems of the contemporary world is the task of preparing citizens *both* technically (that is, capable of serving society professionally or through providing services) and culturally (that is, capable of socially responsible action that improves society). He echoes Habermas's four functions in saying:

> [the university has] provided the foundations of cultural and technological citi-
> zenship: cultural in so far as it has led to the preservation and dissemination of

cultural traditions among the society as a whole, and technological as a contributor to professional society, the demands of the occupational system and the extension of equality of opportunity. (p. 50)

My version of critical pedagogy aims for the transformation of individuals and society by preserving its traditional functions (technical, professional, cultural and critical) and by focusing on a broad definition of citizenship that is yoked to those functions.

The investigative approach

Now that I have set out my stall by making explicit my goals and interests, I need to justify the methods I apply to investigate possible answers to the questions about university pedagogy that I have posed. Broadly, I take a socio-historical approach and incorporate insights from the daily lives of university teachers and students. I explore the culture and politics of university learning and teaching at a particular historical moment and base a commentary on future choices on my understanding of current issues and problems. An historical starting point to any serious issue has been propounded by many social investigators: Habermas continually reminds us of the 'historical dependency' of society. There is an affinity between history and sociology; they are often concerned with the same sets of problems, whether in the past, present or future. The constant is the drive to understand the relationship between personal life, on the one hand, and, on the other, social, political and economic organization.

I am not seeking a definitive tool of explanation, rather a set of core ideas, concerns and questions that are theoretically informed. As I have explained, my analyses centre around Habermas's ideas about the connections between the colonization of the political, cultural and social lifeworld by technical-rational imperatives; about the capacity for communicative reason; and, about an emancipatory democratic project for the contemporary world. So my values and my understanding of the nature of knowledge and theory influence my approach to empirical evidence. My starting point is that outlined by Ozga (1994):

Teachers at all levels find themselves faced with dilemmas relating to the 'delivery' of agendas with which they do not agree. Researchers face similar problems, which make adherence to the critical tradition more important than ever. It was that I had in mind when I talked about the need for 'policy sociology rooted in the social science tradition, historically informed and drawing on qualitative and illuminative techniques.' (p. 222)

So a social science method connected to critical theory selects and interprets empirical data about a particular cultural world with a view to placing it into a wider discourse of history and power and with the aim of transformation. It is, therefore, openly committed; Habermas puts it like this:

> No matter which approach is taken, an anticipatory interpretation of society as a whole always enters into the selection of the fundamental categories. Significantly, this is a prior understanding of how the society is and, at the same time, of how it ought to be – for the interested experience of a situation in which one lives separates the 'is' from the 'ought' just as little as it dissects what it experiences into facts, on the one hand, and norms, on the other. (in Outhwaite, 1996, p. 75[7])

Locating myself in this tradition of thought, necessitates acknowledging personal convictions and preferences which cannot always be supported by unequivocal empirical evidence. Edward Said insisted that critical theory demands a 'politics of interpretation' (1993, p. 157) that refers to large economic, social and political trends and a better future: 'Instead of non-interference and specialization, there must be interference, crossing borders and obstacles, a determined attempt to generalise exactly at those points where generalisations seem impossible to make' (*ibid.*).

As one would expect, open commitment to political and social values has been the subject of critique. There are objections made to critical theory's abandonment of the principle of value neutrality[8] but Pierre Bourdieu argues quite the reverse:

> If the sociologist manages to produce any truth, he does so not *despite* the interest he has in producing the truth but *because* he has an interest in doing so – which is the exact opposite of the usual fatuous discourse about 'neutrality'. (quoted in May, 1997, p. 45)

Which side of the argument one takes depends on what one believes about the nature of knowledge. From Bourdieu's position the production of social knowledge cannot be beyond experience or value free. I regard knowledge about university pedagogy as uncertain and changeable even if I am seeking truths by intercalating insights drawn from inquiry, experience and informed by values. In *Reflexive Methodology* (2000) Mats Alvesson and Kaj Skoldberg engage in substantial discussion about what research methodologies might be suitable for critical theory. They explain that researchers' interest in large questions and issues tends to leave them lying 'at some remove from the questions, concepts and interpretations that typify empirical research' (p. 111). My aim, though, is to tackle this problem by integrating theory with data about everyday life and by focusing on illuminating the problems with university pedagogy and possibilities for it. This is achieved by a two-way process. I use the theory to provide a general orientation, as well as a basis for interpretation of data; but, at the same time, accounts of everyday life clarify the strengths and weaknesses of the theory.

The investigation of university pedagogy I undertake is a reflexive endeavour at the intersection of personal, social, economic and historic formations, so no easy correspondences with any one theory can be made, but, equally I cannot rely on empirical data alone. Alvesson and Skoldberg (2000) give three reasons why: empirical data is too limited for the purposes of critical theory rarely addressing 'social context as well as meaning/consciousness on an individual level'; it is usually ambiguous but conventional interpretations often take too much for granted; and, the act of focusing on what exists now can draw attention away from 'what *can* be' (p. 134). So empirical data is tricky and the act of interpretation involves uncertainties and risks. I am assisted by a range of 'meso' theories which are more specific, but in keeping with critical theory. For example, I have already drawn on Gerald Delanty to ground Habermas's ideas in the contemporary university and I use his history of universities extensively in the next chapter. So, in the course of the book I shall similarly use a wide range of theories about, *inter alia*, the state, policy, identity, professionalism, the role of the university and pedagogy.

Caution about the neutrality of empirical data does not render it irrelevant; on the contrary, it is essential that generalizing theory is illuminated by the particularities of everyday life. Despite his own abstractions, Habermas is clear about this: he identifies 'interdependence between the basic concepts of social action and the methodology of understanding social actions' (1984, p. 102). He recommends an 'interpretative sociology' as a 'theory of everyday life which can also be linked up with historical research'[9] (1987, p. 377). The goal is to tackle the difficult task of articulating the relationship between the general and instances, or, to be more sociological, between structure and agency.

My approach, then, is to make eclectic use of a wide range of empirical material. Alvesson and Skoldberg (2000) explain: 'Given the more expansive range of possible observations ..., it then becomes natural to adopt a freer approach in which imagination, creativity and the researcher's own learning together with his or her analytical capabilities can all be called upon' (p. 130). I have used first-hand accounts of university teachers and students wherever I can find them; I have returned to my own empirical work some published as articles or reports and some unpublished and still in the form of transcripts; I have examined relevant policy documents; and I draw on articles from the educational press and published statistical tables. I view all this material as communications – in Habermas's terms 'speech acts' – or texts about university pedagogy, which are interwoven. It is an unruly tangle of texts which I have interpreted, reinterpreted, written and rewritten to examine critically the intersections between global trends, state interventions and the everyday lived experiences of university students and teachers.

Notes

1 As Martin Parker (2002) puts it 'utopianism has a bad name' (p. 211).
2 I will expand on this point in Chapter 5.
3 At different times Habermas has related his ideas to Piaget, Chomsky, Dewey and R. S. Peters.
4 Habermas often uses the term 'communicative competence' but I have chosen to use the alternative phrase 'communicative reason' to retain the focus on pedagogy as an activity which is aimed at developing minds to think rationally. I also want to avoid any confusion with the use of 'competence' as technical skill.
5 See in particular the 'Habermas/Foucault Debate' (Habermas, 1995a and 1995b).
6 The information was found at *www.msu.edu/user/robins/habermas/said.hyml.*
7 From *Theory and Practice* (1974).
8 See for example, Hammersley, M. (1995), *The Politics of Social Research.*
9 His example is E. P. Thompson's *The Making of the English Working Class* (1963).

3
Socio-historical options and constraints

Unless we have a constructive outlook on the past, we are drawn either to mysticism or to cynicism. (E. H. Carr [1990] *What is History?*, p. 100)

Introduction

University pedagogy arises out of and is enacted within socio-historical contexts. My intention in this chapter is to grapple with these contexts in order to provide a backdrop against which to construct a university pedagogy which is both feasible and critical. While Habermas's large and abstract theories are ever-present and informing, I will anchor them to other theories and analytic histories about crises, shifts, ruptures and transformations of state and society in which universities are implicated. On the one hand, I resist analyses which conclude that there are causal connections between – at the macro level – current global economic and political pressures; at the meso level, the adoption of particular strategies and systems by particular governments; and, at the micro level, the experience of citizens, including university students and their teachers. On the other hand, I believe that an understanding of the experience and meaning of everyday working practices – in this case university pedagogy – can be illuminated by an understanding of how action is made possible or constrained by social, political and economic contexts.

I start the chapter with a brief and general analysis of the crises for welfare nation states today; turning then to a specific history of the university in terms of its relationship to state, society and knowledge and picking up how contemporary societal trends play out in universities in different socio-historic circumstances. The main points are that the past provides us with a set of resources with which to think about universities for critical purposes; and, that contemporary circumstances hold both options and constraints.

The crises for modern welfare nation states

There is fairly widespread agreement among social commentators that the accelerated pace and the quality of change in every aspect of society today amount to a rupture with the past – for some, it is the 'end of history'. This is understood as a global phenomenon and is variously described as post-Fordist, post-industrial, late capitalism, postmodern, depending on the writer's theoretical orientations and whether economic, cultural, social or political restructuring is the focus. I find useful Anthony Giddens' (2001) term 'stretched' to describe the new relationship between 'local involvements' and 'interaction across distance' (p. 245). In this sense 'globalization' is a neutral phenomenon, the result of stretching is that 'modes of connection between different social contexts or regions become networked across the earth's surface as a whole' (*ibid.*). But the effects of the phenomenon are contested, seen as leading paradoxically either – to uniformity, standardization and homogeneity (sometimes called 'Macdonaldization') or to fragmentation and differentiation. It is worth noting here that critical commentators argue that the picture of global markets quite out of the control of nation states is painted by neo-liberals with vested interests who want an excuse for not thinking about alternatives (Apple, 2000; Mouffe, 1998).

So views vary considerably about what constitutes the 'break with the past', and whether it is as dramatic as it is often portrayed. I prefer Habermas's view which emphasizes the inherent instability of states in the late modern world as they attempt to deal with crises that result from an indissoluble tension between the imperatives of capital accumulation and the imperatives of politics intending to expand social welfare. Governments 'have to secure the trust of private investors and of the masses simultaneously' (1987, p. 346). This configuration allows us to think in terms of new equilibria being found at all historical conjunctures and to question how far current social phenomena are ever discontinuous with history and with the idea of 'modernity'.

The founding ideas of modern society were formulated in the Western world in the late eighteenth century and their meanings are open to interpretation. Habermas (1985) informs us that the term 'modernity' was coined in the 1950s to mean:

> . . . a bundle of processes that are cumulative and mutually reinforcing: formation of capital and mobilization of forces; development of the forces of production and increase in productivity of labor; establishment of centralized political power and the formation of national identities; the proliferation of rights of political participation, urban forms of life, formal schooling; secularization of values and norms. (p. 2)

He objects that this definition of modernity is disassociated from its Enlightenment roots. His concept of 'modernity' links a new autonomy to the disintegration of religious and traditional world-views.[1] As human beings learned to control the natural world and to develop new forms of production, they also became capable of different ways of thinking and acting, thereby creating new social relations. A secular society enlarged social contexts and options: it became possible to reflect rationally on traditional norms.

But the potential for autonomous thought and action is constrained by the inevitable contradictions that arise when capital accumulation is confounded by the contradictory imperatives in society for efficiency, for equality and for the pursuit of personal happiness. No policy programme can resolve these contradictions. All solutions bring their own contradictions: for example, bureaucratic models are wasteful; technical-rational models may be efficient but rouse resistance; and participative models can become subversive. Policy begins to 'oscillate[s] hopelessly between increased central planning and decentralization' (Habermas, 1987, p. 382) and changed relationships occur: '... between system (economy and state) and life-world (private and public spheres), around which the roles of the employee and the consumer, the client of public bureaucracies and the citizen of the state, crystallize' (*ibid.* p. 349).

In recent times unrestrained growth and expansion of markets has led to an increase in volatility and fragmentation; and social, economic and political life is constantly reconstructed, making everything appear contingent. From Habermas's perspective, this state of affair results in legitimation and steerage problems for the state, which it attempts to put right by what he calls the 'pacification' or 'neutralization' of the citizen role: class antagonism gives way to citizens as consumers or clients 'cleansed of political participation' (Habermas, 1987, p. 50). Modernity has brought options and the capacity to choose, yet as the horizon of choices available to citizens becomes larger, the state reacts by becoming more inflexible and rigid. The dual process of de-politicization and regulated autonomy is brought about by the invasion of cultural, social and personal life by systems of power (or administration) and money (or the market) that are only subject to rational evaluation within their own truncated terms.

If we accept Habermas's version of the large socio-economic and political trends in contemporary society, there has not been a decisive rupture with the past. From the beginning, modernization has been compelled towards giving and taking away freedoms because removal of the constraints of tradition and religion has necessitated the need for limitations. Yet, there is a significant change: modern and late capitalism has reached a point where it is no longer possible to equate the development of productive forces and human emancipation. But for Habermas the very threatening of the lifeworld has within it the possibility of 'rehabilitating [rationality] through the minds of politically enlightened citizens' (1974, p. 253). Of course, this idealistic view has been challenged by those who point out that gains in autonomy within the modernization processes are largely nominal.[2] Part of the problem in understanding what would mobilize new capacities is that Habermas does not specify the conditions necessary for an autonomous, collectively responsible and morally motivated citizenry. Surely one of the conditions must be education, and Habermas is specific about university pedagogy: the condition he seeks and thinks is not beyond reach is a 'communicative relationship of professors with their students [which is] sustained by the stimulating and productive forces of a discursive debate' (1989, pp. 124, 125).

The story of modernization, nation states and capital accumulation is inextricably linked with the rise and growth of universities. In most countries responses to economic and political instability in the latter part of the twentieth century have taken the form of a series of realigned relationships between the state and citizen, economy, and institutional or organizational structures. The universities have been a crucially important part of this realignment. With this in mind, I move now to a more contextualized and focused discussion of the history of universities in which I draw on Gerald Delanty's *Challenging Knowledge: the University in the Knowledge Society*, which charts the history of the university in terms of its relationship to the state and the public.

The 'idea of the university'

In sharp contrast to schools, universities tend, even now, to be discussed in grand and idealistic terms in which can usually be recognized the vision set out by Wilhelm von Humboldt in the early nineteenth century: the function of universities is to 'lay open the whole body of learning and expound both the principles and the foundation of all knowledge.'[3] Even though most of the Enlightenment philosophers were not part of the academy, universities are identified with the Enlightenment's grand narrative of a necessary connection between reason and progress for they were established as an integral part of the great modern project of producing and reproducing knowledge for the good of society and the economy.

In order to envisage university pedagogy that is both feasible and radical, we must understand what the possibilities are and, for this we need an historical sense of the place of universities in society. The history I tell here emphasizes the 'idea' of the university in terms of its fluctuating relationship to society and the state; and, the parallel transformation of the role of knowledge in society and the role of universities. It also emphasizes struggle and local variation.

Delanty (2001) tells us that debates about the 'idea of the university' date from 1798 when, in the context of state reform, the philosopher Kant pleaded with the King of Prussia for academic freedom for philosophers. Shortly afterwards, on the founding of the University of Berlin (1810), the philosopher von Humboldt wrote a proposal about the University's constitution in which he set out his 'idea' that the university would be granted autonomy from the state in return for 'cultivation of the character of the nation' (p. 33). The next landmark in the debate is also a text in the form of a series of rousing lectures – published as *The Idea of a University* (1960) – given by Cardinal John Henry Newman when he was invited to be rector of the new University of Dublin in Ireland (1852). As a liberal catholic he articulated an oppositional alternative to the modern utilitarianism that had accompanied state formation by calling for universities to be sites where intellects were cultivated by pursuing knowledge as an end in itself. Again the state was put at a distance.

Almost a hundred years later, in 1946, another book called *The Idea of the University* was published. It was by Karl Jaspers, rector of the University of Heidelberg, Germany, and was a reprint of a book originally published in 1923. The occasion was the reopening of the University after World War II. In this tract the education of the whole person (*bildungsideal*) is offered as the goal of universities whose role is to provide a world view based on knowledge generated through research and transmitted through teaching. Habermas writes his essay 'The idea of the university: learning processes' in 1986,[4] as a response to a 1961 revision of Karl Jaspers' book which calls for a renewal of the idea of the university as the embodiment of an ideal form of life which connects science, scholarship and truth. Habermas's starting point is Jasper's frustration that universities are putting themselves in danger of becoming 'giant institutions for the training and development of specialized scientific and technical expertise' (1989, p. 100). His argument is for 'critical renewal' of the traditional idea. He exhorts his colleagues not to identify with what universities 'once claimed to be' (*ibid.* p. 103) but rather to disrupt traditional thinking. He argues for 'self-understanding' of the learning processes which are organized within universities. His hope of renewal – the inspiration for this book despite its focus on pedagogy – lies in the essentially intertwined nature of university functions which, despite increasing specialization and fragmentation, are bound together by 'communicative forms of scientific and scholarly argumentation' (*ibid.* p. 124).

But universities must persuade both state and the public of the usefulness of their argumentation and scholarly processes. Despite universities' insistence on autonomy from the state, the 'idea of the university' has always pragmatically contained a relationship to both the state and society, with different emphases in different countries at different historical junctures. Habermas proposes that, in the past, protection of knowledge generation within the university depended on a 'defensive' relation to society and an 'affirmative' one to the state (*ibid.* p. 109). But Delanty's (2001) account is more nuanced, so, for example, he argues that by the end of the nineteenth century two broad models can be discerned: the Anglo–American civic tradition that emphasized society and the European state-centred model. Nowadays, the notion of *an* idea is debunked, nevertheless, it is also constantly returned to as a starting point for debates about the role of universities.[5] But, of course, there was not really only one 'idea' but a plurality of powerful and attractive 'ideas' which can be traced down the centuries from the medieval universities. I want to show how these ideas not only resonate today but are also of some utility for thinking about the contours of critical pedagogy for universities.

Charting historical ideas about the university

Delanty's (2001) history of universities takes us from the medieval period through three periods of modernity: 'classical', 'liberal' and finally 'organized' or 'late' modernity. He argues that modern universities, which are linked to industrialization, have no real links with medieval universities which were completely separate from politics and society, though with strong allegiances to the Church. Nevertheless:

> Even to this day the monastic origins of the university are evident in the cultural practices of the university (such as the conferring of degrees and honours, the role of ceremony, the belief in an underlying principle of harmony and the notion of faculties of knowledge), suggesting that the legitimation of knowledge is still tied to the legislating role of intellectuals. (p. 29)

Furthermore he highlights the global and cosmopolitan nature of medieval universities which distinguishes them from modern universities, but which might link them to the contemporary universities of late modernity, though, of course, in an entirely different form: a medieval scholar could read everything in print; while today technology allows almost instant access to knowledge across the world.

Universities have been powerful over the centuries. From the seventeenth century, during the period of classical modernity, the state perceived the need to benefit from the new empiricism, so while the social basis of the Enlightenment was the public sphere in the form of 'free floating intellectuals' in a variety of fora, 'a struggle for institutionalization emerged [between] the foundation of royal academies and state-supported institutions of research' (Delanty, 2001, pp. 20, 22). Gradually, knowledge became institutionalized in the universities which at the same time became the sites of education and training for the experts necessary to nascent modern society:

> Isolated in the academy, knowledge was detached from social struggles and made its peace with the state by offering to its cadres its degrees of distinction and accreditation. In this way the university was able to be a powerful actor in the social distribution of cultural capital. (*ibid.* p. 29)

By the end of the eighteenth century we enter liberal modernity when universities were 'serving the nation state with professional elites and as a codifier of national culture' (*ibid.*, p. 22). It is during this period that the vision of universities as protectors of critical reason was voiced by Kant and elaborated by von Humboldt. Developing critical reason was connected to the notion of *Bildung* or individual character formation. At this time, too, the ideal of knowledge as pursuit of truth which should be perceived of as autonomous or 'an end in itself' is articulated. But reality was messier. The differentiation of knowledge and sciences' separation of fact from value challenged the ideal, 'the actual nature of this truth and the possibility of its attainment became increasingly obscure as the century progress' (*ibid.* p. 23). Furthermore, religion held on to some influence by academicizing theology. At the same time the 'idea of the university' was already playing out differently in different countries. For example, the Grandes Ecoles in France had been created by the post-revolutionary state and did not incorporate the idea of *Bildung*, they were entirely secular and strongly emphasized their role in building the nation state; in Germany, the autonomy of the intellectual was stressed; in England, universities were influenced by Oxbridge's elitism and anti-industrialism; whereas Scotland's universities were modelled on Europe.

Throughout modernity the relationship between universities and states has been very strong. Delanty, though, distinguishes between universities in 'liberal modernism' which served the state by providing 'a national culture and professional elites' and universities in 'organized modernism' – from the nineteenth century until the 1970s – which 'serviced the occupational order of mass society while enhancing the power and prestige of the state' (*ibid.* p. 6). As we move closer to our own age universities grow enormously in number and become responsive both to the state in the form of 'providing a trained labour force to serve in the expanding and changing occupational system that the technologically dependent economies required' (*ibid.* p. 49) and also to mass society in the form of education for social citizenship. The different functions can be seen in the establishment of University College London as a civic university dedicated to public utility of knowledge and, by contrast, the London School of Economics and Political Science 'created for the purpose of training social administrators for the future social welfare state' (*ibid.* p. 46). The universities of today, which by and large combine functions, are the product of industrialization, urbanization and mass society. The state protected universities' autonomy in return for their 'servicing economic needs, national prestige, technological expertise ... central to a range of social, economic and political goals' (*ibid.* p. 44).

I believe that 'ideas' about the purposes of universities have accumulated and are available to us as resources which may or may not be taken up. Certainly such ideas are discernible in national and historical variations of the university. For example, as Delanty (2001) points out, during liberal modernity the 'neohumanist' German model and French 'technocratic models' existed side by side in universities, even if one was more evident than the other in particular cases. And, arguably, these ideas are tenacious to this day. As embodiments of an ideal, universities are still places where students learn to think critically, to cultivate themselves and to prepare for life and work; and, where academics produce knowledge both for the benefit of society and for its own sake. What is much less evident, though not, in my view, entirely disappeared, is universities as 'custodians of culture' or as producers of 'universal truth'.

Socio-historical 'cognitive shifts' and universities

Universities deal in knowledge; so any analysis of the role and purpose of universities needs to be based on a view of what knowledge means for society and for the state. My premises are that knowledge, like modernity, possesses the 'two horns' of the potential for emancipation and for exploitation,[6] and that knowledge and power are linked: from the time of the Enlightenment universities developed under the auspices of nation states and provided them with a system of knowledge, 'which was, at the same time, a system of power' (Delanty, 2001, p. 30).

Gerald Delanty's book is structured around the implications of the changing nature of knowledge production for universities. His 'theory of cognitive shifts' in the different periods of modernity provides a framework for thinking about critical university pedagogy in what is often termed the 'knowledge society'. He makes use of Habermas's distinction between knowledge as cognition (how we think or *Erkennen*) and knowledge as science (what we think about or *Wissen*) to argue that knowledge should be apprehended as both *Erkennen* and *Wissen* and also as a 'mode of social organization' (*ibid.* p. 19). From this point, he proposes that universities mediate between the two types of knowledge and that the form of mediation is influenced by cognitive shifts in society.

The theory of cognitive shifts intertwines knowledge, culture and society in the following way. At any time the *mode of knowledge* is a:

> ...set of discourses cutting across the institutional and the epistemological [which] occurs in social and cultural contexts; it is a system of social relations and a category or cultural self-understanding and communication; [it accumulates] in groups, institutions and organizations. (*ibid.* pp. 17–8)

Changes in the mode of knowledge cause changes in *cultural models* which are:

> ...the interpretative models by which a society gains knowledge of itself [they] are represented in major principles of rationality, imaginary significations, cultural value spheres, such as those of morality, religion and art, and historical narratives [they are found in] the cognitive, the normative and the aesthetic structures. (*ibid.* p. 18)

They also cause changes in the *institutional framework* which is:

> ...the mode of production and the accumulation of wealth, the regulation of populations and social relations, and government ... social practices that make up the economic and political structures of society as well as the social institutions of the life world. (*ibid.* p. 18)

In summary, Delanty's theory of cognitive shifts explains how changes in how and what knowledge is produced (the mode of knowledge) always shifts the potential for learning at the socio-cultural level (in the form of cultural models) and at the level of society's institutions. Therefore, knowledge is 'linked (largely through the institution of the university) to the cognitive complexes of culture and to social practices and institutional structure' (*ibid.* p. 18). An important aspect of a theory and history of cognitive and cultural shifts is how the shifts throw up 'new cultural imaginations' (*ibid.* p. 13) which carry hope for social renewal and transformation.

New cultural imaginations can be historically charted and always involve crises. In classical modernity, from the Renaissance to the Reformation, the mode of knowledge production was revolutionary encompassing geography, medicine, astronomical discoveries; new techniques in painting, architecture and music; and, philosophical and religious argument. The effects on cultural models and institutions led to the formation of nation states and forms of governance. But the vision of a perfectly ordered and unified society was not sustainable: the first crisis of modernity began with the French Revolution and the emergence, in liberal modernity, of hierarchies of knowledge and the separation of facts and values, which

31

philosophy had not allowed. After World War I, in organized modernity, a second crisis was precipitated by the beginnings of rejection of truth, autonomy and rationality; a change in the mode of knowledge to positivism; and the move to having experts who specialized within disciplines, and who were the foundation for building welfare states. According to Delanty we are now in the throes of a third crisis. Late modernity is associated with 'colonial liberation, the rise of new social movements and postmaterialist values, democratization, population growth and migration, ecological crisis ... globalization and complexity' (*ibid.* p. 21). We have seen that, while there is a consensus about what characterizes contemporary society, there is little agreement about what the changes signify. The most influential work about the nature of knowledge in a postmodern world is *The Postmodern Condition: A Report on Knowledge* (1989) by the French philosopher Jean-François Lyotard in which he argues that knowledge is 'delegitimized' both as a narrative of freedom and as a narrative of the disinterested pursuit of learning.

Delanty, however, is more cautious. He claims that in the 'knowledge society', the mode of knowledge – characteristic of organized modernity – that is based on specialization and routinization is being dissolved by four specific and closely related changes:

1. Knowledge is produced by many institutions in society, not only universities.
2. We need knowledge for economic production, political regulation and everyday life more than previously.
3. Knowledge is more publicly available and disciplinary knowledge is breaking down, so the boundaries between lay and expert knowledge are becoming blurred.
4. Growing contestability of knowledge claims has led to crisis for the 'culture of expertise'.

While this cognitive shift amounts to universities no longer being 'privileged sites' (*ibid.* p. 3) of knowledge production and reproduction, it does not mean, as Habermas points out, that 'the university is dead' (1989, p. 103) and that the learning processes it engages in cannot contribute to the moral and political liabilities of our time. With this in mind, I resume the history of universities in our time of late modernity.

A current diagnosis

There is a considerable amount of contemporary commentary on the state of universities. Much of it is negative and I will discuss these views in more detail in relation to evidence of 'colonization of the lifeworld' in the next chapter. But here I will attempt a hopeful account by drawing attention to options as well as constraints. So, while there is strong evidence of colonization, as I will show, the current conditions hold possibilities that social justice and concern about global conditions could be become the animus of university pedagogy.

Whoever the commentator, there is agreement that universities are in some sort of crisis, even if there is disagreement about its nature and severity. Delanty (2001) ascribes an 'identity crisis' because the 'founding idea' of a single identity based on a belief in universal knowledge, the quest for truth, and unity of culture is no longer tenable. In *The University in Ruins* (1996) Bill Readings' analysis is the same but he also conveys the sadness of the identity crisis: for Readings what is lost or 'ruined' is the story of 'modernity's encounter with culture, where culture is positioned as the mediating resynthesis of knowledges, returning us to the primordial unity and immediacy of a lost origin' (p. 169). Both Delanty and Readings are grappling with what a renewal of the idea of the university would look like.

Current crises in the universities are connected to the more general crisis of welfare states outlined earlier and, in particular, to the thesis of the decline of the influence of nation states as the guardians of national character and culture. During the modern era universities have, on behalf of the state, monopolized the field of knowledge as well as conferred rights on political and professional elites. However, the 'delicate balance [of] steering a middle course between reliance on the state and serving the functional requirements of capitalism' (Delanty, 2001, p. 50) was unlikely to last. In the context of what Delanty sees as the slow 'unravelling' of the alliance between state and universities, the history of the university that I want to draw attention to here is the one in which during the late twentieth century universities become spaces for the expression of democratic citizenship and the encouragement of 'radical imagination' (*ibid.* p. 19).

Habermas (1989) remarks that the expansion of university education has been a world-wide phenomenon in the mid- to late twentieth century, and that this expansion has brought with it voices from more sections of society. Contemporaneously, the significant cognitive shift for universities after the 1960s was a 'reflexive turn' (Delanty, 2001, p. 6) whereby students and teacher/researchers, for the first time, thought critically about knowledge and progress. During this period universities emerged as 'zone[s] of interpenetration lying between the culture system and society' (p. 19). While universities have put up resistance periodically,[7] it is only during the twentieth century that they have become locations world-wide in which democratic and progressive values have been articulated and protected. From the nineteenth century onwards students across the world have exercised political pressure[8] and what Delanty (2001) refers to as the 'adversary culture' (p. 61) became international news during the wide-spread student movements of the 1960s and 1970s. The 'campus revolts' connect to a cognitive shift in society, there were:

> ... revolutionary cultural undercurrents [that led to] a new cultural ethos for the university which had to accept the politicization of knowledge and its public role in society. ... It is a time of deconstruction [of] established wisdom, fixed cultural identities and the traditional values of the bourgeois epoch of modernity. (*ibid.* pp. 61, 63)

In Habermas's terms, it can be seen as a time when the taken-for-granted lifeworld of university academics and students was threatened. Students and academics in universities began to conceive of knowledge as having the critical function of transforming society as well as the conservative one of transmitting received culture.

New cultural voices that emerge at this time are the women's movement, black and ethnic cultural movements, national liberation movements, Marxism and the postmodern avant-garde. In Europe, the student move-ment is associated with May 1968 in Paris, and, after the onslaught on democratic freedoms during the 1950s 'McCarthy era', American uni-versities were also major sites of political opposition focused on the Vietnam War and the civil rights movement (Delanty, 2001, p. 62).

We know that mass student socialist political activism in Europe and the West has not lasted. Nevertheless, since then there have been 'ongoing battles' in other countries: for example, South Korea, Iran and China (de Groot, 1998). There is not space here for detailed analyses of the failure of the movement to sustain its momentum. However, Habermas wrote at the time about student protest in Germany and posited three reasons for the politicization of students that have a bearing on a critical pedagogy. He claims that for students to be political they must understand themselves as influencing the future; they must experience their universities as agents of social change; and, finally, they must experience parallels between their own education and societal change, linking 'private destiny with political destiny' (1971, p. 14). The reason for the failure of momentum is suggested by Delanty, and is pertinent to my project: finally, the movement 'did not force the university to reflect on its role in society, thereby opening up new possibilities [that recognize] the connection between knowledge and power' (Delanty, 2001, p. 72).

The crux of my argument is that while a critical university pedagogy is 'going against the grain' it is also practically possible and in keeping with the role and function of universities. For this to be plausible it is essential to accept Delanty's point that the radical moment in the history of universities has reverberations today:

'The politicization of the university was irreversible. Even in the postrevolutionary period of the 1980s, when neoliberalism and managerialism penetrated the universities, the university had become a site of cultural plurality ... a more indirect, mediated politics of contestation, subversion and irony continued to be central to the identity of the university in the age of advanced capitalism.' (*ibid.* p. 63)

There is no denying, as I will discuss in the next chapter, that, in Habermas's terms the lifeworld of universities has been distorted, but still extant are resources in the form of discursive practices which are progressive and can be preserved and built upon.

'Golden age'?

Today much academic debate about the condition of universities tends to despair and cynicism, and carries an implication that matters were much better in the past. This might be because many of us who today work in universities and write about them are of the generation of 1960s university students who are now disappointed. Yet it might be useful to abandon mourning and 'romantic nostalgia' (Readings, 1996, p. 169). While the promise of the university uprisings has not been fulfilled, it has been carried forward into possibilities for universities all over the world. It is important to grasp that the experience of the 1960s was an historical moment and that from the Enlightenment until this moment universities had not involved themselves in the public realm. Delanty sums up the position: 'The great social movements of modernity – the workers' movement, the anti-slavery movement, colonial liberation – had little to do with the ivory tower of the academy and its posture of splendid isolation' (2001, p. 2). Maintaining a close relationship to the state and serving political elites meant that the pursuit of truth could be kept from society as a whole. So, for example, in Russia in the early twentieth century 'the professorate saw the students, who included revolutionary intellectuals, as an obstacle to their own objective to gain autonomy. The professorate were highly successful in constituting themselves a neutral ground between students – that is society – and the state' (*ibid.* p. 51).

While the Enlightenment had stood for the liberation of humanity from tradition and ignorance, the role of universities in liberal and organized modernity has been to place knowledge at the service of nation state building in the post-Enlightenment era. For the most part of their history, far from being progressive, universities have legitimized the dominant social and political values and in latter times 'degenerated into the ideology of a professional class with a high level of social prestige' (Habermas, 1989, p.

114). Germany provides a salutary reminder. Renewals of the debate about the 'idea of the university' in Germany occurred before and after WWI in the period 1890–1933. Following von Humboldt's articulation of universities for the autonomous pursuit of knowledge with spiritual and moral underpinnings, university professors gradually became referred to as 'mandarins'. Habermas describes the legacy of von Humboldt's 'idea of the university':

> In the inwardness of these mandarins, sheltered by official power, the neohumanist ideal of education had taken the distorted form of the intellectually elitist, apolitical, and bureaucratically conformist self-understanding of an educational institution that was removed from practice, internally autonomous, and intensively research-oriented. (1989, p. 114)

After WW II universities in Germany 'stood convicted in all eyes' because of their 'demonstrated impotence in the face of, or even complicity with, the Nazi regime' (*ibid.* p. 115). Destructiveness came from the separation of knowledge, culture, politics and power.

We should remember, too, the historic struggles of women and working-class men to gain entry to universities and how for centuries university students were subservient and how universities have always reproduced class structures. Habermas warns that nostalgia can signal 'the idealistic tendencies of an educationally elitist bourgeois cultural pessimism' (1989, p. 102) and, tells us that it was always unclear how universities' 'mission of enlightenment and emancipation was to accompany the abstention from politics that was the price [they] had to pay for state authorization of its freedom' (p. 113).

Expansion and differentiation

To return to the present day, recent transformations in universities can be summarized as: expanded access; a more diverse student body; changes in funding sources; organizational change, including new governance in the form of audit and 'new public management'; changes in curriculum and pedagogy; new forms of institutional competition and stratification; and challenges to the teaching and research role of the universities. Additionally, as I have indicated above, these developments intersect with wider economic, social and intellectual changes associated with a globalized, information-based and post-modern era.

To close this chapter, I will discuss two trends in contemporary higher education which appear as two sides of a coin: they represent a 'cultural model' which has dual potential. I shall return to the issues the cultural model raises as the book progresses. On the one hand, there has been the thrust from governments all over the world to provide university education for a larger proportion of the population and more people are seeking it. In the UK this policy trend carries the shorthand 'access and widening participation'. On the other hand, there is increasing stratification of universities which mirrors hierarchies in society; the shorthand is 'diversification'.

One story, though short, is hopeful and progressive. Welfare states can be seen as placing equality as well as economic growth at the centre of their missions, the poorer people and countries are, the less they are educated (Stewart, 1996). In the last fifty years we can see universities gradually becoming central to a political agenda of social inclusion and social citizenship. During this time, UK participation in higher education has increased from approximately 8% to over 30% of the school-leaving cohort (and this does not include large numbers of 'mature' students). The increase had been more substantial in other European countries and in the USA there has been a five-fold increase in participation (Delanty, 2001).

The other story is bleak and longer. The main purpose of 'massification' has been to produce technically exploitable knowledge and create a trained labour force, rather than for personal transformation or a critical educated citizenry. The expansion has been almost exclusively middle class so it has not impeded the reproduction of class structures and the persistence of socio-economic inequalities.[9] Furthermore, socio-economic inequalities are maintained by institutions being divided along class lines. In the case of higher education institutions in the UK, in 1992 former 'polytechnics' became part of one system of degree-granting higher education institutions, but the system preserves the divisions of the past and prevents radical transformation. The former polytechnics tend to have fewer resources and more students, and do less research which lends credence to judgements that pedagogic standards are lower. In fact what operates is 'a crude reputational model of higher education which favours the elite and already advantaged' (Lucas and Webster, 1998, p. 112). The stratification of universities according to wealth and class has been discussed by Peter Ashworth and his colleagues. They demonstrate that universities that are placed high in published league tables are those which do not have large numbers of working-class students. Thus 'quality' measures are, in fact, 'status measures' and league tables are persuasive because they conform 'to a general supposition about the status hierarchy of universities' (2004, p. 6). This observation is illustrated by figures about three contrasting universities extracted from publicly available tables:[10] a former polytechnic with 33% of students from lower socio-economic classes (SEC) comes 79th in overall rankings in league tables; a university established in the 1960s with 23% of students from lower SEC ranks 52nd; and an 'elite' university with 9% of lower SEC students ranks 2nd. So, on the face of it, working class students go to 'worse' universities. Courses, too, are differentially taken up by students: Van de Werfhorst (2002) found that, after weighting for ability, students from a 'professional' background are more likely to be studying the 'prestigious' subjects of law and medicine. There are also well-documented sub-plots of inequality which concern the numbers and treatment of women and part-time university teachers; and, disabled and black students and academics (Law *et al.* 2004; Morley, 1999).

Conclusion

Notwithstanding the black and white stories sketched above, literature about the meaning and impact of the transformation of universities emphasizes contradictions, tensions and complexities. Despite grand ideas, the history of universities is one of struggle, ambivalence, resistance, compromise and reconciliation. Habermas (1989) says that 'countervailing developments' are all there have ever been to count on. Importantly, though, he believes that universities are 'still rooted in the lifeworld' (p. 107), that is, the core of their business is the production and reproduction of the lifeworld (culture, personality and integration into society) through the 'bundle' of functions of research, preparing professionals, educating citizens and contributing to public understanding. Even so, I believe with Bill Readings that we must accept that the university has 'outlived [itself as] producer, protector and inculcator of an idea of national culture' (1996, p. 3), it is no longer possible to claim one big 'idea of the university'.

Universities, then, appear to have lost direction and face a legitimation crisis, but crises produce possibilities: for Delanty the situation is 'interesting' (p. 3); for Readings it is 'up for grabs' (p. 2); for Habermas (1989) salvation lies in 'the communicative forms of scientific and scholarly argumentation' (p. 124). It is remarkable that an 'essential core' of what universities are about resonates from medieval times and is today present and persistent in accumulated beliefs and values, even if some cause tension and some are muted. The ideas of the Enlightenment university can be summarized as: the autonomous pursuit of knowledge and truth; the connection of science and progress; the critical and emancipatory power of knowledge and reason; the usefulness of knowledge for society; and, provision by the state. To add to these are the ideas of the modern university: equality, citizenship, democracy, critique and the unity of teaching and research. My argument is that these ideas and the 'cognitive shift' we are experiencing today carry 'promissory notes' (Habermas, 1989, p. 125) and can be used as resources, perhaps even as weapons, whether or not at present there is more to be worried about than to hope for.

Grandiose ideas about the role and purpose of universities must be eschewed in favour of more modest ideas: for example, from Delanty is the idea of thinking of universities as 'incubators' rather than 'prime originators, of cultural change' (2001, p. 64); or from Readings (1996) is the idea of the university as one place among many in which thinking can take place. Readings believes that there is 'considerable room for manoeuvre, provided that students and teachers are ready to abandon nostalgia and try to move in ways that keep questions open' (*ibid.* p. 192). Depending on how people act, we could be witnessing either 'the the twilight of the University's critical and social function [or] a new age dawning' (*ibid.* p. 5). Critical university pedagogy would take up the function of universities to educate citizens and professionals who can tackle injustices and social problems, the current socio-historical conditions carry constraints on achieving this ambition, certainly, but also options.

Notes

1 In this Habermas follows classical social theorists, for example Weber and Mead.
2 See, for example Claus Offe's commentary of Habermas's ideas in *Modernity and the State, East West.*
3 Quoted by Lyotard on p. 33 in *The Postmodern Condition: A Report on Knowledge*
4 This time the occasion is a lecture series in celebration of the six-hundreth anniversary of the founding of the University of Heidelberg.
5 Examples are Ronald Barnett's *The Idea of Higher Education* (1990) and *Beyond All Reason* (2003); and, Anthony Smith and Frank Webster's collection *The Postmodern University?* 1997.
6 Michel Foucault, the hugely influential philosopher, is not so optimistic: for him knowledge is produced by discourses which are closed systems of power.
7 For example, Delanty (2001) tells us that the University of Paris dissolved itself in 1259 rather than submit to a papal bull.
8 Habermas (1971) sums up the position up to the late 1960s: 'They played a revolutionary role in nineteenth-century Russia, in China in the twenties and thirties, and in Cuba in the fifties. In 1956, the revolts in Budapest and Warsaw were set off by student protests. Students are of great political significance especially in the developing areas of Southeast Asia, Latin America, and Africa. Governments in Bolivia, Venezuela, Indonesia and South Vietnam have been overthrown by students' (p. 13).
9 For an excellent discussion see *Higher Education and Social Class: Issues of exclusion and inclusion* (2003) by Louise Archer and colleagues.
10 From the *Times Higher Education Supplement* 12 December 2003.

4

Accounting for pedagogic quality

Interest and inclination are banished from the court of knowledge as subjective factors. The spontaneity of hope, the act of taking a position, the experience of relevance or indifference, and, above all, the response to suffering and oppression, the desire for adult autonomy, the will to emancipation, and the happiness of discovering one's own identity – all these are dismissed. (Habermas, 1974, p. 305)

Introduction

The story of the 'colonization of the lifeworld' of university teachers by economic imperatives and government interference is privileged by the characters and the raconteurs being one and the same: critical academics have written scholarly books and articles about the restructuring of higher education; and write indignantly to the educational press about the effects of cuts in resources and of regulatory systems. So the connections between broad socio-historical and political trends and everyday experiences working in the universities are not hidden. Despite the narrative of decline being well known, it is necessary for me to retell it in terms of the 'symptoms' or 'pathologies' of the colonization of the lifeworld as outlined by Habermas and also in terms of its effect on university pedagogy. In the next two chapters, I will explore two interleafed strands of colonization. In this chapter I will take the ideas or, more accurately perhaps, the ideals discussed in the previous chapter as signs of a unified lifeworld of academics and examine the effects on academics-as-teachers of the 'audit culture' which has arisen out of the practices of what is known as 'new public management'. In the next chapter I will argue that technical-rational constructions of university pedagogy distort both the essential nature of educational endeavours and create conditions in which it becomes difficult to envisage and enact critical university pedagogy. The overriding imperatives of money and power have adversely affected university pedagogy and the academic psyche; but, academics are not ciphers. I suggest that our actions have not always been exemplary and that now, in a situation in which universities are transforming and principles are thrown into question, it is incumbent upon us to be self-reflective and critical. There are options: embracing agency is a basis for grounds for hope of a university education which is transforming for both individuals and society.

Colonization of the lifeworld and university pedagogy

In pre-modern times the components of the lifeworld – culture, society and personality – were not separate from the systems that maintained it. In modernity the lifeworld is, potentially, freed from superstition, religion and tradition and becomes more rational. Lifeworld and system become uncoupled as increasingly complex steering and legitimating systems of governance and law are needed (Habermas, 1987). This causes tensions which can be analysed through the theory of the colonization of the life-world. In order to proceed I must elaborate the theory which was intro-duced in Chapter 2. As mentioned, in his work as a whole, Habermas appears to construe the lifeworld as a complex world of practices, customs and ideas, which, when not under threat, tend to be taken for granted. He asks us to think of the lifeworld as a *'resource'*[1] made up of culture, society and personality and to accept an idealized 'theoretical description of a balanced and undistorted life-world' (1985, p. 344) as follows (the italics are his):

> I call *culture* the store of knowledge from which those engaged in communicative action draw interpretations susceptible of consensus as they come to an under-standing about something in the world. I call *society* the legitimate orders from which those engaged in communicative action gather a solidarity, based on belonging in groups, as they enter into interpersonal relations with each other. *Personality* serves as a term of art for acquired competences that render a subject capable of speech and action and hence able to participate in processes of mutual understanding in a given context and to maintain his own identity in the shifting contexts of interaction. (*Ibid.* p. 343)

The three elements that constitute the lifeworld are reproduced by processes that correlate to them and which are made possible by communicative action. Habermas describes the processes:

> *Cultural reproduction* ... secures the continuity of tradition and a coherency of knowledge sufficient for the consensus needs of everyday practice. *Social*

integration ... takes care of the co-ordination of action by means of legitimately regulated interpersonal relationships and lends constancy to the identity of groups. Finally, *socialization* ... secures the acquisition of generalized capacities for future generations and takes care of harmonizing individual, life-histories and collective life forms. (*Ibid.* pp. 343–4)

Each of these processes ensures renewal, or that new conditions connect to existing conditions: 'Thus interpretative schemata susceptible to consensus (culture), legitimately order interpersonal relationships (society), and capacities for interaction (personal identity) are renewed in these three processes of reproduction' (*ibid.* p. 344).

Universities' teaching role can be seen to be primarily concerned with cultural reproduction, social integration and socialization as defined above by Habermas which is why he is sure that universities are 'rooted in the lifeworld' (1989, p. 107). I am also in this book applying 'lifeworld' to the culture, solidarities and identities of academics themselves so that I can use the concept of 'colonization' to make sense of what is happening to university teaching and the concept of 'communicative reason' to explore what might be possible.

From Habermas's perspective, the improvement of any social, political or ethical matter requires conditions in which undistorted communication can take place. Central to the argument of the book is the premise that university pedagogy *is* such a matter. It is, in Habermas's terms, a 'communicatively structured activity' or an 'area specialized in cultural transmission' (1987, p. 330). Teaching, therefore, is 'dependent on mutual understanding as a mechanism for co-ordinating action [because it is] an ethical–political [rather than a] pragmatic issue' (*ibid.*). This means that better teaching is not simply a matter of personal preference or of technique and skill. I will argue that the extent to which institutional conditions allow for rational discussion (what Habermas calls ideal speech conditions) influences the quality of teaching because it depends on the quality of negotiated understandings about the nature and purposes of our teaching and of our students' learning.

Habermas variously attributes colonization of the lifeworld to different rationality or means. The lifeworld can be threatened by technical, economic, bureaucratic or cognitive-instrumental rationality (1985, p. 348), and by 'state intervention with monetary and bureaucratic means' (1987, p. 355). He appears to use terms loosely and interchangeably: I will focus on money and power translated as state pressure to be 'accountable' for pedagogic practice and to construct teaching as a technical-rational rather than practical-moral activity. I have interpreted Habermas's colonization theory as an invasion of the 'communicatively structured' lifeworld of university pedagogy by the state's managerial and technical imperatives which impose foreign ways of relating and working; suppresses the freedom to take positions on how and what to teach; and, places constraints on the capacity to enter into authentic dialogues about teachers' teaching and students' learning. The most devastating symptom of such colonization of the lifeworld is the distortion of communication that is essential to its health. When participants are making use of their communicative reason, they are reflective, accountable to each other; and able to take 'yes' and 'no' positions (Habermas, 1984). I will argue that distorted communication is evident in universities these days when, in Habermas's terms, background consensus is lacking and the sincerity, truth and the rightness of the expressed intentions of interlocutors are dubious.

There are other severe symptoms of a colonized lifeworld. Habermas builds on Weber's ideas that disenchantment and loss of a sense of meaning are a necessary part of modern bureaucratic life and also on Marx's notion of 'alienation' of the proletariat to propose psychological effects of 'anomie [and] phenomena of alienation and the unsettling of collective identity' (1987, p. 386). He makes clear, though, that he does not think that such symptoms are an inevitable part of the condition of late capitalism: attacks on culture and identity can be resisted, in particular by withdrawing legitimation from the invading imperatives. In my account of colonization in the universities I will attempt to point to fissures and permeability that allow choice to be exercised.

Policy to embed technical-rationality in universities

To re-cap, according to Habermas all institutional forms have been subject in modernity to a two-sided process of change, which is summarized by Outhwaite (1996):

> On the one hand, more and more areas of social life are prised out of traditional contexts and subject to rational examination and argument. On the other hand, the expansion of markets and administrative structures leads to what Habermas calls the colonization or hollowing-out of the lifeworld by autonomous subsystems which are removed from rational evaluation, except within their own highly circumscribed terms. (p. 269)

I believe that this analysis helps us to understand what is happening in our universities in the twenty-first century; put simply, at present the subsystems of money and power are overpowering the capacity for rational examination and argument.

Within this particular story of colonization, a description of what has led to the decline of the condition of universities can be brief: over the last two decades or so universities have submitted to pressure from government to embrace the values and norms of the marketplace and have conformed to a range of measures designed to monitor and control core academic work. This trend is evident in education policy across the world and is more marked in some countries than others. The case of the UK can be illustrative of how policy history shapes education systems. This history shows how universities followed schools and further education colleges in having their mission narrowed to concentrate on economic returns. In general, the current discourse about education can be contrasted to that of the immediate post-WW II period in which there was evidence of what can be termed a 'social-democratic discourse'. Official documents about schooling promoted the ideas of 'the democratic ideal as the objective and inspiration of all our educational activities [and] the liberation of the creative spirit in every individual'.[2] It is commonly agreed that the end of this era was heralded by a defining speech by the Labour Prime Minister, Callaghan, in 1976 (the 'Ruskin Speech') in which it was suggested that schoolteachers overemphasized social ends at the expense of the needs of the economy and industry, and in which the teaching profession was challenged to make the curriculum more responsive to the 'world of work' (Avis *et al.* 1996; Jones, 2003).

In the UK, the 1988 Education Reform Act (ERA) came as the apotheosis for school education of the market ideology of the government and of the intention directly to regulate schoolteachers' work which since 1945 had been carried out with an apparently high degree of autonomy.[3] The Act introduced a cluster of measures that at first sight appear contradictory. On the one hand, it decentralized by dismantling local-level power and devolving financial responsibility to the schools. On the other, it took over central control of the curriculum in the form of a National Curriculum and associated assessments; and, relegated the responsibility for 'quality control' to a government agency that inspects schools. This contradiction is evident in universities today in which entrepreneurial activity and open competition is encouraged at the same time as strenuous efforts are made to standardize teaching and the curriculum. So in all sectors we can see deregulation and 'marketization' coexisting with state regulation and funding. Further education colleges, which are now sometimes part of higher education, were dealt with a little later and differently from schools. The government took colleges from local government control and converted them into corporations with non-elected boards of governors who are, in the main, from local business and industry. A government agency is responsible for inspecting the curriculum and auditing financial arrangements, including the imposition of funding formula based on student numbers (Randle and Brady, 1997).

Higher education in the UK has a parallel and connected history. In the

1960s, the 'Robbins Report' (Robbins, 1963) was seen as the state's first attempt explicitly to connect the sector to economic requirements, but, at the same time, it equally stressed the 'transmission of . . . common standards of citizenship' (p. 6). Some years later, the 'Dearing Report' (Dearing, 1997) dealt with a raft of higher education issues and emphasized the role of universities in supplying what was needed for the national economy. The emphasis is even stronger in the most recent government 'White Paper', *The Future of Higher Education* (DfES, 2003), which is an unequivocal statement that higher education is for the economy and, as a corollary, for individual prosperity (through which social justice will be achieved). The social-democratic discourse of the post-war years has disappeared from official documents about education; social and transformative purposes are barely mentioned. The pattern of policy bringing about the economizing of higher education is being repeated across the world.

In all education sectors these policy transformations have been met by a critical literature. In sum it argues that prescriptions about curriculum and pedagogy have redefined quality and standards as quantitative and technical; and that the emphasis on markets, consumers, deregulation, diversity, choice, competition and accountability 'commodifies' the education of students and is making inroads into traditional teaching professional identities. So, for example, headteachers, principals and vice-chancellors are no longer expected to be inspiring educational or moral leaders but rather line-managers who brand, budget, market and monitor; while at the level of everyday practice teachers have become deliverers of a commodity, testers, technicians and operatives.

There are, of course important differences in how policy affects different sectors and the same sectors in different social and geographic locations. Furthermore, it can be argued that, however much governments might want to control universities, they only ever partially succeed. Pertinent examples from England are the effective resistance to extreme forms of competency-based and standardization of education and training for university teachers; and in a number of institutions a quiet return to year-long courses from 'modularization' which has been roundly condemned for being inimical to learning (Brecher 2005). Studies indicate that institutions and teachers have a range of ways of dealing and coping with the new policy environments: some creative, some compliant and accommodating, and some resistant and distancing. Despite the overwhelming evidence of colonization, I want to attempt a reading of the restructuring of university education which opens spaces for envisaging alternative futures.

The 'audit culture' and 'quality regimes' in universities

At the heart of thinking about critical pedagogy is a stance on the business of defining and assuring the quality of 'learning and teaching'. In Jill Blackmore's (2004) words, quality business has become the 'discursive orthodoxy of university life' (p. 383) and makes incursions into the lifeworld of academic teachers that are strongly felt. The phenomena can be understood in the broad context of what Michael Power (1994) has called the 'audit explosion'. He argues that in contemporary society auditing as a practice and an idea is ubiquitous and connected to a fundamental shift in patterns of governance. His argument is echoed by commentators who see the university as taking on the values and norms of business and as becoming 'corporate' (Giroux, 2005; Readings, 1996) or 'entrepreneurial' (Barnett, 2003). For Bill Readings the forms of regulation in universities comprise a cultural shift in which 'the intellectual has been taken over by the administrator and the academic entrepreneur' (1996, p. 106). We can also see the audit explosion as a cognitive shift in society and culture which attempts to resolve the tensions that arise with the complexities of late capitalism:

> Audit is a way of reconciling contradictory forces: on the one hand the need to extend a traditional hierarchical command conception of control in order to maintain existing structures of authority; on the other, the need to cope with the failure of this style of control, as it generates risks that are increasingly hard to specify and control. (Power, 1994, p. 6)

Power does not reject entirely the need for control and accountability, but rather argues that the particular style that prevails – 'quantified, simplified, ex-post by outsiders' ('Style A') (pp. 8–9) – has detrimental effects, three of which are of particular relevance: it is abstracted from first-order activities and obscure; it makes it difficult to envisage alternative styles which involve 'civic dialogue ... direct accountability and active interaction' (p. 27); and, it shapes the social context which is the subject of audit to fit the parameters of the audit.

The development of contemporary quality systems, procedures and discourses in universities has national and international social, economic and political dimensions. In Europe, North America, Australia and New Zealand as well as in in developing countries, the adoption of quality systems is linked to the perceived need to compete in a global market and to harmonize national and global higher education systems. Nevertheless, local circumstances and contexts throw up different configurations and contradictory trends. So while Rhoades and Sporn (2002) suggest that the European quality systems are focused on the standardization of higher education across Europe, Barroso (2003) highlights variation and contradiction.

The UK's case has been particularly disreputable. It has been through three major iterations and all involve teams of 'peers' visiting and inspecting. The first iteration ('Teaching Quality Assessment') was not thought discriminating enough so the second ('Subject Review') attempted quantitative judgement. Both of these 'methodologies' have been described by Vidovich (2004) as the most intrusive in the world and are said to have the international reputation of being a lesson in 'how not to implement quality procedures' (Harvey, 2002). At the same time, UK universities are perceived as more complicit than those in Australia and Canada (Vidovich and Slee, 2001, Morrow and Torres, 2000). In 2001 and 2002, during the time of the Subject Review, a series of articles in *The Times Higher*[4] revealed that the system was blighted by elitism, favouritism, gamesmanship and grade inflation.[5] Finally, accusations of 'cartel abuse' when philosophers across the country gave each other's departments the top scores[6] signalled the need for a change in 'methodology'. The crescendo of complaints resulted in what is called a 'lighter touch' ('Institutional Audit') which returns to qualitative comments but is still experienced as oppressive. Constant adjustments like this can be expected for audits are concerned with 'image management rather than ... substantive analysis' (Power, 1994, p. 48) and, as academics learn to 'play the game' of image management, crises will occur:

Audits are usually publicly visible when they fail. Their benefits are often ambivalent and a source of controversy. Audit reconstitutes itself in a syndrome of regulatory failure: it emerges from crises institutionally secure despite processes of blame allocation within the regulatory world. (*Ibid.*)

So the audit method, designed to reassure the public and the state is intrinsically flawed but instead of being thrown out it is merely adjusted. The objectives of any methodology use a similar discourse and appear reasonable: to contribute to the enhancement of teaching quality; to give students, employers and others access to information so that they are assured of standards and appropriateness; to rectify institutional practices which are not up to standard; and, to provide accountability for the use of public funds. But, at present, 'Style A' is relentlessly pursued and there is no debate about whether quality objectives could be met by pursuing Power's 'Style B' model of control and accountability, which is characterized by being qualitative and high trust; and by involving internal agents and public debate. Instead of considering pedagogy in the context of broad social and psychological issues, universities, as 'service providers' are required to follow hefty 'codes of conduct' about numerous areas of practice as well as adhere to 'programme specifications' and 'benchmarking'.

The discourse of 'new public management'

Quality systems in universities are operated by an orientation and set of practices known as 'new public management' or 'managerialism'. In *The Managerial State* (1997) John Clarke and Janet Newman argue that in the UK managerialism has been used by the state to displace the public service professional identity and values constructed by a post-WW2 consensus: 'Managerialism is the ideology that ... promises to provide the discipline necessary for efficient organisation, particularly in relation to welfare professionalism's claim to exercise discretionary judgement' (p. 30). They characterize managerialism as the imposition on the public sector of a cluster of private sector practices and orientations: emphasis on quality and excellence and systems for being accountable for it; a focus on economy, efficiency, effectiveness, being enterprising and satisfying the demands of service users; the adoption of the principles of commercialism, mixed economies, flexible accumulation and market relations; and, representation by non-elected boards and agencies. Managerialism masks the ethical-political nature of public service problems by presenting them as if they are amenable to direct management solutions within neutral institutions.

According to Clarke and Newman (*ibid.*) managerialism has reformed public service institutions and work through the devices of 'subordination', 'displacement' and 'cooption'. We can see all three at work in universities. Universities have become like corporations, displaying 'market behaviour' (Delanty, 2001, p. 122): management must, therefore, take account of the realities and responsibilities of budgetary management and competition. Consideration of how to achieve the complex intellectual, social and emotional ends of education becomes subordinate to improving efficiency and performance. Displacement is evident in the managerial notion of 'transparency': attempts are made to make educational offerings unambiguous by demands to set clear targets, and to develop performance indicators to measure the achievement of those targets so that the students as customers (and increasingly their parents) can choose between good and bad. This binds universities to ensuring that their place in the publicly available league tables is attractive enough to sell their courses; and this means that they must accept and do well in inspections and audits.

No story of colonization would be complete without reference to control of the discourse. 'Cooption' refers to managerial attempts 'to colonise the terrain of professional discourse' (Clarke and Newman, 1997, p. 76) by stressing flexibility, responsiveness, self-management and teamwork; and by appropriating such terms as 'justice', 'choice', 'opportunity', 'student-centred', 'empowerment' and 'ownership' that have a progressive appearance. Despite the all-pervasiveness of this discourse, I must confound any suggestions that the question about the role of discourse is settled.

The French philosopher Michel Foucault is the theorist to whom is most commonly attributed the formulation of the complex and difficult idea that subjects and subjectivities are dominated through discourses. However, Habermas, who has engaged extensively and critically with Foucault[7] concludes that:

> There is some unclarity ... of how discourses ... are related to practices: whether one governs the other, whether their relationship is to be conceived as that of base to superstructure, or on the model of a circular causality, or as an interplay of structure and base. (1995a, p. 51)[8]

He does not accept the degree of autonomy Foucault attributes to discourses to reproduce technological, economic and political conditions (1995b).

I accept Habermas's uncertainty about the power of discourse to shape the lifeworld, nevertheless, language sends a strong message which we can decipher by attending to what is sayable; what is talked about and how; who can say what; what is consented to; what is construed as possible and impossible; what is and can be envisaged; and, what is silenced, excluded or lost. In terms of critical university pedagogy the concept of discourse is useful in two broadly related ways. First, as used by Habermas, to refer to 'validity claims' made by the prevalent discourses of managerialism and technical rationality about the nature of teaching and learning; and secondly, as discourse combined with actions (discursive practices) to become a set of conditions which enables or constrains possibilities for transformatory change. So, if historical ideas about the function of universities are to be drawn on as resources for thinking and acting, they must be talked about in a language which challenges the language of managerialism.

University teachers' experience of quality

How is the audit culture and managerialism experienced and reacted to at the micro-level of everyday working practices? The case I make is that the systems, procedures and practices associated with attempts to ensure pedagogic quality in universities are an invasion of the lifeworld of academics-as-teachers. I take lifeworld to mean the values, traditions, practices and ideas of university teachers, individually and as an occupational group. Lifeworld refers to the way everyday work is done and talked about; to formal and informal personal relationships with students, colleagues, managers and officials; to what inspires commitment, interest, satisfaction, and a sense of security; to how academic teachers position themselves in relation to different actors' demands on them; and to the degree of control over their own work that they experience. It is possible to discern an idealized academic lifeworld. However sceptical one might be, there are beliefs and values that have the imprint of the Enlightenment which academics as an occupational group appear to hold tenaciously: engaging students in developing the capacity to think; the integrity and worth of disciplines or interdisciplines; the wish to resist, in one form or another, the standardization and technologizing of teaching; antipathy towards an instrumental version of university education; the unity, at some level, of research and teaching; and, the desire for autonomy.

There is little doubt that academics regard the quality industry's incursions into their working lives with distaste. Evidence that many of us feel uncoupled from a lifeworld that is expressed by the ideals of the modern university can be found in 'no' positions as expressions of outrage, for example: 'a new managerial ethos has invaded the scholar's space' (Delanty, 2001, p. 107); 'We have to stop the QAA[9] monster or it will eat us alive';[10] 'The result is a vague, persistent and crippling sense of failure' (Strathern, 1997, p. 318); and, 'The university ... is a machine for the creation of the next generation of "entrepreneurs" and "innovators"' (Robinson and Tormey, 2003, p. 25). Such resistance might be expected when taken-for-granted ways of working are disturbed. However, I want to go further and focus more closely on the effects of regimes of regulation on university teaching by drawing attention to two clusters of reactions that tally with Habermas's description of 'pathologies' that accompany lifeworld colonization: symptoms of stress and false speech acts.

A recent survey (Kenman and Jones, 2004) has made rather sensational education news: '[university workers] make more serious professional errors, suffer more stress-related problems, are more likely to resort to drink and have less sex as a result of overwork compared with other workers.'[11] Be that as it may, Louise Morley's book *Quality and Power in Higher Education* (2003) demonstrates how quality systems influence subjectivities and social relationships. While Morley's interviews of institutionally and structurally differentiated academics and administrators reveal some ambiguities, a large part of the story is of negative emotions particularly of multiple bereavements: loss of confidence and equanimity, loss of a sense of security, loss of control over one's own work, loss of interest in core teaching and research work, and loss of academic identity. Grief, humiliation and anxiety can be heard in this quotation:

I didn't feel like an academic, I felt like, I felt like the prey to the QAA, that whatever they wanted they must have, whatever they wanted I must produce a document, and I must get all the documents and put them all in boxes for them. And I felt that was my job, and everything else came second, and I had to do their bidding, and do it as well as possible, because otherwise, I don't know what the otherwise would be. There is ... in a sense there is a silence on the other side of what will happen, both to you as an individual and your institution. And there is that threat, the unspoken threat. And that's the other side of accountability and the audit society, the unspoken threat that ... you can be a failing university. And you know, again if you're in a more prestigious position you can lose that prestigious position. (p. 68)

Creativity is needed to teach well whatever pedagogical rationale is operating, and critical pedagogy requires the capacity to dream. The psychotherapist Andrew Cooper (2000) claims that harsh regimes of accountability can produce in individuals a punitive super-ego which stifles creativity. This process is illustrated clearly in another response from Morley's academics: 'And it's just the whole thing is so unutterably awful ... it's like some form of torture. It's like, you know, beat yourself up before they come to beat you up, and then you will get beaten up again' (p. 90). If university teachers feel like Morley's (2003) respondents, they are unlikely to mobilize their communicative reason in relation to teaching.

The experience of stress is often related to 'loss of personal professional control and the feeling that demands outweigh capacity' (*ibid.* p. 80). The concept of 'intensification' is helpful. It is drawn from theories of labour process and developed by Michael Apple (1988) to discuss schoolteachers' experience of their work. He explains how having more and more work to do faster results in a chronic sense of overwork and of not coping which has a variety of negative effects: for example, interfering with sociability; negatively affecting the quality of work done; causing tensions between staff; engendering a sense of disenchantment with work; and, not having enough time to do one's work properly. Morley's respondents report all these symptoms. Yet I believe that in terms of the thesis of colonization it is important to distinguish the 'intensity' of work from what makes it feel empty and valueless. Andrew Hargreaves (1994) contrasts types of time in terms of subjective responses: time spent on managerially determined objectives (technical-rational time) and on demonstrating good performance (micro-political time) is unrewarding in contrast to time spent on one's own genuine professional concerns (phenomenological time). Time accounting for the quality of teaching (as it is currently being demanded by government agencies) is technical-rational and micro-political. Perhaps the most important point here is that work being done in micro-political time is not authentic, it is a legitimating device which carries with it very little evidence of genuine improvement. Cooper (2000) argues that a 'crisis of authenticity' in welfare work, including education, is the result of government's 'disturbed ... obsessional anxiety about loss of control' (p. 122). This is a very serious crisis because being inauthentic damages the 'capacity to discriminate what is fake and what is authentic, what is true and what is false, what is good and what is corrupt' (*ibid.*).

From Habermas's point of view the most serious damage that can be inflicted on the lifeworld of culture, society and personality by inappropriate invasions of the imperatives of money and power is the distortion of communication itself. It is often remarked that new public management has developed a climate of mistrust and blame and that this has damaging effects on public service work.[12] It is clear that to be of any genuine use, systems devised to define, improve and ensure pedagogic quality in universities require relationships of sufficient trust between the academic labour force, managers and policy makers, and the public: these groups should not routinely be lying to each other or avoiding the truth. Strategic action is a sociological concept that Habermas employs to explain the processes of distorted communication such as mendacity. Strategic action is focused on self-interest or self-preservation and the relationship between interlocutors is adversarial: a 'basic value [is] successful self-assertion against an opponent'[13] who is perceived as pursuing competing interests. Strategic action is not concerned with genuine motivation; it aims to produce the desired effects so it is feigned or cynical impression management. Clearly, then, when action is strategic the sincerity, truth and the rightness of expressed intentions cannot be relied upon. Current conditions encourage strategic action. It is difficult to have open, rational discussion or conversations about the ends and means of teaching in which university teachers can make sincere claims about what is right to do. The specifications, prescriptions, quasi-contracts and technical-rational discourse of current forms of accountability signal the colonization of the lifeworld of university pedagogy which is dependent on interaction and collective thoughts and feeling (intersubjectivity). Moreover, every academic knows that a great deal of time is spent complying and conforming cynically to quality systems' demands by 'stage-managing' (Morley, 2003, p. 73) or 'window-dressing'. Cooper (2000) tells an anecdote which both illustrates and explains what state of mind is encouraged into being by quality regimes. He recounts that a colleague read a draft of an article of Cooper's in which he (Cooper) admits to some 'cheating' during a quality inspection. He reports his colleague's response to this admission:

> [He] advised me against saying anything which might lead others to suppose we had 'cheated' in our preparations or conduct. I see this as a further re-enactment of the state of mind induced by the experience of inspection and audit. Ordinary confidence in truthful states of mind is attacked by a punitive, abnormal super-ego and replaced by an anxiety-driven cover-up in which aspects of reality must

be hidden or suppressed for fear of destructive negative judgements. We did not cheat. It is as simple as that. (p. 134)

A further related distortion concerns the second-order nature of audit. Everyday experience with students continues to remind university teachers that teaching is an uncertain and risky business, characterized by dilemmas and demands and underpinned by norms and values; but quality systems divert attention from this reality because they are devices designed to minimize complexity and risk. Such inauthenticity, in turn, signals difficulties for the pedagogic lifeworld: problems – like the ones I have described earlier – arise when reality is denied or when concern for appearances becomes more important than attention to reality. Cooper (2000) explains how distortion occurs:

> The methodologies and intellectual habits which constitute proceduralism, audit, quality assurance and all the paraphernalia of new public management are notable for the doubly alienating manner in which they can colonise both psychological and social space: they refer us to *external rather than internal criteria* for assessing and evaluating our work, but they also assume occupancy of these internal spaces, so that *externality becomes the principle by which internal life is lived and reproduced.* (p. 128) (emphases in text)

What this means in practice is that we all aim to *appear* excellent but, as Bill Readings (1996) identifies, 'excellence has the singular advantage of being entirely meaningless ... we can all agree upon it' (p. 22). The 'logic of accounting' (*ibid.*) pressurizes us into pursuing the external criteria of a position in the league tables rather than difficult, often unanswerable, philosophical questions about the ends and means of university education.

Nevertheless, in a society in which there is a decline in trust in public services and in which social practices have been transformed by the greater production, availability and contestability of knowledge, publicly funded academics must give accounts to the public and to the state about their work. Why not welcome exchanges about the worth and nature of university education and aim to build trust? We must, anyway, work with the difficult, paradoxical situation to which Marilyn Strathern (2000b) draws attention: 'People want to know how to trust one another, to make the trust visible, while (knowing that) the very desire to do so points to the absence of trust' (p. 310). Mechanistic, regulative approaches to ensuring and accounting for quality are distorting academics' communications about pedagogic work with the state and public. Using Michael Rustin's words (2004) how can we secure an 'occupational culture and mentality' (p. 99) which promotes collective deliberation in open discussion about what is worth teaching, why it is worth teaching and how it should be taught?

Academic complicity

'Auditors are ourselves' Strathern briskly points out (2000b, p. 315). Certainly, in my experience, a frequent topic of discussion among academics is why we 'have done this to ourselves'. The question, then, is what parts of the lifeworld – for example, cultural norms, expectations and values – *allow* the invasion of discursive practices that are repudiated by large numbers of academics? It would not be convincing to present universities as utterly powerless to resist the incursions described here. Some, of course, have more power than others: universities struggling for resources and to attract students have more to lose by not complying than rich universities (Morley [2003] suggests, too, that more quality is 'done' in the ex-polytechnics in the UK). Nevertheless, by way of illustration of how weak active opposition has been across the system, seven economics professors at wealthy, research-led Warwick University published their angry arguments about why the inspection of teaching was 'damaging and destructive' *after* they had gained top marks[14] and there have been flurries of rebellion at the London School of Economics and Kings College London[15] (both elite universities), which have died down with a change in methodology. Related to this, it should be kept in mind that most of the dissatisfactions that appear in scholarly analyses are written by senior academics in the more prestigious universities. Furthermore, there is some evidence that traditionally vulnerable groups have benefited: students, students unions and new lecturers are more positive than established academic staff about the transparency associated with quality systems (Luke, 1997; Morley, 2003) and some academics who are under thirty are reported being 'fed-up with the gripes of the over fifties'.[16]

These observations do not affect the argument here that, on the whole, systems of regulation and inspection waste time, encourage cheating and divert attention from the realities of teaching. Furthermore, most research and anecdotal evidence tells us that academics are highly critical of quality systems. So why don't academics (particularly, one might argue, from the elite universities) insist on the conditions they need to discuss openly and come to authentic agreements? Why are they often not only compliant but also complicit, working hard on administration and policy development for quality systems? There are no simple answers. Authors invoke Michel Foucault's elaboration of the concept of the panopticon to explain academics' 'self-surveillance'. The panopticon was a circular prison designed (though never built) by Jeremy Bentham in the eighteenth century to allow an unseen observer to watch prisoners, therefore, since the prisoners cannot avoid the gaze of the observer, in effect everything they do is subject to inspection: surveillance is continuous and gradually becomes internalized and unconscious. But academics and their managers appear knowing.

Similarly, there is little evidence among academics of the 'colluded self' that Catherine Casey writes about as an effect of corporate culture in *Work, Self and Society after Industrialisation* (1995): 'The current manifestations of collusion [are] compulsive optimism and evangelical espousal of the values and behaviour of the new culture' (p. 191). I believe that the complicity of academics can be explained in good part by self-interest at the levels of state officials, university vice-chancellors, senior managers, heads of department and many successful academics. Of course, this has never been different: universities pragmatically must maintain a relationship to the state and academics have always been motivated by the 'two poles of idealism and competition',[17] (Rossen, 1993, p. 140). Scholarly life has been predicated on a principle of individualism: socio-historical accounts of the establishment, production and reproduction of disciplines show how they function as exclusionary and elitist (Becher and Trowler, 2001).

Nevertheless, current conditions encourage the pole of competition more than the pole of idealism. In a paper entitled 'The Left in the Academy: demotivated, withdrawal, passive complicity or soldiering on? Observations of an early retiree' (2003) Rachel Sharp argues that the crisis of universities is 'within' and claims that as a 'Left academic' she can no longer easily find allies in her Australian university. She identifies the 'types' who now inhabit universities: the 'middle level corporate manager' who is engaged with reaching targets and self-promotion; the 'individual go-getter' who pursues grants and consultancies for career advancement and farms out teaching; the 'old style liberal' who is conscientious, nostalgic and critical but 'goes along with changes'; the 'new style vulgar liberal' who celebrates difference and will not go beyond 'discourse'; the 'not very competent free loader' who, despite managerialism, has not been eased out; and, finally, 'the growing mass of flexible labour . . . a genuine underclass'. These 'types' might be caricatures, but they are recognizable and they highlight what might be internal obstacles to critical pedagogy.

What academic 'type' or identity is being nurtured in the techno-bureaucratic university? One of the managers Morley (2003) interviews comments mildly that academics involved in audits are 'very into what points they get and all of that' (p. 81). Philip Altman goes much further in a newspaper article entitled 'Stench of rotten fruit fills groves of academe',[18] claiming that all over the world the commercialization of higher education and the 'deterioration of the idea of higher education as a "common good"' has led to corruption and fraud. Henry Giroux (1983) argues that critical pedagogy requires us to think 'how we can minimise the effects on our students of those parts of our "sedimented" histories that reproduce dominant interests and values' (p. 241). Surely he is right and as education workers in universities during late or post-modernity, it is apt to be self-reflective and critical about ourselves.

From the perspective of critical pedagogy, alternative constructions of 'pedagogic quality' would be connected to an egalitarian agenda underpinned by notions of empowerment of individuals and the transformation of society. Currently, many managers and academics working in universities accept glaring inequalities and self-interest is evident. The corporate university only cares about itself rather than about inequities in the system as a whole, however impoverishing this might be for culture and society. In parallel, there are the academics – Rachel Sharp's 'individual go-getters' – who focus on their own career advancement, whose mistreatment of younger and part-time colleagues is a symptom of their lack of concern about the effects of a fragmented and stratified workforce.[19] By and large, successful academics are white, male and middle class, while black and female academics or aspiring academics experience discrimination (Law *et al.* 2004, Morley, 1999). Nor must we forget that, despite policies associated with widening access to universities, there are entrenched inequalities in student participation.

I shall return to these matters in Chapter 8, but, in the meantime, even if the academy has always been selfish and competitive, we need now to think about what conditions would encourage solidarity and an interest in justice. It might appear that by knowing what is happening to us and complaining we can remain true, right and sincere in our hearts and minds, yet to make a difference we need to act. But it is difficult to do so in working environments that are not so much sites of trust and interdependence as of anxiety. Andrew Cooper explains: 'In the collective mind the threat of external impingement, or internal disruption, tends to predominate over belief in a capacity to shape political and personal destiny in an uncertain world' (2000, p. 122). I believe that the kind of academic culture and identity that is being invoked in current conditions finds it particularly difficult to focus on pedagogic questions, even if teachers are committed.

Conclusion: alternative critical quality systems

Although I have argued that fraudulence is being encouraged and that real quality has become confused with the appearance of quality, the situation is more blurred and imperfect than I have so far suggested. As Stephen Ball (1993) argues, managerial discourses are: 'complex and polyvalent, empowering and disempowering, intersecting and contradictory' (p. 79). Academic teachers cope variously: they are not only recalcitrant, but also sometimes adopt management practices because they are useful, and, at other times, adapt them so that they become useful. In real-life settings organizational control is made up of a strategic mix of techniques: new managerialism and entreprenuerism alongside old committee structures, consultations and hierarchies. Undoubtedly, the academy displays the pathologies of an invaded lifeworld: lying, loss of belief and apathy. Yet, from Habermas's perspective, this situation opens up spaces for communicative action, for the symptoms of colonization signal a 'withdrawal of legitimation [and] a steering crisis' for governments (1987, p. 386).

If we are to resist constructions of 'quality' that distort academic work and suggest alternatives, then we must not only think but also act collectively and with conviction. Maria Jose Lemaitre (2002) (addressing the National Commission for Programme Accreditation in Chile) expresses it eloquently:

> We say that we want higher education to be an opportunity for equity, for better opportunities for personal, social and professional development, for the better understanding of complex and diverse societies, for the development of truly democratic institutions. This will not happen on its own. It demands imagination and courage; hope lies in the intelligence and collective will of policy developers, government officials, quality assurance agencies and researchers. (p. 37)

Blind resistance to systems of regulation will not be helpful. We need alternative ways of assessing and evaluating pedagogy which promote imagination and courage. We could choose not to be fearful and to engage honestly with our managers. We could accept some form of making accounts of our teaching but, at the same time, put up a strong defence against disfigured academic teaching subjectivities and identities being brought into being. In Bill Readings' words we could seek to make evaluation of teaching 'a social question rather than a device of measurement' (1996, p. 119). In the chapters that follow I shall attempt some ideas about how this might be done.

Notes

1 Italics and those that follow are in Habermas's text.
2 In a tract by a schools' inspector called *Education and the Democratic Ideal* (Hughes, 1956).
3 Despite the discourse, it is argued that schoolteachers were subject to a form of 'indirect rule' (Lawn, 1996). Eustace Percy, appointed President of the Board of Education in 1924, searching for a way to regulate teachers, found his answer in the method of administration the British Empire used in its colonies whereby 'relative autonomy' was granted to the 'natives' (ibid. p. 93). In this version of schoolteachers' history the state was responding to teachers' pre-war demands for more independence by offering status as partners in return for their acceptance of limited or 'licensed' (Dale, 1989) autonomy.
4 In the UK *The Times Higher* is the only weekly newspaper for higher education so it is very widely read and used as a conduit for comment and criticism.
5 For example, 'TQA [Teaching Quality Assessment] devalued by grade inflation',

2 March 2001, 'Analysis: good teachers or great stage managers?', 2 August 2002, 'Quality requires a radical rethink not a quick fix', 30 March 2001, 'Universities are sinking under inspection load', 23 March 2001.

6 Drawing the comment from an inspector 'I suspect philosophers are poking fun at the entire methodology' ('Philosophy scores add to QAA [Quality Assurance Agency] criticism' *The Times Higher*, 22 June 2001.)

7 Kelly (1995) has edited and published the exchanges between Habermas and Foucault.

8 Foucault does not accept Habermas's 'grand narrative' of modern progress and possibilities; and Habermas does not accept a reading of history that is 'seamlessly filled by the absolutely contingent occurrence of the disordered flaring up and passing away of new formations of discourse [in which] the only thing that remains is power.' (Habermas, 1995a, p. 51).

9 Quality Assurance Agency; a UK government agency responsible for the quality of teaching.

10 'LSE leads revolt against QAA', *The Times Higher*, 23 March 2001.

11 'No sex please, we're stressed', *The Times Higher*, 29 September 2003.

12 See for example ONora O'Neill's 2002 BBC Reith Lectures *A Question of Trust*.

13 From Habermas's *Theory and Practice* (1974) quoted in Outhwaite, 1996, p. 88.

14 'Trial by Ordeal' *Guardian Education*, 30 January 2001, pp. 12–13.

15 'LSE leads revolt against QAA', *The Times Higher*, 23 March 2001.

16 'Thirty-somethings are sick of grumpy old staff', *The Times Higher*, 14 January 2005.

17 Rossen (1993) argues that copious fiction about university life reflects the tension created by these two poles and reminds us that in Douglas Adams' *A Hitchhiker's Guide to the Galaxy* a young phycisist is lynched by his colleagues for winning a 'Prize for Extreme Cleverness'.

18 'Stench of rotten fruit fills groves of academe', *The Times Higher*, 21 January 2005.

19 Andrea Abbas and I (2001) discuss the plight of part-time sociology teachers in 'Becoming sociologists: professional identity for part-time teachers of university sociology, *British Journal of Sociology of Education*, 22(3), pp. 339–52.

5
Pedagogic justice

Our reflections of teaching as a practice must insist on a pedagogic scene structured by a dissymmetrical pragmatics, and this unequal relation must be addressed in terms of ethical awareness. The scene of teaching belongs to the sphere of justice rather than of truth: the relation of students to teacher and teacher to student is one of asymmetrical obligation, which appears to both sides as problematic and requiring further study. (Readings, B. (1996) *The University in Ruins*, p. 161)

Introduction

The last chapter focused on the effects of the audit culture on university teachers' lifeworld. It established that to move towards critical pedagogy university teachers must be enabled to focus on the realities of teaching and be trusted to make their own accounts of what and how they teach (otherwise there will be a tendency to treat managers and outside bodies as opponents with whom to be dishonest). This chapter discusses how technical-rational constructions of university pedagogy distort it by denying its intersubjective and ethical–political nature. Habermas's ideas about 'cognitive interests' inform the discussion which is structured around the goals for a university education suggested in Chapter 2.

Critical pedagogy for all three 'cognitive interests'

The organizing idea for this chapter is that instrumental reason or 'technical-rational interest' inappropriately dominates considerations about university education. Habermas connects his theory of communicative action to previously established sociological concepts of action. He draws up a hierarchy of understanding and knowledge by distinguishing between those concepts of action which presuppose only one objective world; those which proposed both the objective and social worlds; and, those which presuppose three worlds of objective, social and subjective. These concepts arise because humans are possessed of three cognitive interests: 'technical interest' in predicting and controlling the workings of the environment; 'hermeneutic interest' in comprehending and communicating with others; and 'emancipatory interest' in being autonomous (Habermas, 1972, pp. 303–6). For Habermas, these three interests are universal and encompass all human interests:[1]

> Orientation toward technical control, toward mutual understanding in the conduct of life, and toward emancipation from seemingly 'natural' constraint establish the specific viewpoints from which we can apprehend reality as such in any way whatsoever. (*Ibid.* p. 311)

Knowledge cannot 'outwit its innate human interests' (*ibid.*). All three interests are evident in the structure of society and expressed in the means of social organization: work (technical interest), language (social interest) and power (emancipatory interest). Habermas and other critical theorists claim that, in modern society, interest in technical control of the objective world is pursued at the expense of interests in communication and emancipation.

According to Habermas modern positivism has become 'scientism' by which he means 'the conviction that we can no longer understand science as *one* form of possible knowledge, but rather must identify [all] knowledge with science' (1972, p. 4). He emphasizes that it is a matter for celebration that modern science allows us to extend our ability to predict and rationalize technical control over objects. But scientism has established 'predictions in the form of technical recommendations as the sole admissible "value"' (1971, p. 306). The results are twofold: only the one interest in taking control of the world is served and, more disastrously, the other interests in intersubjective meaning and social justice are not linked to the appropriate forms of knowledge, leaving moral–political questions unanswered. Habermas's disquiet about the effects of the overriding concern with 'the extension and dissemination of technical knowledge' (*ibid.* p. 310) is shared by critics of the current configuration of higher education (for example, Barnett, 1994, 2000; Giroux, 2001; Walker and Nixon, 2004).

At the heart of the problem with a technical-rational approach to education is a preoccupation with a particular form of economic and bureaucratic utility which can be seen not only in how governments limit the purposes of education to economic considerations, but also in policies and practices of standardization: for example, in the emphasis on the prespecification of educational objectives; in competency-based programmes of education and training for teachers that emphasize behavioural performance; and in the ascendancy of so-called transferable skills development in educational programmes. Such approaches to pedagogy mechanize and atomize a holistic and individual process by treating knowledge and understanding as commodities. Jean-François Lyotard writing about universities in *The Post Modern Condition* (1989) is blunt:

> The question (overt or implied) now asked by the professionalist student, the State, or institutions of higher education is no longer 'Is it true?' but 'What use is it?' In the context of the mercantilization of knowledge, more often than not this question is equivalent to: 'Is it saleable?' And in the context of power growth: 'Is it efficient?' (p. 51)

The effect of commodifying knowledge is that some knowledge is disallowed or marginalized. In the case of pedagogy, knowledge about social, cultural, political, ethical dimensions are underplayed, and the question of values put aside. This affects actors' (students, teachers and managers) capacity to think about learning and teaching in ways which incorporate all three cognitive interests.

Education is an area of life in which communication, agreements and moral judgements are functionally necessary. At one level, values are inescapable – even if they are tacit, they direct people's energies and efforts. Jon Nixon's (1995) explanation of the role and nature of values is closely linked to my suggestion at the end of Chapter 3 that some of the traditional ideas of the university can be revived for progressive purposes:

> Values affect action by satisfying our sense of what feels right or awakening our sense of what is morally offensive. The affective nature of values – the way they cling to feelings and associations – accounts for their resilience and for the continuing influence they exert across generations. Values take us, as individuals and groups, back to our roots for the purpose of reclaiming what is morally alive in our communal pasts; they trace old loyalties but point also to new possibilities for realizing our moral agency. (p. 220)

This view of values resonates with Habermas's taken-for-granted, unreflected-upon lifeworld: the harmony of social formation and individual identity depends on agreed-upon values which engender moral commitment. Applied to university teaching the idea of reclaiming historic ideas ('old loyalties' in Nixon's phrase) might guide thinking about 'new possibilities' that are denied by a technical-rational and managerial discourse. We might then begin to hear a language about teaching which refers to intrinsic dedication to teaching and the dispositions and virtues it requires: for example 'patience', 'wisdom', 'prudence', 'deliberation'. Such words seem hopelessly old-fashioned, but 'creativity' and 'determination' might pass muster. At present, the moral commitment of university teachers to the good of their students is undermined by a discourse which excludes the dilemmas of moral commitment, replacing them by decisions about the best technique or system. This is what Habermas calls 'decisionism' which occurs when 'efficiency and economy are justified as if they were values' (Habermas 1974, p. 261). Of course, any discourse can take on colonizing action if it is stipulated and used for surveillance: during the 1980s and 1990s the vocabularies of anti-paternalism, user-centredness and empowerment, associated with progressive movements, were used to legitimate and gain the consent of potential opponents within education. A new discourse would function differently only if it is used freely as part of a recognizable lifeworld.

Since there are strong grounds for eschewing the technical-rational approach to education and learning, it is worth thinking about its appeal. It is argued that the appeal of technical rationality is that its claims to explicitness, precision, transparency, visibility and clarity *appear* to relieve the anxiety of 'hazardous' work for which teachers must now be accountable (Morley, 2003; Strathern, 2000b). The problem, as we have seen, is that apparent transparency obfuscates pedagogic reality which, as Fred Inglis (2000) puts it, involves 'the inevitably messy give-and-take of human dealings' (p. 424). In a general way, technical-rational approaches are attractive to contemporary nation states grappling with the threats that arise from postmodern chaos; and, to be more specific, the false promise of predictable and demonstrable results offers governments a way of regulating university teachers.

Habermas's assertion that the 'objectivist attitude squeezes the conduct of life into the behavioural system of instrumental action' (Habermas, 1972, p. 317) means that subjective and social matters tend to be treated *as if* they are technical matters. It must be emphasized that there is nothing intrinsically wrong with technical-rational knowledge or know-how – for example, learning mechanical or work-based skills or the 'what works' approaches to teaching. Knowledge arising from the technical-rational area of cognitive interest is necessary but by no means sufficient for pedagogic work. Problems arise when technical-rational approaches to knowledge bounce across the whole spectrum of human interests or operate in the wrong area of interest.

What kind of critical university pedagogy?

Making judgements about whether colonization is occurring involves setting out what might be endangered by the concentration on the technical rationality. In Chapter 2 I argued that the goals of university education should be tied to the urgent moral-political liabilities of our times. With this in mind, I suggested three over-arching issues on which to hang goals for a university education: the current imbalance in the broad goals of university education; persistent social inequalities; and, global problems. The question that I am attempting to engage with in this book is what kinds of institutions, curricula, pedagogies and academic behaviours would go towards addressing these urgent issues? I will expand on the pedagogic implications of each goal.

Rebalancing the broad goals of university education

The central role of university education is the reproduction of the lifeworld: society, culture and personality (or identity). Broadly and simply, education's benign purposes are for personal growth, for an educated citizenry necessary to a healthy democracy, and for producing wealth and services. We can discern Habermas's three cognitive interests in these purposes. They can also be seen in his outline of universities' three main responsibilities towards students. First, he says, universities must equip students with qualifications in the area of 'extrafunctional abilities [which are] the attributes and attitudes relevant to a professional career that are not contained *per se* in professional knowledge and skills' (1971, p. 2). This does not mean that universities do not also teach 'functional abilities' but this is not sufficient for a 'higher' education. Habermas speaks of professional 'virtues' with which the socialization processes of universities must at least be in harmony. So students are being prepared for work, however indirectly. Secondly, universities 'transmit, interpret, and develop the cultural tradition of a society' (*ibid.*). He emphasizes the role of universities in the 'self-understanding of society' pointing out that their function of working with 'active traditions' does not allow them to 'completely escape the constraint of either continuously reproducing them, or developing them or critically transforming them' (*ibid.* p. 3). So universities are responsible for students' understanding of and active engagement in culture and society. Finally, he claims, universities shape the political consciousness of students. This can be ideologically effective but unconscious, as in the liberal and organized modern university when generations of students 'reproduced the mentality of a university-trained professional stratum for which society still intended a relatively uniform status' (*ibid.*). If, in the same unreflective way, universities:

> . . . were exclusively adapted to the needs of industrial society and had eradicated the remains of beneficent but archaic freedoms [they would] stabilize implicit

professional standards, cultural traditions for forms of political consciousness, whose power expands in an uncontrolled manner precisely when they are not chosen but result instead from the on-going character of existing institutions. (*Ibid.* p. 4)

An alternative is for universities to be self-conscious about their role in relation to their influence on the political consciousness of individuals and society. From the perspective of critical theory, the task of forming political consciousness will focus on urgent moral–political liabilities (especially inequality, poverty and the environment). For Bill Readings (1996) (and Habermas) the potential for consciously shaping a more just future arose from student protest: 'What we stand to learn from the events of 1968 is that the emergence of the student who has a problematic relationship to modernity offers a resource for resistance' (p. 150). Habermas (1971) delineates the way that students must experience their university education in order to become politicized: they must come to feel that in the future they will be responsible for and able to act in society; they must perceive their universities as agents of social change; and, they must come to think of changes in social structures as relevant to their private destinies. A university education which results in these outcomes would need to focus on the full range of cognitive interests. However, at different historical junctures different interests appear to be emphasized. At present, policy analyses show us that the technical-rational interest of education for jobs and money is predominating and undermining the development of other interests. Yet, there is absolutely no evidence that an instrumental and vocational education fosters economic growth (Wolf, 2002). Over thirty-five years ago, Habermas saw universities becoming dedicated to the production and reproduction of 'technically exploitable knowledge' and neglecting to take responsibility for 'cultural self-understanding' and ... the norms of social actors' (1971, p. 4). The overwhelming emphasis on university education for economic wealth and individual prosperity should be re-balanced to take in, as equal partners, the two other traditional aims of education: individual fulfilment and transformation; and active citizenship in a democracy.

Addressing inequalities in university education

In our own developed society there is still a need to address the inequities of the connection between origins and destinies or life-paths in terms of class, ethnicity, gender and disability. It is established that educational biographies are largely influenced by social class factors (Power *et al.* 2003). Working-class children (tellingly, Alison Wolf [2002] refers to them as 'other people's children') are more likely to be offered impoverished vocational curricula[2] and, despite the policies on access and widening participation, they are less likely to study at universities, and, if they do, it will be at the less prestigious universities (Archer *et al.* 2003; Ball *et al.* 2002). I want to draw attention to two aspects of this state of affairs which are relevant to university pedagogy: first, is the commonsense belief that the hierarchy of universities reflects true pedagogic quality that was discussed in the last chapter. Secondly, is the quest to ensure that the 'brightest and the best'[3] are placed in the elite universities, which is embedded in 'access' policies. This project detracts from the important task of seeking general principles of pedagogic practice appropriate for all university students that, in the words of philosopher and educationalist John Dewey, aims for 'the development of mind' (1916, p. 16).

Before continuing, though, I want to make it clear that I do not stand with those who think that university education is now provided for too many, I welcome the shift from 'elite' to a 'mass' higher education viewing it as potentially democratizing, despite its continuing and perhaps worsening stratification. Nor do I accuse university teachers of being agents of inequitable social reproduction in society (Bowles and Gintis, 1976; Sharp and Green, 1975). At the same time, I agree with Readings (1996) that now we can no longer hold on to 'grand narratives' about the emancipatory role of the university in society, we must be modest in our ambitions and strive to construct universities as places where people can 'think together' (p. 192) and pursue justice. A starting point is to look at inequities within the system.

On the whole, educational stratification takes place along academic/vocational lines: in the UK the big divide is between the 'old' and 'new' universities which were polytechnics previous to 1992 (there are, of course, subtle gradations within these broad categories). In a book called *Degrees of Difference* (1994) Patrick Ainley uses history to challenge the normal hierarchy. He informs us that the original idea of polytechnics in England derived from the notion of 'really useful knowledge' from the 1830s' working-class self-improvement movement. The ideal of 'practical education ... aimed to use for work, not in the manner of today's vocational education, as a preparation for employment, but as a pedagogical and philosophical principle' (p. 9) is contrasted with the 'medieval flummery and academic obscurantism of Oxford and Cambridge' (p. 27). He worries that, in the competition between universities, 'really useful knowledge' will be lost and that students from poorer backgrounds will be relegated to 'teaching-only' institutions that will concentrate on an impoverished curriculum of 'skills' when 'at rock bottom the real "personal and transferable skills" required for preferential employment are those of whiteness, maleness and traditional middle-classness' (p. 81).

Certainly the 'skills agenda' can be understood as an instance of the hollowing out of the meaning of a university education and it seems at present that no student, whatever the university, can escape (in the US the term 'capabilities' is used). Policy documents shamelessly emphasize the necessity of 'equipping the labour force with appropriate and relevant skills' (DfES, 2003, p. 10) in order to protect the economy from a skills shortage in 'allied professional and technical areas' (*ibid.*). The over-emphasis on utilitarian 'transferable skills' for employability is a clear symptom of pedagogy colonized by technical rationality. Universities are not configured as spaces where students form their identities and develop as citizens.

Of course, becoming 'skilful' is essential, but how it is interpreted is crucial. Bill Readings (1996) discusses the 'university of excellence' and argues that the term 'excellence' is 'dereferentialised' by which he means that it has no meaning independent of particular contexts. The same can be said of the term 'transferable skills' which is empty of meaning until given meaning. Nevertheless, constructing university education as 'acquiring employment skills' is pedagogically ill-informed because it relates to a technical-rational interest only (instrumental versions of 'communication skills' do not amount to an interest in the social world). The skills agenda reduces university education to what Jan Parker (2002) refers to as a 'model based on training' in which the 'role of teacher is narrowed to that of supervisory coach' (p. 373). Most importantly, impoverished constructions of skill divert attention away from the most important pedagogic responsibility to guide students' intellectual growth – which I referred to earlier in John Dewey's phrase as 'development of mind'. These days the student subject to be produced is a 'consumer' and 'investor' or 'skilled technician' which, as many academics observe, encourages an instrumental attitude to education. Louise Morley (2003) demonstrates how students as 'purchasers of an expensive product' (p. 129) are often in favour of inspections, but this manipulates their needs and priorities to focus on 'service level agreements' (p. 132) rather than on curriculum content and intellectual challenge.

The alternative is to return to the idea of university education for initiating students into distinct forms of knowledge and understanding embodied in disciplines and interdisciplines. Although some argue that there are threats to coherent, autonomous disciplines, academic teachers are still strongly motivated by producing and reproducing their disciplines. The advancement of learning and pursuit of truth (however provisional and contingent) needs disciplined modes of enquiry and communities of discursive practice. Richard Pring, the educational philosopher, explains that learning a discipline is 'a matter of learning *how* to do something, to solve a problem, to create something of value, or to produce what is wanted' (1976, p. 25). Each discipline or interdiscipline is a 'community of practice' which models practices, knowledge creation and dissemination, a way of writing and speaking.[4] Treating disciplines as vehicles by which to acquire useful, employment-related skills strips them of their power to develop minds and to contribute to understanding and knowing how to act in the world. I am not complacent about existing practices but, rather, agree with Jan Parker, that a rejection of the reduction of discipline to 'common transferable and equivalent subject-specific skills' should be accompanied by 're-energising' (2002, p. 373) the notion of discipline and linking it to current pedagogical knowledge.

While I agree that the skills agenda is a symptom of technical-rationality, I am reluctant for now to believe that the university teachers of students in less prestigious universities are more influenced by it than those in elite universities. On the whole in the UK, the established universities have reaped the benefits of widening access so, arguably, the pressure to innovate is less than in the former polytechnics that often struggle to maintain student numbers. These universities orient themselves towards the market by creating courses that appear attractive to non-traditional students whose characteristics are that they are from lower socio-economic groups, tend to have lower A-level points, are more mature, are more often the first in their families to go to university and, more often 'drop out'.[5] In an effort to respond to employers' needs and to students' and parents' desire for degrees with an apparent vocational focus these universities are more likely to teach new interdisciplinary degree courses which focus on empirical fields, for example, Leisure, Youth and Sports Studies, and, most popular of all, a range of courses focusing on aspects of 'Media'. Such courses become the butt of moral panic about 'dumbing down'[6] and are routinely derided by politicians and academics.[7] Easy generalizations are made that 'better' learning and teaching is taking place in the 'good' elite universities. The contradiction is ignored that all university courses are working to the same 'benchmarking' and other quality standards, as well as being scrutinized through audits and external examiner processes. I do not think that we have the evidence yet to pronounce on the quality of pedagogy in different institutions, wherever they are in the academic hierarchy. I want to accentuate this point: people speak and write glibly of 'good' universities by which they mean traditional universities with a reputation (I have already pointed out in the last chapter how league tables simply reproduce society's expectations). Students believe that their place in the hierarchy is deserved: 'Because anyone can get into [university name], it's an inner city polytechnic for God's sake! Like you don't have to be academically elite to get into [University] because that is why I'm here. Because I live locally and I am basically stupid' (Neil, 31, white male HE student) (Archer *et al.* 2003, p. 129). It would be fitting to have as the first aim of critical pedagogy the production of students who are confident of their intellectual abilities.

Nevertheless, universities cannot in any direct manner 'compensate for society' (to use Basil Bernstein's famous phrase) especially when wealth is so unevenly distributed between them and the hierarchy so entrenched. The market-return of degrees for graduates from the elite universities is patently greater than for graduates from universities low down the league table hierarchy. Even if, as now in the UK, policy rhetoric promotes paying attention to 'all aspects of the student experience'[8] it is, at best, disingenuous to think that poor universities can offer the same resources to students as rich universities. But we can think about equality in terms of how to engage students in the experience of academic learning ('academic engagement'[9]) and I think that this involves a search for *general* pedagogic principles. I realize that this might be a contentious statement. University teachers with critical interests tend to resist prescriptions about teaching, but I want to suggest that guiding principles might take us further than thinking about what specific practices might accommodate the 'difference' of 'non-traditional' students.

The extent to which we emphasize similarities or differences in the capacity to learn is a key component of ideas about pedagogy. Habermas's work points to the similarities between learners: the capacity to learn which resides in language is universal and so is the potential of communicative reason to reflect on and reason about one's circumstances with others. In his seminal essay 'Why no pedagogy in England' Brian Simon (1999) draws attention to the 'amateurish and highly pragmatic' (p. 34) character of educational theory and practice especially in the universities. He calls urgently for a pedagogy that is systematic and focused on the commonality of learners.

Taking an historical perspective, he argues that in England a 'science of teaching' has been 'shunned' in large part because of the 'contemptuous rejection' of the idea of professional training for teaching by the public schools and elite universities, and because of the rise, over fifty years ago, of the intelligence tests which invited a focus on ability and individualism. It is arguable that neither of these attitudes has been shaken off. Jerome Bruner similarly argues that 'education goes forward today without any clearly defined or widely accepted theory of instruction' (1974, p. 114). Both Bruner and Simon propose a version of 'perfectibility of the intellect' (*ibid.*) which emphasizes both that the similarities of humans as learners are more important than individual differences, and that pedagogic theory should help us estimate what is possible in terms of capacity for learning. At this point I am making the broad point that I believe that pedagogic efforts could be guided by principles which are likely to draw the best from students. I will return to Brian Simon and Jerome Bruner in the next chapter in which I attempt to sketch the contours of a general pedagogic theory that is in keeping with critical pedagogy.

In the early part of the twentieth century, in an inspiring passage in *The Aims of Education* (1967), the philosopher A. N. Whitehead set for university education an 'idea' which focuses on the role of imagination in developing minds:

> The justification for a university is that it preserves the connection between knowledge and the zest for life, by uniting the young and the old in the imaginative consideration of learning. ... This atmosphere of excitement, arising from imaginative consideration, transforms knowledge. A fact is no longer a bare fact: it is invested with all its possibilities. It is no longer a burden on the memory: it is energising as the poet of our dreams, and as the architect of our purposes. [Imagination] enables men [sic] to construct an intellectual vision of a new world, and it preserves the zest for life by the suggestion of satisfying purposes. ... Fools act on imagination without knowledge; pedants act on knowledge without imagination. The task of a university is to weld together imagination and experience. (p. 93)

I know that in today's universities many will snort with derision at such an image, yet still, as teachers, we long for students' passionate engagement with subject matter, even if it seems beyond reach. Part of the problem is the intrinsic difficulty of abstract and analytic thought. Diana Laurillard (2002) clarifies how academic knowledge deals with both first-order knowledge (direct experience of the world) and second-order knowledge ('our experience of our experience of the world' [p. 2] or knowledge which is abstracted from everyday experience). It is the latter that causes problems because it *is* difficult to consider matters that are disembedded from experience. But not out of reach for anyone. *Children's Minds* (1978) is a seminal work in which the author, psychologist Margaret Donaldson, challenges the acceptance, on the grounds of a spurious 'ability', that so few people acquire 'a taste for the intellectual side of life' (p. 82). She critiques and builds on Piaget's work to demonstrate that even small children are capable of disembedding thought from everyday activity. But she shows how abstraction, which is so highly valued by society, is difficult both to teach and to learn.

In late modernity, the capacity to grasp and generate second-order knowledge amounts to being 'included' for it is a source of power and emancipation. According to Dewey, the emancipation of an idea from its immediate context is a representation of the emancipation of the individual and society: '[freedom] designates a mental attitude' (1916, p. 305). Donaldson makes the same point from the perspective of a psychologist: 'in order to handle the world with maximum competence it is necessary to consider the *structure* of things. It is necessary to become skilled in manipulating *systems* and in abstracting forms and patterns' (1978, p. 82).

My conclusion here is that a just and inclusive university pedagogy should attempt to articulate principles which apply to all students and which are likely to engage them academically and promote intellectual growth, specifically the capacity for difficult abstract thought. This assertion will justifiably draw accusations of elitism and naivety for it appears to contain the beginning of a 'grand narrative' based on old ideas about reason and truth. In defence, I refer the reader to the quotation from Readings (1996) at the beginning of this chapter that asserts that 'the scene of teaching' is always in need of 'further study'. His chapter 'The scene of teaching' in *The University in Ruins* (1996) argues that we cannot make large claims for training 'a certain kind of student subject: critical, well-rounded, or empowered' (p. 151), we can only attempt to 'rephrase teaching and learning as *sites of obligation*, as loci of *ethical practices*, rather than as means for transmission' (p. 154, emphasis in text). Following Readings, I am interested in a just pedagogy yet want to emphasize the tentativeness and also the modesty of any claims that I make: there are no guarantees and pedagogy can only attempt to open dialogical spaces for what Readings (1996) calls 'Thought'.

University education for contemporary social problems

There is a consensus that the world has changed and that we are living in an uncertain and risky society.[10] Globally there are complex, serious and threatening problems to address: millions of people around the world do not have enough to eat and are deprived of basic health care and education; evidence that our lifestyle is doing irreparable damage to the natural environment becomes almost daily more convincing; many people live under repressive regimes; and, conflicts worldwide appear to become more entrenched, including the 'war of terror' instigated by the USA and taken up by the UK. In such a society Ainley (1994) claims that survival must now supersede any form of utopianism and others describe the state of affairs as 'supercomplex' (Barnett, 2000; Wheeler, 2005). What do supercomplex problems of survival imply about university pedagogy? It does not seem enough in a complex and risky world to educate only to increase the wealth of nation states and the prosperity of individuals. So what knowledge, understanding and attributes will assist students to live with others in such a world? For this discussion we need to return to the epistemological shifts that Delanty (2001) identified.

Delanty 'leans heavily' on the distinction between 'knowledge as science' and 'knowledge as a mode of social organization' because it allows a 'theorization of the university as a mediatory site between these two levels of knowledge' (p. 19). According to his theory of 'cognitive shifts' when knowledge as a mode of social organization changes, cultural models and institutions are transformed. Cognitive shifts can explain historic crises:

Enlightenment revolutionary, emancipatory and humanist knowledge was challenged by nineteenth-century reform, historicism and positivism; which in turn was challenged by the rejection of truth, autonomy and rationality at the end of WWI. In organized modernity the mode of knowledge became 'specialization, within disciplinary boundaries administered by experts and which was part of wider processes of societal modernization' (ibid. p. 20). Now in late modernity we are in the throes of a crisis in which 'The cultural model of integration has been challenged by new forms of exclusion and fragmentation; the mode of knowledge, the self-legitimation of expertise, has been challenged by the universal risk society (ibid. p. 21). This crisis has precipitated four specific changes in the 'mode of knowledge': knowledge is produced by sources other than the university; we need knowledge more than ever for economic production, political regulation and everyday life; knowledge is more publicly available – the boundaries between lay and expert knowledge are becoming blurred; and, there is growing contestability of knowledge claims.

Universities in the risk society need to consider the implications for pedagogy of the current mode of knowledge, even if, as Barnett (2000) puts it, 'there is no end to [the] proliferation of definitions of knowledge' (p. 36). There is a pessimistic and prevalent view that discourses emanate from power and produce knowledge which traps subjects in systems, the only escape from which is a struggle for supremacy. Delanty (2001) takes an optimistic stance (in keeping with Habermas). Knowledge 'is neither a tool of domination, an ideology, nor a neutral category but is embedded in contemporary cultural models and in much institutional framework' (p. 21). Moreover, the current mode of knowledge denotes 'a movement towards social reflexivity and discursivity which comes with the opening up of new public spheres and the empowering of social actors' (ibid.). From Delanty's point of view, universities can take up the options presented by engaging with four types of knowledge: research, education, professional education, and intellectual inquiry and critique. These are identical to Habermas's 'bundle of functions' of the university which refer to a full range of technological and cultural interests: accumulation of information; human experience/formation of personality/Bildung; accreditation and vocational training; and public issues/intellectualization of society. So my first point is that universities can make a contribution, through their students, to problems in society if their education is not over-specialized, for the next generation will be able to handle complexity and risk only if they are reasonable in three worlds: objective, intersubjective and subjective.

I want to bring this discussion back to pedagogy by drawing on the idea that the university produces knowledge of use to society. For this I employ the term mentioned previously, 'really useful knowledge', which was coined by nineteenth-century workers' movements because, at the time, it encompassed different interpretations of knowledge that I think I can apply to critical university pedagogy. 'Useful knowledge' serves as shorthand to denote three ideas about knowledge: knowledge which transforms and uplifts the individual; knowledge for the improvement of occupational skill; and, questioning about what type of knowledge counts as genuinely 'useful'.[11] Delanty (2001) asserts that 'knowledge is increasingly being tailored to a use rather than being an end in itself' (p. 108). But we do not have to defend the idea of 'knowledge for its own sake' if we construct university learning as fulfilling functions for society *because* it self-consciously produces in future citizens a lifeworld of identity formation, socialization and culture that is empowered to negotiate and act in the direction of solving social problems in the contemporary world. The new 'utility' of a critical university education would take into account the interests of living with others in the world and social justice, as well as interest in knowledge which produces goods and services.

In terms of the content of a university education for tackling moral–political liabilities, unlike some who write about critical pedagogy, I do not propose particular 'radical' knowledge nor that students should necessarily reflect on their own socio-political circumstances. Instead, I take on Bill Readings' cynical point that in the techno-bureaucratic university 'radicalism sells well in the market place' (1996, p. 163). Hope lies in the development of minds that are in tune with cognitive shifts in society and capable of tackling contemporary urgencies. In this respect, the work of Gibbons *et al.* (1994) has been influential: they argue that transdisciplinary, heterogeneous, fluid knowledge which is generated in contexts of application and is socially accountable and reflexive (Mode 2 knowledge) is taking over from disciplinary, transcendent, self-referential, homogeneous, hierarchical knowledge which is governed by a small group of scientists, generally academics (Mode 1 knowledge). I think the trend is exaggerated and that what is perhaps more accurate, as Barnett (1994) identifies, is that knowledges are 'intermingling'. From the point of view of critical pedagogy the key issue is what is the purpose of knowledge: Delanty (2001) makes the case for the democratization of knowledge whereby more and more social actors are involved in the definitions of problems and the application of solutions. But such democratization can only be achieved through public reflexivity, above all we need citizens who can reason.

Unfortunately, though, the potential for rational thought bequeathed by modernity ideals is often squandered. The British author and journalist Francis Wheen has written a popular book, *How Mumbo-Jumbo Conquered the World: A Short History of Modern Delusions* (2004), which rails against the many manifestations of unreason in contemporary society. He claims that reason is on the retreat both as an ideal (for he identifies a reluctance to defend it) and as a reality (for which he gives ample evidence in his book). The result is disastrous:

> The sleep of reason brings forth monsters, and the past two decades have produced monsters galore. Some are manifestly sinister, others seem merely comical – harmless fun, as Nancy Reagan said of her husband's reliance on astrology. Cumulatively, however, the proliferation of obscurantist bunkum and the assault on reason are a menace to civilisation, especially as many of the new irrationalists hark back to some imagined pre-industrial or even pre-agrarian Golden Age. (p. 7)

The 'new irrationalists' come in many guises: 'holy warriors, anti-scientific relativists, economic fundamentalists and radical post-modernists' (p. 311) and Wheen elaborates on the irrationality of them all. He pleads for the re-establishment of the values of the Enlightenment before these groups 'consign us to a life in darkness' (p. 312). Wheen (2004) is not the only person to raise the alarm about the rise in society of 'mumbo-jumbo' as a substitute for knowledge: Critchley (2001), discussing the marginalization of philosophy in contemporary society, remarks on the enormous number of books in bookshops on 'new age' ideas and other alternative lifestyle issues and describes them as evidence of 'obscurantism'.

What attracts people to unreason? Perhaps it is because knowledge is losing its ability to provide a sense of direction for society[12] or perhaps people reject what is commonly understood as 'knowledge' based on reason because as scientism it ignores lifeworld interests in understanding the meaning of life and in ethical matters. Critchley argues that human beings need a 'third way' between scientism and obscurantism: 'The universe expresses no human purpose, it is simply governed by physical laws that we can do our best to ascertain, but which are indifferent to human striving. The universe is vast, cold, inhuman, and mechanical' (2001, p. 8). People become anxious because there is an 'experiential gap between the realms of knowledge and wisdom, truth and meaning, theory and practice, causal explanation and existential understanding' (ibid.). We need knowledge that builds bridges across these gaps. We also need to revive reason so that we can discern which knowledge is true, moral and humane; knowledge is not entirely contestable (even if we must be very cautious) for some knowledge is more likely to help us address problems in the risk society. Critical university pedagogy will therefore attempt to engage students' minds in connecting academic knowledge to culture and society. This would be 'useful'.

Realizing social goals in everyday teaching interactions

My discussion so far in this chapter has focused on broad educational goals achieved through the intellectual development of students, but there are also implications for process. If we accept that knowledge is diffuse and contested and also that knowledge needs to be evaluated for its applicability to problems in society and culture, then, in Ulrich Beck's words, 'traditional "lecturing societies" [should be replaced] with dialogic attentiveness and the courage to disagree' (2000, p. 138). Understanding pedagogy as a dialogic process is key to my concept of critical pedagogy. In part this is to accept that it is 'communicatively structured' and that there is no escape from the need for dialogue or conversations. But it also involves an appreciation of how very messy and uncertain such pedagogy is, which brings me back to the realities of everyday teaching, what Readings (1996) called the 'pragmatic scene of teaching' (p. 153). By way of illustration, I quote from Felicity Rosslyn's (2004) first-hand account of teaching university English. In keeping with my theme, she wants to 'cleave to the actual' to avoid 'vague formulations of the kind forced on us by our managers'. Her question is 'What *does* happen in a seminar?' (p. 3) She describes what happens as a first-year one-hour seminar progresses: her thoughts, who speaks when and what about and so on. She then evaluates the seminar, first drawing attention to its departure from the goals set out in the course handbook:

> The words that spring to mind for the academic content of a seminar like this are not 'rigorous and critical'. The most that can be said is that students have been encouraged to think generically – they have heard me assume that Shakespeare's comedies resemble one another, and that the characters in the plays are not just themselves, but representatives of something else in suggestive patterns. Compared with the way they were encouraged to work at school, however, this is a leap forward, and it would be unwise of me to try to move much faster. It might be easier to make a claim for this hour in terms of its therapeutic content, its contribution to the students' general well-being as young people in an anxiety-provoking new environment. At the most basic level it has been a display of trust. A few students have trusted one another, and trusted me, enough to say things they genuinely mean. The ones who did not manage to speak have perhaps felt encouraged enough to speak next time: we are now engaged in a joint activity (except, of course, for those who did not attend and will somehow have to be engaged next time). At a more complex level, some of the students now have words for things they might not have named themselves, and a sense of permission to think about them – ambivalence in love, the proximity of love and hate, the combination of the ideal and the real in physical passion. They have also just experienced the value of peer-group learning: the girl who is at home with ideas of humiliation and bestiality has raised the whole level of discussion,

and if they can contain their envy (which may be disguised as disapproval) they have the chance of acquiring a similar level of abstraction. (p. 4)

It is not my intention to comment on Rosslyn's approach, but simply to draw attention to how much is going on that cannot be captured by the technical-rational discourse of 'learning outcomes' and 'skills'. Bill Readings (1996) argues that teaching is dialogic: the student is an 'addressee' whose 'head is full of language ... all his experiences encoded in inner speech' (p. 155) so she or he is not 'a mute, wordless creature' (*ibid.*) receiving messages from the sender teacher. He describes a state of affairs in which no one has much control and in which the great difficulty of 'coming to agreements' is revealed:

Understanding and misunderstanding, as it were, are entwined as the conditions of linguistic interaction. Communication cannot be the transfer of a prefabricated meaning, since the meaning of words does not remain the same from one utterance – or more precisely idiolect – to the next. What a sender says takes its place amid a crowd of idiolects in the listener, and their conversation acquires its sense in a discursive act of which neither is master. (p. 156)

Rosslyn (2004), the university teacher, knows all about this, but is, nevertheless, hopeful:

In the course of any hour's discussion value-systems clash, taboos surface and lose their compelling secrecy, bewildering states of mind are canvassed, and 'foreignness' is discovered to be not unfamiliar. For each student the memorable content of each seminar is likely to be quite different – but the overall effect may still be the same, the discovery that the world is much bigger and more various than they ever supposed it was. (p. 4)

What we see happening in Rosslyn's seminar room is what the Russian linguist V. N. Volosinov describes as 'the *strife*, the *chaos*, the *adversity* of ... psychical life' (quoted in Morris, 1994, p. 39, italics in text) and I believe that this plays out at the 'scene of teaching' in all universities. Teaching requires a special kind of 'alertness to otherness' (Readings, 1996, p. 162) on the part of both students and teachers, even if the obligation on teachers is heavier than on students. Such attentiveness cannot be fostered by technical-rational means.

Conclusion

Whatever the intentions of 'quality watchdogs', the essential nature of university education shapes pedagogic work as social and cultural action.

Whatever the contested ideas about what constitutes a good university teacher, teaching is intellectually and emotionally complex and demanding. It involves finely honed judgements about content; about the process of giving students access to content; and, about relationships in and out of seminar and lecture rooms. University teachers are inevitably embroiled in the cognitive, social and emotional development of their students. The climate of mutual obligation in classrooms and institutions affects the capacity to learn. There are many constraints: teaching requires creative responses to multiple demands in a turbulent higher education environment.

All the same, when pedagogic processes are denuded of substance and value, they become dreary and demotivating for teacher and student alike. The bleak official discourse about 'good' or 'excellent' university teaching presents it as banal, simple, technical, self-evident, value-free and apolitical: for example, we read the oxymorons that university teachers are required to 'demonstrate' that they 'think critically' or that they are 'ethical' in relation to 'capability statements' or 'standards'.[13] It is also a travesty of the task in hand. A whole vocabulary is missing which relates in everyday language to the real business of teaching students; and which allows 'further study' about what is right and wrong at the 'scene of teaching'.

It is true, as Readings (1996) argues, that in the new 'corporate' university difficult questions of value and justice are put aside because 'what gets taught ... matters less than the fact that it be excellently taught' (p. 13). As a communicatively structured area of the lifeworld, the education of university students is being colonized inappropriately by technical-rational considerations. But the very nature of pedagogic work militates against a smooth completion of a project to instrumentalize completely university pedagogy.

Notes

1 I have found the question of art and aesthetic experience problematic in respect of the 'three interests'. Bernstein (1985) suggests that Habermas appears to 'have slighted the complex issues' involved in this area (p. 28). However Habermas (1985) replies to his critics: 'If aesthetic experience is incorporated into the context of individual life-histories, if it is utilized to illuminate a situation and to throw light on individual life-problems – if it at all communicates its impulses to a collective form of life – then art enters into a language game which ... belongs to everyday communicative practice' (p. 202).

2 The Labour government in the UK has recently ignored proposals for an overarching diploma for 16-year-olds which addressed the 'academic/vocational divide'; instead there will be specialized vocational diplomas ('Diplomas fail to heal 14–19 split' and 'Did A-level reforms fall victim to election fever?', *The Times Higher*, 25 February 2005 p. 2 and p. 14).

3 From a UK government White Paper *The Future of Higher Education* (DfES, 2003).

4 Jan Parker (2002) develops these ideas.

5 Woodward, W., 'Top universities still failing working class', the *Guardian*, 18 December 2002, p. 8

6 *The Times Higher* conducted (19 November 2004) a poll among academics and reported that 84% 'agreed' and 50% 'strongly agreed' that 'The squeeze on resources is having an adverse effect on academic standards.' The next week (26 November 2004) Angela Morgan from the University of Teesside (a 'new' university) wrote to point out that 'the poll may (or may not) represent the views of a small minority of academics who are responding to a set of biased questions. The article's value is limited to the provision of a useful lesson to my undergraduate students in how not to report survey findings.'

7 For example, Utley, A., 'Those "Mickey Mouse" degrees are having the last laugh', *The Times Higher*, 15 November 2002, pp. 6–7; Brockes, E., 'Taking the Mick', the *Guardian* 15 January 2003; and, Tysome, T., 'Do they deserve to be degrees?'' *The Times Higher*, 23 January 2003, pp. 8–9.

8 The Higher Education Academy website: www.hea.ac.uk.

9 Paul Ashwin uses the term 'academic engagement' (Ashwin and McLean, 2005).

10 See Ulrich Beck's *Risk Society* (1992).

11 In the 1830s all these interpretations of 'useful knowledge' were not made by all interested groups committed to the idea. Vincent (1981), analysing working-class autobiographies, demonstrates that for working-class self-educators 'useful' 'amounted to a secularised conversion experience' (p. 136). It did not coincide with the interpretation made by middle-class educators (specifically, The Society for the Diffusion of Useful Knowledge (SDUK) who promoted the idea of 'useful' as generating and having knowledge which applied to the mechanical trades. There was also a disparity about what constituted 'useless' knowledge – implied by the term 'useful': the SDUK was inclined to doubt the worth of imaginative works; while the working-class readership – keen to delight its spirit – was more eclectic. For both groups, though, the pursuit of knowledge was linked to emancipation of the working classes.

12 A point made by Gerald Delanty (2001).

13 'Proposals for national professional standards for supporting learning in Higher Education' www.hea.ac.uk.

6

Student experience as the development of communicative reason

I want to suggest that the crucial feature we need to take into account is the subjective experience of the educand – his or her activity and its effects on consciousness; and this in the large historical sense. (Brian Simon, 2005, 'Can education change society?' p. 148)

... the value of enquiry, the ferment of doubt, a willingness to dialogue, a spirit of criticism, moderation of judgement, philological scruples, and a sense of the complexity of things (Terry Eagleton, 2001, *London Review of Books*)

Introduction

The last two chapters have examined the obstacles to achieving critical university pedagogy. I now turn to discuss grounds for hope even if we live in 'dark times'.[1] I build on the notion of developing minds to discuss the ends and means of students' learning and to consider what kind of approach to generating general pedagogic theory might be congruent with educational goals suggested by critical theory. For Habermas, all grounds for hope in society today reside in the mobilization of the human capacity for communicative reason, which is 'self-consciousness, self-determination, and self-realization' for individuals and collectives (Habermas, 1985, p. 338). My task is to translate this apparently simple, though abstract claim made at the 'macro' level into theoretically informed practice that is feasible at the 'meso' level of institutions and at the 'micro' level of everyday pedagogy.

Expressed as simply as possible, my main argument is that there is no *direct* educational route to achieving the goals of critical theory in contemporary society. I believe that our hope for educating people with the capacities to tackle today's 'urgencies of society' lies in insisting with Dewey (1916) that to educate is to develop minds towards the dispositions Eagleton identifies in the quotation above. Furthermore, for my purposes, developing mind or intellect or the capacity for thinking beyond everyday concerns is synonymous with mobilizing communicative reason. Three quotations taken together draw attention to the main characteristics of communicative reason.

First, Robin Barrow uses Dewey's expression 'mind' to emphasize the idea of education for intellectual capability being a form of enculturization into the history of rational thought:

> To be educated is, as far as we know, a peculiarly human possibility. It is to have a developed mind, which means a mind that has developed understanding such that it can discriminate between logically different kinds of questions and exercise judgement, critically and creatively, in respect of important matters. . . . It has everything to do with entering the world of understanding traditions of thought we humans have so far achieved. (1999, p. 139)

Secondly, Dewey himself draws attention to the capacity to use one's mind to shape the future:

> To foresee a terminus of an act is to have a basis upon which to observe, to select, and to order objects and our own capacities. To do these things means to have a mind – for mind is precisely intentional purposeful activity controlled by perception of facts and their relationship to one another. To have a mind to do a thing is to foresee a future possibility. (1916, p. 103)

Finally, Victor Soucek defines a communicatively reasonable person as one whose motivation is improvements in society:

> [s/he] is characterised by an orientation towards the understanding of a given social problem rather than by orientation towards achieving technical success. (1994, p. 94)

The graduate who I envisage as being communicatively reasonable can, then, be summed up: an analytic, critical and imaginative thinker who is committed to working with others for the public good. This does not seem a wildly radical goal for university education, but it is far from the mission statements which refer only to the 'employability' of their students.

Certainly some version of communicative reason is necessary for students to be prepared to be agents in their own lives and in society as a whole. We can configure university education as assisting students in becoming more fully human: that is, university learning – whether or not it has 'critical' purposes – mobilizes the resources of the lifeworld (culture, society and identity) by developing epistemological, ontological and practical interests; or, put in other words, university education concerns developing knowledge, realizing a self or being, and acquiring skill and technique. I believe that the goal of communicative reason for university students (though it might be expressed differently) is recognizable to university teachers and desired by them. I think that this is because developing minds for communicative reason is intimately connected with historic 'ideas' of a university: the pursuit of knowledge and truth for the betterment of society; and, the critical and freedom-bestowing power of knowledge and reason. Most importantly, perhaps, is the 'idea' that university education prepares democratic citizens. Gerald Delanty (2001) reminds us that democracy consists of three central spheres: the rule of law, representation of social interests and the participation of the public in the polity, which is citizenship. Citizenship is about rights, duties, participation and identity and it can be oppositional. Delanty points out that 'Without citizenship, democracy is purely formalistic. Confined to the institution of parliament and the negotiation of social interests' (*ibid.* p. 47). He proposes that the contemporary cognitive shift makes it incumbent on universities to produce a 'new' type of citizen who is both cultural and technological, for rights and the uses to which technology is put are now closely connected. I am interested in the 'critical' aspect of being a citizen.

In constructing ideas about university pedagogy we must constantly guard against technical solutions. I believe that the route to achieving the goal of communicative reason is to generate general pedagogic principles which aim to develop unity between the three human interests in control over the external world, in communication and in social transformation. 'Drawing out'[2] dispositions of mind and character requires attending to the realities of the lived experience of university students and teachers and attempting to understand what is possible by making use of the cultural and theoretical resources that are available.

Habermas's theory of communicative action

Hope for a possibly more-critical university pedagogy in the future lies in Habermas's theory of communicative action. The theory must be understood in the context of the two trends in modernization: on the one hand, the economic and political system is steered by money and power, which leads to colonization of the lifeworld; on the other, there is the trend towards communicative action the potential for which has been released by the 'unthawing' of the pre-modern elements of the lifeworld by the critical consciousness of the Enlightenment (Habermas, 1985). Given this potential, Habermas wants to retrieve the, as yet, 'unredeemed promise [of] self-conscious practice' (*ibid.* pp. 337–8) to work towards the common good. The invasion of capitalist economic imperatives militates against communicative action, but simultaneously rouses subjects to defend it. Contradiction and antagonism in society are caused by a collision between technical or purposive rationality systems, mediated by money and power, and the lifeworld (culture, society and identity) which resists, releasing new capacities for rational action (that is, communicative reason). Language is the key to Habermas's hopeful ideas about the future.

For Habermas there is a universal human capacity for making and communicating meaning in 'speech acts'[3] with the *telos* of cognitive interests in control of the external world, coming to agreements with others and emancipation. Yet, language capacity and interests would be worthless unless human agency is accepted as a challenge to deterministic accounts of human activity. How (2003) puts the position of critical theory succinctly: if we accept that human subjects are not wholly determined by the discursive conditions in which they find themselves, we can talk meaningfully about 'enabling conditions which either enhance or distort human potential' (p. 152). We can apply this to university pedagogy by allowing Habermas to guide our thinking about the process of coming to agreements about conditions which might enhance or distort students' potential for developing their minds and becoming communicatively reasonable.

Habermas observes that 'Participants in communication ... by no means refer only to things that happen or could happen or could be made to happen in the objective world, but to things in the social and subjective worlds as well' (quoted in Outhwaite, 1996, p. 84). He means that those acting communicatively with the intention of reaching understanding with another or others make three claims: that they are communicating a true proposition about the objective world; that they are sincere in their claims, which relates to the subjective world; and that they intend to express something justifiable, which relates to the social world. These 'validity claims' give us a framework for making judgements about how far we might be from ideal speech conditions in which exchanges are comprehensible, true, sincere and just:

> We can examine every utterance to see whether it is true or untrue, justified or unjustified, truthful or untruthful, because in speech no matter what the emphasis, grammatical sentences are embedded in relations to reality in such a way that in an acceptable speech action segments of external nature, society and internal nature always come into appearance together. (quoted in Outhwaite, 1996, p. 129)[4]

Pedagogic endeavour is always communicatively structured. Myriad, incessant, utterances about the ends and means of university education take place all the time: explicitly and implicitly, formally and informally; students communicate with teachers, teachers with students, managers with teachers, teachers with managers, teachers with policy makers and so on, endlessly. There are attempts to understand and to come to agreements, but we also witness obfuscation, deliberate lying and subterfuge. As Habermas points out 'Typical states are ... incomprehension and misunderstanding, intentional and involuntary untruthfulness, concealed and open discord' (quoted in Outhwaite, 1996, p. 120)[5] which evokes the chaotic, dialogical nature of pedagogy (Readings, 1996). Nevertheless, language carries a universal human potential which is the basis for grounds for hope which justifies attempts to make judgements about whether 'speech acts' are true, sincere and just; and, also to think about what conditions are more likely to allow true, sincere and just utterances. I realize that this assertion appears to be far removed from actual pedagogic practices; in the rest of the chapter I will attempt to draw theory and practice closer together.

Communication and university pedagogy

'Speech acts' (including texts and non-verbal communication) make up university students' educational experience but this is not precise enough for my purposes. Alvin Gouldner's *The Future of Intellectuals and the Rise of the New Class* (1979) introduces the concept of the 'culture of critical discourse' which is a discourse that has evolved in modernity. The main modes of the discourse are argumentation and justification. Speakers within the culture of critical discourse, on principle, agree to keep everything open for discussion. The distinctive features of the discourse are it is relatively context-independent, it values explicit utterances, and it allows theory-making and reflexivity. The culture of critical discourse cannot justify claims based on the basis of the speaker's position in society. The connection to Habermas can be seen in Gouldner's assertion that the culture of critical discourse 'is the grounding for a critique of established forms of domination and provides an escape from tradition' (p. 85). This discourse, according to Gouldner, is the common bond of a 'new class' of intellectuals. I shall return to discuss the notion of intellectuals in the next chapter, but for now I want to establish that the development of university students' minds towards communicative reason requires them to learn to communicate within the culture of critical discourse. I also want to sound Gouldner's warning that as well as potential for freedom, the culture of critical discourse 'bears the seeds of a new domination. Its discourse is a lumbering machinery of argumentation that can wither imagination, discourage play, and curb expressivity' (p. 85).

There is one digression about communication and education that I think is worth taking. Denis Hayes (2003) makes Habermas's theory of communicative action responsible for a 'therapeutic turn' in pedagogy that manifests itself in a preoccupation with the notion of self-esteem, particularly of students from poorer backgrounds. While I hope I have demonstrated that it is far-fetched to accuse Habermas of any form of low expectations, there *is* evidence of an 'it's good to talk' pedagogy which has its roots in a justifiable concern for the fate of individuals, but is, in fact, limiting and oppressive (Cameron, 2000; Ecclestone, 2004). It has some connections with critical, radical and feminist pedagogies, yet constructs the student subject as weak, vulnerable and incapable of agency. By way of illustration, a young lecturer in his first full-time post judged that most of his first years' first essays were so poor that the students would benefit by re-writing them in the light of his feedback: the second essays were dramatically improved. When colleagues heard of his action, he was castigated for upsetting first-year students (there was also, of course, anxiety about extra work if all students came to expect their essays to be marked twice). Misplaced sympathy for nervous first-year students deprives them of an opportunity to tackle their difficulties and become competent thinkers and writers in their disciplines, which are expressions of the culture of critical discourse. My understanding of mobilizing communicative reason is distant from the unreflective idea that 'it is good to talk'. It is also far from an interpretation of 'coming to agreements' that is about always seeking consensus. With Readings (1996), I think that in present conditions hope for universities probably lies in 'a second-order consensus that dissensus is a good thing, something, indeed, with which Habermas would be in accord' (p. 167).

When I say that communication structures what is university pedagogy, I am referring to all forms of communication in many locations: in the teaching room; but also in meetings; in institutional and national documentation; in press releases and so on. As I illustrated in the last chapter, even at the level of the teaching room communication is dialogic and polyphonic (Volsinov, 1973). So trying to hear all the speech acts about university pedagogy can take the form of a multi-voiced cacophony in which powerful voices are louder and in which it is difficult to know what to believe and act on. If communicative reason means developing the capacity to make judgements and act reasonably, I see a parallel between university teachers developing communicative reason about pedagogic matters and students developing communicative reason in relation to subjects, disciplines or professional fields.

Whatever the caveats, the role of language cannot be over-estimated: as Diana Laurillard (2002) puts it, university learning and teaching allows 'no escape from the need for dialogue' (p. 71). However, communication is not straightforward in today's conditions. If we take the example of students learning from talking to each other (quite an acceptable pedagogic idea these days), we can draw on an older idea of Cardinal John Newman that 'conversation' is the heart of university communities: ' [the students] are sure to learn from one another, even if there be no one to teach them; the conversation of all is a series of lectures to each, and they gain from themselves for themselves new ideas and views, fresh matter of thought, and distinct principles for judging and acting, day by day' (1960, p. 110). Is this vision completely lost today at undergraduate level? If not, would it be so difficult to arrange? It often seems as if students' living arrangements rather than their discipline departments dictate their social relationships. Discussion about the focus of study does take place inside teaching rooms in tutorials, seminars and group work arrangements, but it is not clear to me how far this is taken up outside teaching rooms in the spirit described by Newman.

I have been trying to stress that the communications of a critical pedagogy must keep questions open. I think this can happen in two ways. The first evokes ideal speech conditions: in principle, the more honest, trusting and open the dialogue, that is, the less it is distorted by power and interests, the more transforming the effects of learning. The second concerns the role of language in learning. In educational settings language is a tool for exploring ideas and thinking aloud with others, which is illustrated by the work of many educationalists. The use of language allows knowledge and thought processes to be available for reflection and revision, so learners can both receive knowledge and re-make it for themselves. Nevertheless, Jerome Bruner worried about the importance of accumulated knowledge being underestimated and warns against 'overestimating the importance of social exchange in constructing knowledge' (1999, p. 15). He proposes that students 'talk' with bodies of knowledge as long as 'the encounter is not worship but discourse and interpretation' (p. 17).

Having established the pivotal role of communication in pedagogy, I turn now to the notion of the 'student experience' as a prelude to discussing what kind of pedagogic theory might guide us in judging pedagogic communications at all levels.

The 'student experience' of university pedagogy

It has become commonplace for educationalists specializing in higher education (often called 'education developers') to exhort teachers to be 'student-focused' or 'student-centred' which, broadly speaking, means understanding pedagogic matters from the students' point of view. Building on this, in the UK the term 'student experience' has become a slogan used to convey the espousal of good practice. The professional body for higher education teaching, the Higher Education Academy (HEA), asserts that it will become, in the UK and abroad, 'the first choice of the sector for knowledge, practice and policy related to the student experience in higher education'.[6] The question 'What do we mean by the student experience?' is answered like this:

> Learning and teaching will always be at the heart of the student experience. But it is important to recognise that today's students engage with the institutions in which they study in a way that is different from the past. Higher education is but one part of their lives as workers, carers and citizens of the world. Efforts to improve the student experience therefore need to embrace a wider view of the whole learning environment – research and scholarship, administrative support, ICT, libraries, student services and facilities – as well as teaching and learning.[7]

Policy statements such as these can be understood as speech acts in need of interpretation and in need of exploration about the extent to which they are true, sincere and just. As it is presented, the notion of the student experience is, to follow Readings (1996), meaningless (like 'excellence' and 'transferable skills'). The student experience, proclaims the HEA, must be 'the best possible on-campus and off-campus educational experience'[8] but we are given no clues as to what 'best' might comprise. From the point of view of my argument about critical pedagogy, this situation is both constraining in that it proposes a discourse which focuses away from education as the development of minds (in fact, in this case it appears to play down the principal role of cognitive development); but also offers opportunities to define and give meaning to the notion of the student experience.

While it is clearly not possible to give a definitive account of the current student experience a range of theoretical and empirical studies provide glimpses from which I select in order to discuss the type of experience which might contribute to the development of mind for communicative reason. One of the most important insights which should tax the minds of critically inclined university teachers is that academic culture is differentially experienced as engaging or alienating (Mann, 2001) and the extent to which students feel they 'belong' in university is often an effect of social stratification (Leathwood and O'Connell, 2003; Read *et al.* 2003). Costello (2001) provides an illustration with quotations from three students at the same Law School in the USA:

> 'Do I feel comfortable here at the law school? Sure. It's, well, a comfortable sort of place to be – I mean, I can grab a cappuccino at the café, and go right out into the courtyard and hang out with some friends – studying, yes, but also just talking, arguing, enjoying the sunshine.' – Grant (a straight white man of upper-middle-class origins)

> 'At first I used to feel weird walking around the halls, like I didn't belong. I couldn't really believe that I was here. Now I'm used to it, but sometimes I still kind of look around myself and think, "you really did it, girl" and it's sort of

weird but good.' – Cheryl (a straight African-American woman of lower-middle-class origins)

'I hate this place. Just walking into the building depresses me. I avoid hanging around this place, and try not to let it get to me.' – Wei (a gay Asian man of upper-middle-class origins) (p. 43)

The recondite ways in which institutions reproduce patterns of social stratification are explored in research which reveals the difficulties that some students more than others encounter in formal education settings because of the ways dominant discourses and power operate (Lea and Street 1998, Jones *et al.* 1999 and Margolis, 2001). But, as I pointed out earlier, we must be wary of pedagogic solutions that imply *some* groups of students are fragile and delicate and in need of special care. We know that students from *all* social backgrounds experience social and academic difficulties in the transition from school to university (Ballinger, 2003; Lowe and Cook, 2003) and that 'being and becoming a student' is hazardous even in elite universities (Barnett, 1996; Perry, 1999).

Reproduction in Education, Society and Culture by Pierre Bourdieu and Jean-Claude Passeron (2000) contains the influential proposition that education operates in its structure and processes to reproduce existing social categories. Brian Simon (2005), though, argues that education systems will change patterns of social mobility only very slowly and that even small changes can be counted significant. For him, the crucial feature is the experience of education and I believe that the experience of university learning is far more unpredictable and nuanced than structural accounts often allow for. The next quotation is by a mature student from a British inner-city polytechnic:

'There's one thing I must mention about higher education: once you've experienced it, it seems to open a lot of areas you've never thought about; it seems to show you that there are different ways of being satisfied in your life, because now I've thought to myself that whatever job I do I can enjoy, following my own interests and reading and doing other things. Once you've studied the world becomes a smaller place and you tend to look at people as more a single society. You begin to find common values between individuals. You can talk to anyone'. (Ainley, 1994, p. 75)

As a contrast, this is a student from a more prestigious university:

'It's probably made me more analytical. I'm able to sit back and analyse things. It also means that I've read virtually every book that any sort of fairly intelligent person is meant to have read. I've just read them all, I haven't enjoyed many of them.' (Thomas, 1990, pp. 96–7)

It seems to me that the former student has both had a more authentic experience of learning and been more aroused to act for good in the world, whereas the latter has experienced a degraded form of learning.

I do not deny that students whose social origins might have placed them further away from the culture of critical discourse than others will struggle more with academic learning; nor do I deny the struggle of their teachers who are likely to be teaching in universities with the least resources (Leathwood and O'Connell, 2003). For this reason, we should certainly protest against the worsening stratification of universities which takes place under the guise of 'diversification'. Nevertheless, we must avoid easy judgements and distinguish sharply between the potential of students; their current experience and conceptions of academic learning; and the conditions in which they are attempting to learn. University pedagogy informed by critical theory will always focus on potential. We cannot extrapolate from the type of university what is the student experience; teachers in all universities can ask the question of whether, and if so how, university education and pedagogic practices can contribute to the development of communicative reason.

A symptom of lack of belief in student potential is the despair that many university teachers express about their perception that students are becoming more instrumental: students are treating their degrees as means to ends rather than relishing learning for its own sake, as they used to; they are interested only in what marks they achieve towards a degree which they see only in terms of securing a job. If this is so, it is not surprising: commentators have pointed out that treating students as customers is likely to result in their treating their degrees as products (Morley, 2003; Naidoo, 2003). 'Golden ageism' is at work too: it is probable that to varying extents students have always been interested in their marks and in getting work after university[9] *as well as* in 'learning about what's happening in life.'[10]

While contemporary discursive policies and practices promote instrumentalism, there are some questions for university teachers. Do students know about their teachers' despair and if so how do they experience it? Are the effects of instrumentalizing policies and practices entirely out of the control of university teachers? Even within constraints are there options? Could adjustments be made to the curriculum of the science degree which challenge the ideas of the student who values it because: 'we're always going to make weapons of some kind, ships of some kind, boats, we're always going to drive some kind of vehicle, and we're always going to need hospital equipment'[11]? Is acquiescence necessary? Some university teachers have responded to current pressures by treating their disciplines as vehicles by which to acquire useful, employment-related skills (McLean and Barker, 2004). In an economized higher education most of us succumb to practices that we know encourage strategic approaches (for example, reduction of formative assessment, design of modules which do not make connections; 'condoning' of poor performance; fewer opportunities for discussion and so on). In these circumstances, students are being castigated for being instrumental when being offered an instrumental version of the curriculum.

By way of refuting students' reputation for pragmatism, there is evidence that students seek a transformative experience of learning. Jan Parker (2002) reports that in two institutions (in which, by quality assurance measures, pedagogic matters are going well) third-year students claim that their lecturers are 'not sure why they were teaching what they were teaching' (p. 376) and record disappointment at not having engaged more with the discipline (at the same time, their lecturers complain that students are 'dependent and lacking in motivation' (*ibid.*). Kym Thomas (1990), too, reports that in two degree courses in three universities she found that many students were disappointed that their degrees had not engaged them or made them more broad-minded. I believe that most university students want to be well taught and engaged in subject matter that gives them some purchase on life further than acquiring skills and getting a job.

A further aspect of this is what has been called 'teacher expectation'. During the 1970s in relation to school education, much was made of what was known as the 'self-fulfilling prophecy' which referred to a concept developed by Robert Rosenthal and Lenore Jacobsen (1968) which demonstrated that attainment was significantly improved when teachers expected improvement. Later Rosenthal and Jacobsen and other researchers who built on their work emphasized both the complex and subtle ways in which expectation is conveyed and the important role of changing the method of teaching if educational goals were not being met, that is high expectations alone are not enough (Child, 1981). While university teachers need to be convinced of the educability of their students, they must also have knowledge and understanding about giving students intellectual access to subject matter. University teachers already express loud 'no' positions towards student instrumentalism, it could be further resisted in quite practical ways that are educationally sound.

'Student experience' for critical ends

In thinking about the question of what kind of student experience for what kind of ends, I want return to Readings' (1996) idea of a dual obligation on students and teachers to tackle the difficulty of the 'scene of teaching'. Possibly the most important thing that I have to say about the experience of university pedagogy is that it should cause some trouble on both sides. This is to say that higher learning should be intellectually demanding for students; and that university teachers need the context and resources to be able to think about how to make difficult subjects accessible (rather than easier), in itself a difficult task. A pedagogic example of the difficulty of communication between students and teachers, as speakers and hearers is, I think, familiar to all teachers – it is, in other words, part of the pedagogic lifeworld. How do we know whether students are genuinely engaged in subject matter or simply aping what they think we want of them? This is central:

> Nearly every subject has a shadow or imitation. ... One can learn imitation history – kings and dates, but not the slightest idea of the motives behind it all; imitation literature – stacks of notes of Shakespeare's phrases, and a complete destruction of the power to enjoy Shakespeare. (W. W. A. Sawyer quoted in Ramsden, 2003, p. 39)

Imitation subjects are communicative distortions. Not to make this dual effort to think about 'real' subjects is an abrogation of the asymmetrical obligation that Readings (1996) advocates. But what kind of student experience might encourage students to pursue real subjects?

Assuming that students' potential for communicative reason resides in learning real subjects, the question can be phrased as 'What kind of student experience will develop minds and an appetite for thinking?' During the 1970s in Harvard, William Perry (1999) conducted a seminal, longitudinal study of the intellectual and ethical progression of undergraduate students. He found students progressing within nine positions from one in which all knowledge is right or wrong to one in which knowledge is understood as contingent, but in which, nevertheless, principled commitments are made. This development, according to Perry, requires courage on the part of students and teachers who support 'sustained groping, exploration, and synthesis' (p. 237). The question about student experience which Perry regards as the most pressing is this: 'What environmental sustenance most supports students in the choice to use their competence to orient themselves through Commitments – as opposed to using it to establish a nonresponsible alienation?' (p. 238). His answer is comparatively simple: an environment in which students experience 'the realization that in the very risks, separateness, and individuality of working out their Commitments, they were in the same boat not only with each other but with their instructors as well'[12] (p. 239). This answer yet again recalls Readings' (1996) point about the need for teachers' and students' 'mutual obligation' to engender 'Thought'; it also connects to currently popular ideas about universities and disciplines and interdisciplines as 'communities of practice' (Lave and Wenger 1991, Wenger, 1998). Most significantly for my argument, it reveals pedagogy as a 'communicatively structured' activity which relies on and ties together the human interests in intersubjectivity and transformation to create solidarity.

However, while Perry's study is inspiring, it might well be argued that whatever experiences he found students to have long ago in an elite university cannot be replicated in the wide range of contemporary universities. But his advice about pedagogic practice chimes with contemporary constructivist ideas as well as those from critical pedagogy which propounded that, put simply, we must not any more conceptualize learning as the *transmission* of knowledge into empty heads (Freire calls it 'banking'), by which teachers have merely to make the facts clear and correct students; but, rather as complex patterns of *interpretation* and 'making sense' actively undertaken by students.[13] Here Perry describes a situation which he has heard recounted by 'hundreds' of university teachers and which, I risk asserting, is familiar to all university teachers today:

> Typically [the teachers] enter their classrooms ... looking at the section meeting or tutorial as an opportunity for the students to develop initiative and scope in their own thinking. No sooner do the students get started, however, and some error or inexactness is voiced, than the older form of responsibilities imposes on the instructor the imperative of 'correcting'. In the hours where this tendency gets into motion, three to five corrections of this kind appear sufficient to defeat the students' initiative for search and the flow of their exploration. The initiative for conversation then falls back upon the instructor, who then finds himself in a monologue or lecture, with the sensation of being somehow trapped, compelled, by powerful forces, in himself and in the students, to do what he had never intended to do. (p. 237)

The scenario describes a distorted communication. Of course, as Perry himself points out, errors need to be corrected but the problem is timing and manner because what is most important is to 'encourage risking, groping, analytic detachment, and synthetic insight' (p. 238). The contemporary shift to accepting that knowledge and knowing are now inseparable – as suggested by Delanty's (2001) analysis of the cognitive shift to a knowledge society in which knowledge is 'up for grabs' – engages students in quite a different manner than when knowledge could be viewed as something passed down intact. This point is central to the pedagogy for critical purposes that I propose and it is about how engagement in real subjects has moral implications:

> The forms of knowing entwine with the forms of the known, and this involvement includes the forms of the knower's responsibility. The alienated student ... may imitate or parody the forms of other people's knowledge, but he [sic] is as sterile intellectually as he is socially. (Perry, 1999, p. 238)

My definition of the 'student experience' then is one which allows intellectual, ethical and social progression at the heart of which is communication with peers and teachers and results in communicative reason.

Generating pedagogic knowledge

For me, the search for general pedagogic principles is also a quest for a praxis – a theoretically and politically informed practice – which challenges technical-rational approaches to university education and addresses the problems of social justice and educating for a critical citizenry. The praxis I seek must also help university teachers in a wholly practical way to create environments in which students are exposed to experiences likely to develop their minds and their communicative reason. As I argued in the last chapter, I think that university teachers, individually and collectively, should seek some general pedagogic principles; at the same time, I accept (in fact, embrace) the enormous difficulties in coming to agreements about what these might be and at what level of generality. My position is precarious. So it is important to be as precise as possible about where I am positioned as regards knowledge claims about university pedagogy. Michael Young (2000) distinguishes three arguments that derive from the sociology of education and apply to the curriculum and pedagogy:

- The 'postmodernist' argument that there are only at best pragmatic grounds for distinguishing knowledge from experience; hence knowledge, in the sense that the word is normally used, is impossible.
- The 'voice discourse' argument that knowledge claims are always the political claims of dominant groups. The voice position follows from the postmodernist argument. It asserts the claims of experience and the equal validity of the perspectives of all groups, whether expert or not, on the grounds that claims for knowledge, to be in some objective sense independent of the social position of the knower, are untenable.
- The 'multi-dimensional' argument that the objectivity of truth claims always depends on their external validity – that they do explain something in a convincing way, on the support they invoke from a particular community of experts and on the legitimacy of the particular community involved. (p. 528)

I place myself with the third argument. Knowledge claims about pedagogy should do justice to teachers' teaching and students' learning and be seen to do so by these groups. I believe that if the first two arguments were adopted in policy and practice teachers and students would be let down because in the attempt to link theory and practice there is nowhere to go: as Young puts it, we are left with 'the white middle-class biases and prejudices of teachers or curriculum policy-makers, on the one hand, or what students want, a kind of consumerism, on the other' (*ibid.* p. 529). The 'multi-dimensional' argument carries grounds for hope: '[it] is concerned with how communities construct, challenge and modify knowledge, and how they are challenged from within and from without' (*ibid* p. 528).

How then is knowledge about university pedagogy to be generated? I think that the process can be construed as an expression of communicative reason aimed at communicative action. Knowledge and understanding about university teaching and learning inevitably draws on the lifeworld of university pedagogy as experienced by students and teachers which includes cultural ideas and values about the purposes and functions of university education, personal beliefs and assumptions about university learning, and, the actual day-by-day experience of teaching and of learning. Simultaneously, because this lifeworld is under threat – as outlined in previous chapters – it must be subjected to critical reflection in the light of theory so that practices and policies can be defended, challenged or justified. Pedagogy as an area of knowledge is particularly tricky, we must accept with Leach and Moon (1999) that 'it will be in a constant process of renewal, taking evidence and ideas from all available sources,[14] riven inevitably with controversy,' (p. 275). But I believe that the push should be towards a more intellectualized pedagogy which has purchase on actual, everyday practices in teaching rooms. This ambition is as difficult to achieve in today's conditions in universities as it was in schools during the early part of the twentieth century when Dewey wrote that instruction 'is plagued by a push for quick answers. This short circuits the necessary feeling of uncertainty and inhibits the search for alternative methods of solution .... ' (quoted in Leach and Moon, 1999 p. 275).

Stephen Rowland (2000) provides a model which demonstrates how knowledge about teaching is generated in three contexts (which he also calls 'resources for learning'): the 'personal context' of one's own experience; the 'shared context' of discussion with colleagues and students; and, the 'public context' of theories deriving from a range of disciplines. From my point of view, none of these resources for learning should be privileged: each is examined in the light of the other; and both tacit and codified knowledges are equally subject to critique. The aim is to evolve what Stephen Brookfield (1990) calls a 'critical rationale' (p. 15) which he describes as 'a set of values, beliefs and convictions about the essential forms and fundamental purposes of teaching' (*ibid.*) in which are embedded criteria for judging the quality of teaching. This is both an individual and a collective enterprise. As Young (2000) reminds us: 'it is a mistake to imagine [that] "theory" [is] best developed independently of the exigencies of policy and practice ... meanings are created in the public domain in the context of collective situations and activities' (p. 531). I draw on Young and Rowland in defining pedagogic knowledge as the 'shared procedures' of university teachers and pedagogic researchers (to whom I will return in Chapter 8). I accept too that the 'the process of embedding and giving meaning to knowledge is subtle and difficult' (*ibid.*) and that we should not make 'premature moves to theory' (p. 532). Nevertheless, there is an urgent need to go beyond both our own experience as university teachers and beyond narrow, technical rational definitions of 'evidence-based' practice.

Theoretical resources for general pedagogic principles

Some criteria for what would count as general pedagogic principles are proposed by educationalists. In the last chapter I discussed the argument found in Brian Simon's essay 'Why no pedagogy in England?' (1999) that entrenched elitism has been an obstacle to taking pedagogy seriously. In the same essay, he insists that effective pedagogy starts with drawing up general principles of teaching based on what students 'have in common as members of the human species' (p. 42). This is quite a different starting point from those who emphasize the differences between learners. It does not mean that specific individual needs are not considered, only that such considerations arise from understanding the similarities between learners. Jerome Bruner contributes specific criteria for a pedagogic theory: that the theory is 'correct' (and as he points out most theories are not 'flat wrong'); echoing Simon, that it is 'relevant' to all students, not just those who are highly motivated or alienated; that it is 'manageable' by which he means that it makes practical sense and does not obscure what needs to be done, and that it should relate 'to the urgencies of society' (1974, pp. 114–15). To these criteria I would like to add Simon's (1999) dictum that 'the process of learning [should relate to] the process of teaching' (p. 42). I am, then, seeking principles which are characterized by constructing teaching as socio-political action; offering university teachers a chance to base their practice on reasoned, universal precepts, rather than on the idiosyncrasies of the classroom; by an emphasis on human potential for abstract learning; by feeding as directly as possible into the teaching act; and by suggesting how the full range of attributes of a critical citizen should develop. This is not a straightforward task and what *I* present as manifestations of such principles are not by any means the only ones.

Although literature about university pedagogy is still slight compared with school, college and adult education, the array of theoretical resources from many disciplines is both bemusing and causes antagonism. This can be because underpinning beliefs about the nature of mind and learning are different and people have allegiances; and sometimes it is because career progression is invested in one approach or another (Young, 2000). In this section I discuss critically some theoretical resources which, if taken together, both fulfil the criteria set out above and are congruent with Habermas's abstract ideas about communicative reason. I must be cautious. First, space compels me to simplify which risks misrepresentation; secondly, as I have already mentioned, the selection is not intended to imply that there are no other general principles based on theories that would not also be convincing and useful;[15] thirdly, commitment to principles or theories *do* carry prescriptive implications, but these must be generated by university teachers themselves, tempered by the actualities of teaching.

I take the position that, while no one theory is the ultimate truth, all theories are not equal, some are more true and just than others, even if they must remain provisional. However, I take the view, too, that theories are often partial and that what John Stuart Mill had to say about philosophy also applies to pedagogic theory:

> It is not so much a matter of embracing falsehood for the truth, as of mistaking part of the truth for the whole. It might plausibly be maintained that in almost every one of the leading controversies, past or present ... both sides were in the right in what they affirmed, though wrong in what they denied; and that if either could have been made to take the other's view in addition to their own, little more would have been needed to make its doctrine correct. (quoted in Critchley, 2001, p. 47)

In general, then, I am interested in the possibilities of syntheses.[16] I bring together the following: theories which suggest that university education is a socio-cultural phenomenon; research about developing critical thinking; ideas about discipline-specific pedagogy; research which connects student perceptions of their learning environment with their learning outcomes; and, theories about identity formation and emotion. Again – to underscore the point – this attempt at synthesis should be taken as an experiment in seeking general principles of pedagogy which are in keeping with critical pedagogy.

Socio-cultural pedagogic theories

An obvious resource for exploring university pedagogy from the perspective I am interested in is the tradition of 'critical pedagogy' which encompasses a wide range of theoretical perspectives. The common features of radical or progressive pedagogies are critique of current conditions; a focus on transformation and emancipation; emphasis on the value-laden and political nature of education; and, interest in culture, identity and subjectivity.

The most celebrated writer on critical pedagogy is Paulo Freire (1996) whose work I introduced in the first chapter. He developed a pedagogic theory for use by teachers in literacy programmes in Brazil in the 1970s. At first sight, it is difficult to see how his methods are applicable to universities today[17] but his underpinning ideas are congruent with the aim of developing the minds of all for critical purposes. I draw attention to three. First, individual consciousness and the world stand in relation to each other and to be educated is to come to grapple with the relationship. Secondly, teachers are endowed with the central role of creating environments in which students are likely to engage in learning that is 'authentic'. A condition of this is that teachers identify with their students in order to bring about (in Jerome Bruner's (1999) succinct phrase) a 'meeting of minds'. Finally, education is about becoming more fully human by coming to see the world 'as a reality in process' (Freire 1996). Such learning occurs as the learner develops the capacity to discern and separate elements of a whole and to integrate the parts back into wholes; and, simultaneously, to be aware of the process of 'reinventing'. Freire (1996) conjures a wonderful vision which refers to the three human interests: 'Knowledge emerges only through invention and reinvention, through the impatient, continuing, hopeful inquiry human beings pursue in the world, with the world and each other' (p. 53). He is also quite clear about the role of communication: 'It is not our role [as educators] to speak to the people about our own view of the world, nor to attempt to impose that view on them, but rather to dialogue with the people about their view and ours. We must realize that their view of the world, manifested variously in their action, reflects their *situation* in the world' (p. 77).

Importantly, Paulo Freire's work establishes firmly that, from the perspective of critical theory, teaching is profoundly moral (or in Bill Readings' words 'teaching becomes answerable to *the question of justice* rather than to the criteria of truth' 1996, [p. 154]). Part of the question of justice is about teachers seeing themselves as having a role within the wider society, (especially for my purposes in relation to the purposes of higher education.) Another part is the weight of responsibility on teachers to assist students in the transaction between the inner and outer worlds. Although not 'critical', the philosopher of education, Richard Pring, draws attention to how the practice of 'scaffolding'[18] students' communicative reason incorporates the moral responsibility of integrating inner and outer:

Teaching, therefore, is more than a set of specific actions in which [students are helped] to learn this or that. It is an activity in which the teacher is sharing in a moral enterprise, namely, the initiation of [students] into a worthwhile way of seeing the world, of experiencing it, of relating to others in a more human and understanding way. In so doing, it is a transaction between the *impersonal* world of ideas embodied within particular texts and artefacts and the *personal* world of the [student] as he or she struggles to make sense, searches for value, engages in discovery, finds ideals worth striving for, encounters ideas. (2001, p. 112, emphasis in text)

Freire provides principles and inspiration for thinking about how to connect personal and impersonal, but some radical pedagogies fall into the two paths of critique identified by Young (2000) that either all knowledge is relative or it is an expression of 'the unjustified dominance of Western white, male knowledge and expertise' (p. 524). The final result of both claims is that: 'They deny, to the subordinate groups with which they claim to identify, the possibility of any knowledge that could be a resource for overcoming their subordination' (*ibid.*). Other versions of critical pedagogy offer an emancipatory rhetoric and theoretical insights, but can be obscure and abstract, and treat pedagogic practice cursorily or unrealistically (for example, Castells *et al.* 1999). The suggestions for practical enactments of theory which are offered can be summarized in three broad categories of action: demonstrating respect for students and their knowledge; using informal and participatory methods; and, making explicit the cultural values, beliefs and epistemological standpoints that frame academic expectations of students.[19] These principles of practice are helpful but insufficient because they do not connect teaching and learning closely enough. Examples of work that has more purchase on practice are Andy Northedge (2003a, 2003b) who uses a socio-cultural lens to analyse precisely how he assists students to participate in academic discourse in a social work course; and Sarah Mann (2001) who uses social theory to demonstrate that the central problem is whether students are engaged in or alienated from their studies.

Participation in an unfamiliar discourse and culture is the basis of what is known as the 'academic literacies' school of thought which, like Paulo Freire's work, stems from literacy programmes in a developing country. During the 1970s, Brian Street made an anthropological study of literacy programmes in rural Iranian villages which demonstrated that 'literacy events must ... be interpreted in relation to the larger sociocultural patterns which they exemplify or reflect' (1984, p. 125). Since then his ideas have been used to show how, similarly, students' writing at university is related to broader social and institutional imperatives (Lea and Street, 1998; Jones *et al.* 1999). An interest in the idea of university students being encultured into a community has led to educationalists drawing on the work of Jean Lave and Etienne Wenger (1991) which has resulted in the notion that learning at university is becoming a participating member of a 'community of practice' (Wenger, 1998). Leach and Moon (1999), for example, use the concepts 'setting' and 'arena' to think about the elements of a context in which learning takes place: 'An arena [is a] physically, economically, politically and socially organised space in time' (p. 267) while classrooms and institutions are settings. From their point of view, teachers determine the quality and nature of learning through creating and sustaining pedagogic settings in communities of practice that are arenas. Pedagogical settings need to take into account the complexities of academic learning in institutions: the prior knowledge of learners, how learning tasks might engender motivation; the effects of discourse, affective and cultural dimensions; and, particularly the inarticulate values that reproduce inequalities.

Developing critical thinking

Germane to the argument about the purposes of a critical university education are ideas drawn from the book *Higher Education: A Critical Business* (1997) in which Ronald Barnett proposes 'criticality' defined as: 'a human disposition of engagement where it is recognized that the object of attention could be other than it is' (p. 179). Contemporary society calls for this kind of critical capacity and it is universities' business to develop it. Barnett takes on Habermas's challenge that we need some large, universal ideas to counter the repressions, distortions and fragmentations of contemporary society: critical standards *could* have a transformatory effect by uniting us as critical citizens in a unified world. Barnett's 'criticality' encompasses 'forms', 'levels' and 'domains'. The forms are critical reason, critical self-reflection and critical action and can operate in the three domains of knowledge, self and the world. Forms and domains can in turn operate at four different levels: critical skills, reflexivity, refashioning of traditions and transformatory critique. These ideas are in harmony with the notion of universal cognitive interests, but, like Habermas, they do not connect to the 'micro' level of university pedagogy.

A research group at Southampton University in the UK is taking up Barnett's abstract ideas in an empirical study.[20] They seek to generate theory about the development of criticality which will inform practice and, though their work is not yet complete, they have formulated ideas about how to encourage students to progress from 'pre-criticality' through 'criticality in use' to 'criticality and world knowledge' (Johnston, 2005). They demonstrate how this progression relates to students' command of different types of knowledge (declarative, procedural and 'knowledge of what it is to be'); and also to personal qualities (robustness, confidence and a questioning attitude). They suggest concrete 'vehicles for encouraging critical development', for example, in the context they are researching (Modern Language and Social Work) 'out of university experiences' appeared to assist progression (*ibid.*). The researchers emphasize that they are not proposing 'isolated techniques' but the relationship of techniques to context and knowledge cannot be clarified outside the understandings of particular disciplines and professional fields.

Discipline-specific university pedagogy

There is growing interest in going beyond generic principles of practice to an understanding of how specific disciplines and topics are organized, adapted and represented for the purposes of learning. The US educationalist Lee Shulman is attributed with the concept 'pedagogical content knowledge' to express the intersection between discipline-knowledge and knowledge about how to teach the discipline. This is how he defines pedagogical content knowledge in a presidential address to the American Education Research Association in 1985:

> Within the category of pedagogical content knowledge I include, for the most regularly taught topics in one's subject area, the most useful form of representation of those ideas, the most powerful analogies, illustrations, examples, explanations, and demonstrations – in a word, the ways of representing and formulating the subject that makes it comprehensible to others. ... Pedagogical content knowledge also includes an understanding of what makes the learning of specific topics easy or difficult: the conceptions and preconceptions that students of different ages and backgrounds bring with them to the learning of those most frequently taught topics and lessons. If those preconceptions are misconceptions, which they so often are, teachers need knowledge of the strategies most likely to be fruitful in reorganizing the understanding of learners, because those learners are unlikely to appear before them as blank slates. (in Wittrock, 1986, pp. 9–10)

This is a challenge to the view that sound content knowledge is enough to teach well and also to Bill Readings' anti-modern idea that there is nothing to know about teaching except that it is an obligation: to do their students justice teachers need to understand how students learn subjects.

Phenomenography: approaches to learning

Probably the most influential theory about higher education in the UK and Australia is what is commonly known as 'approaches to learning' (for example, Biggs, 2003; Prosser and Trigwell, 1999; Ramsden, 2003[21]). As well as being ubiquitous (seen in courses, policy statements as well as referred to in many books and articles), it is empirically well grounded and coherent and holds out the promise of being practically useful: Diana Laurillard claims that it 'offers the best hope for a principled way of generating teaching strategy from research outcomes' (2002, p. 71). Put simply, the research has demonstrated that students' conceptions of learning will influence approaches to learning which, in turn, are strongly related to learning outcomes. Conceptions of learning are represented on a continuum of increasing sophistication from 'a quantitative increase in knowledge' to 'an interpretative process aimed at understanding reality' (Prosser and Trigwell, 1999, p. 38).[22] The key variation in approach to learning is expressed as the dichotomy 'deep' and 'surface': 'The motivation associated with a deep approach to learning is to understand ideas and seek meanings. [Students adopting a surface approach] are instrumentally or pragmatically motivated and seek to meet the demands of the task with minimum effort' (Prosser and Trigwell, p. 91).[23]

The research is rooted in phenomenography which combines data from interviews with individuals to derive categories of student perceptions by searching for variation in responses. It builds on Ference Marton and Roger Saljo's (1976) research which found that students set about reading texts with two broad intentions: to make sense of the text or to complete task requirements. Since then 'approaches to learning' research has developed questionnaires, investigated large populations of university students and been replicated many times in different contexts.[24] The finding that students who conceive learning as an interpretative process aimed at understanding reality are more likely to take a 'deep' approach to learning is exceptionally tenacious.

Furthermore, the apparent usefulness of the research resides in the finding that student perceptions of their learning environment have an influence on their approach to learning: if students perceive clear goals, appropriate workload and assessment, opportunities to study independently and teachers who respect them, they are more likely to take a 'deep approach' to learning. It is a theory with two distinguishing features: first, it identifies the student experience and intentions as the critical factors; and, secondly, the teacher's task is expressed as creating an environment for learning. The latter is significant because as Dewey (1916) put it 'attitudes and dispositions ... cannot take place by direct conveyance ... it takes place through the intermediary of the environment' (p. 22). The theory hands the teacher, as mediator of second-order academic knowledge and understanding, the specific task of creating an environment which is likely to engage the student in the subject matter so that s/he seeks meaning. Laurillard (2002) says that the only 'prescriptive implication' she discerns in the findings set out above is that there must be 'a continuing dialogue between teacher and student, which reveals the participants' conceptions, and the variations between them, and these in turn will determine the focus for further dialogue' (p. 71). Although, Prosser and Trigwell (1999) insist that findings are 'descriptive and analytic, not ... causal and explanatory'

(p. 172), it seems rational when searching for practical guidance to use such findings to justify attempts to manipulate students' perceptions or to change the learning environment.

However, 'approaches to learning' is criticized as an under-challenged orthodoxy which is overused uncritically so that the complexities of the educational endeavour are oversimplified and important issues ignored (Haggis, 2003, 2004; Malcolm and Zukas, 2001; Mann, 2001; Webb, 1997). In part the objections can be seen as a contemporary suspicion of any theory that smacks of a grand narrative in an era when difference is celebrated. One aspect of the criticism is that 'approaches to learning' is elitist because it promotes 'deep' learning as 'good' learning without acknowledging that such learning is a construction of the Western Enlightenment tradition, which excludes certain types of students. I reject this criticism on the grounds that being inclusive involves thinking about commonality and searching for general pedagogic principles which serve all students: 'deep' learning is shorthand for learning which engages students in a search for understanding and meaning and I accept this as a good educational goal for all students because it prioritizes intellectual growth. As a theory it offers the possibility of a practicum that challenges 'intellectual elitism' (Lawton, 1977).

On the other hand, if 'approaches to learning' is to be regarded as a perspective to help teachers improve pedagogy, its abstraction from educational purposes and values, and from political and social realities poses severe problems. Phenomenographic researchers will argue that they cannot be criticized for what they do not set out to do: the focus on the learning of 'phenomena' abstracted from 'situation' is deliberate. For example, Marton and Booth (1997) state that 'the thematic field that surrounds the [phenomena being studied] is made up of aspects of a wider, more general global world, with roots in the current culture and branches that reach out to the learners' future world' (p. 142). They clarify that the choice not to engage with critiques of society or alternative futures is conscious. But from the point of view of developing communicative reason, deliberate severance from a consideration and evaluation of *why* (whether at the level of the system as a whole, or a university or an individual teacher) it is worthwhile to engage students 'deeply' in their academic subjects is a moral choice – to choose not to consider why lays the theory open to technical-rational interpretation. As Bruner puts it '[the] educator who formulates pedagogic theory without regard to the political, economic and social setting of the educational process courts triviality and merits being ignored' (1999, p. 116).

Identity and emotion in pedagogic processes

Finally, following Habermas, I have argued that university education should reproduce the lifeworld of culture, society and personal identity. It should, too, refer to all human interests: in knowledge, in intersubjectivity and in autonomy. Since the whole person is involved, general pedagogic principles must incorporate notions of identity-formation and the role of affect in learning. The concept of identity is elusive. Several social theorists assert that human identity is complex, flexible, hybrid, diverse and constantly reconstructed in interaction with discursive practices in particular historical, political social and economic conditions (Castells, 1997; Craib, 1998; Hall, 1996). In these accounts structure/agency inflections differ. Some stress the idea of identity as constructed through discourses to which the individual, embedded in social organizations, is subjected; while others incline towards a process of endless self-re-creation. Neuroscience has now combined with social theory to examine the question of identity and suggests a more unitary, stable self but which nevertheless, has potential. For example, Damasio (1999) explains the development of an 'autobiographical self':

> The image we gradually build of who we are ... of where we sit socially, is based on autobiographical memory over years of experience and is constantly subject to remodeling. ... The changes which occur in the autobiographical self over an individual lifetime are due not only to the remodeling of the lived past ... but also to the laying down and remodeling of the anticipated future. ... The potential to create our own Hamlets, Iagos, and Falstaffs is inside each of us. Under the right circumstances, aspects of those characters can emerge. (pp. 224–5)

Damasio's version of identity-formation encourages the view that we can continue to make ourselves, and also meshes with Habermas's idea that to become agents in the world, students must believe themselves capable of action.

There are strong emotional dimensions to identity formation. The sociologist Arlie Hochschild's *The Managed Heart* (1983) is a seminal book on the sociology of the emotions. She theorizes a relation between social rule and private experience that shows us how emotion orients our purposes, action and thinking. Her theory incorporates two main ideas: that emotions reflect what is relevant to the individual in any situation; and, that emotion is best understood in relation to its social context. So, while she conceives of emotion as a biological sense which 'signals' our relation to the world, the social context is central: '*Social factors enter into the very formulation of emotions*, through codification, management, and expression' (p. 207, Hochschild's emphasis). She demonstrates how institutions 'control us not simply through surveillance of our behavior but through surveillance of our feelings' (p. 218). Work in institutions, Hochschild argues, always involves the management of emotions as the self struggles with and against institutional rules, what she calls 'emotional labor'. Others have built on Hochschild's work and, in harmony with notions of the 'making' of identity, stress the blurred, provisional, and socially, politically and culturally situated nature of human emotions (Fineman, 2000; Smith, 2002).

In general, these ideas connect to those of the 'academic literacies' tradition which identifies the struggles which students might have to become university students and enter into Gouldner's culture of critical discourse. University education, whatever its quality, will have an influence on the identity of students and a university education will evoke emotions. While much about the interplay between biology, psychology and political and economic society remains mysterious, cognizance that the psychic lives of students enter the pedagogic relation might influence practices that establish the interpersonal relationships between students and teachers. We might also consider how to encourage the traits of character that contemporary society needs: for example, resilience, tenacity and the disposition to work on behalf of others.[25]

Summary of theoretical resources for critical pedagogy

In the sub-sections above I have drawn on research and theories about learning in order to demonstrate how we might derive some general pedagogic principles which are also relevant to the interests of critical theory. Radical pedagogies remind us that formal learning (especially in a university) can be alienating and excluding. The task is to give access to the academic culture as a form of personal and social empowerment. Emerging practical ideas about how to develop different forms of 'critical thinking' can provide a framework for university teachers interested in critical goals to think about how they teach. The notion of pedagogical content knowledge directs attention to the central importance of being a strong discipline expert at university level, but also to how it is an insufficient knowledge base for teaching; teachers also must know how their teaching might make possible to learn their discipline or professional field. Similarly, well-established research, generally called 'approaches to learning' offers a handle for thinking about how to influence students' perceptions so that they are more likely to seek meaning in their academic studies. And we must take account of the profoundly emotional nature of forming an identity as a critically thinking university student.

Though I cannot pretend that I have satisfactorily synthesized these theories as praxis, I do think that the principles derived fulfil the criteria that I set out earlier: they could be persuasive to university teachers; they refer to all students; they can be translated into practices; and, they are connected to broader societal goals. I believe that progress towards a synthesis of peda-gogic ideas is iterative through critical engagement with all three contexts of knowledge generation about teaching (one's own practice, communications with others about teaching, and theory and evidence). Each teacher needs to work on their own critical rationale.

Conclusion

Universities' pedagogic role in achieving the critical objectives of social justice and the capacity to address the problems of a globalized society is to develop minds capable of communicative reason. The capacity to exploit the potential in modernity for transformation requires certain dispositions, as well as expert knowledge and understanding and the means of commu-nicating it. University teachers and managers could seek to agree what student experience would enhance communicative reason. But it would mean eschewing quick fixes: the only way forward is in the: 'diffuse, fragile, continuously revised and only momentarily successful communication' (Habermas, 1984, pp. 100–1). When communicating about university pedagogy we must consistently attempt both to be true, sincere and just and to develop judgement about whether we are dealing with true, sincere and just utterances.

I started the chapter by defining communicative reason and explaining Habermas's theory of communicative action. I established that university students need to become part of a culture of critical discourse and empha-sized the primacy of language in pedagogy. I problematized the notion of 'student experience' to propose that we should not make structural inequalities an excuse for not thinking about how to mobilize the com-municative reason of all students. The latter part of the chapter described my search for general principles of pedagogic practice which both serve critical ends and have a purchase on how to educate students capable of communicative action. I propose that thinking collectively and critically about such theorized general principles is a large part of what I call 'intel-lectualizing university teaching' in the next chapter.

Notes

1 From Walker and Nixon, 2004.
2 I refer to the Latin roots of education – *e ducere*, a drawing out.
3 For the purpose of analysis, the 'speech acts' of participants may be any verbal or written communication: a conversation, a political debate or a decision-making process.

4 From *Communication and the Evolution of Society.*

5 *Op. cit.*

6 'Shaping the Academy – Consultation Paper – November 2004': www.heacademy.ac.uk.

7 *Ibid.*

8 *Ibid.*

9 Perhaps less so during the perceived 'golden age' of the 1960s and 1970s because there was plenty of work to be had.

10 Simon, a first-year student of English quoted in Thomas, 1990, p. 88.

11 Lesley, a first-year science student quoted in Thomas, 1990, p. 53.

12 This could be one explanation of why many students find that final year projects or special subjects engage their commitment.

13 For example, Freire (1996) criticizes the 'banking concept' of education whereby education becomes 'an act of depositing, in which the students are depositories and the teacher is the depositor' (p. 53).

14 They cite 'psychology, ethnomethodology, philosophy, sociology, literary theory, anthropology, science and linguistics'. During the period from the end of WWII until the 1980s, teacher education involved study of four 'foundation' disciplines: history, philosophy, sociology and psychology.

15 For example, Leach and Moon (1999) draw on Lave and Wenger's (1991) idea to claim that pedagogy is concerned with 'the construction and practice of learning communities' (p. 268) and from here make five assertions about 'effective pedagogic settings'.

16 In the sections that follow I draw extensively on work done with Paul Ashwin (2005) in which we attempted to bring together the critical pedagogy of Paul Freire and the phenomenographic approach as set out by Marton and Booth (1997).

17 The method involved 'generative themes' which emerge from contacts with communities and which are discussed using a dialogic process. A 'thematic universe' arises from these discussions and from this the teachers extract a vocabulary which is socially and culturally relevant to the particular community (Freire, 1972a). This method was adopted by literacy programmes across the world, including, in London during the 1970s.

18 The idea of 'scaffolding' is taken from Lev Vygotsky's (1896–1934) work and means the guidance of teachers which is directed towards moving a learner from where s/he is to what they are capable of.

19 The final stipulation is a particular feature of practice arising from the perspective of the tradition of 'academic literacies' (see, for example, Lea, 2004)

20 www.soton.ac.uk/\simcriticality/TheProject.htm.

21 Also see Marton *et al.* (1997) for the practical implications of research which is broadly psychological.

22 In an 'inclusive hierarchy' individuals holding the most sophisticated conceptions will simultaneously hold other conceptions.

23 There is a parallel literature that links teachers' conceptions of teaching and students' approaches to learning (Trigwell *et al.* 1999 and Trigwell and Prosser, 2003).

24 It is important to keep in mind that, naturally, some studies are of a better quality than others.

25 Richard Sennett discusses the worth of such attributes in *The Corrosion of Character: Personal Consequences of Work in the New Capitalism* (2000).

7
Intellectualizing university teaching and student learning

There is great danger for students, parents, faculty members, and politicians when we come to rely on simple models of the world of human beings in order to explain how things work, how education educates, how and when students learn. (Benson R. Snyder, *The Hidden Curriculum*, p. 183)

Introduction

The next two chapters focus broadly on the issue of how to realize a university pedagogy that connects knowledge and human interests. The main question is if all grounds for hope of pursuing the ideals of the Enlightenment reside in the mobilization of communicative reason, how might this apply to the public sphere of university education?

Underpinning this chapter are two main ideas: university teaching is an activity for intellectuals who are educating intellectuals; and teaching is essential to the integrity of universities as places of intellectual activity. The argument is that to resist technical-rational versions of university pedagogy, academics-as-teachers need both to accept these ideas and to convey them to government and to the public: the possibility of critical university pedagogy depends on the identity of academic teachers and on their reputation. The concepts of 'intellectual' and 'professional' are explored in relation to how academics-as-teachers interested in critical pedagogy might use them to make arguments about the configuration of their teaching. The chapter also returns to the four functions of universities (research, professional training, general education and public enlightenment) to discuss why they should remain 'bundled' and to emphasize that all the functions, including teaching, are characterized by what Habermas calls the 'scientific and scholarly learning processes'. I start, though, with an attempt to reflect the everyday thoughts and practices of university teachers. First, I caricature

Hastings Campus Library
University of Brighton
TN34 1BE

01273 644640

08163057 Pedagogy and the universit
                    Due: 06/02/2015
08163057 Pedagogy and the universit
                    Due: 06/02/2015
08413223 Bourdieu and education : a
                    Due: 06/02/2015
05675073 Class strategies and the e
                    Due: 06/02/2015
05968550 The education debate / Ste
                    Due: 06/02/2015
37109778 Critical theory and educat
                    Due: 06/02/2015
06784968 The power of critical theo
                    Due: 06/02/2015
04118043 Asylums and after : a revi
                    Due: 06/02/2015
04482700 Mental health policy in Br
                    Due: 23/01/2015
3501429X Decarceration : community
                    Due: 06/02/2015
38063445 Class and civil society :
                    Due: 06/02/2015
07157481 The social organization of
                    Due: 06/02/2015
0810851X Asylums : essays on the so
                    Due: 06/02/2015
05330246 Medical power and social k
    Due: 06/02/2015

6/01/2015 12:57

You may have other items on loan.
Please check your library account on
the library catalogue:
http://capitadiscovery.co.uk/brighton-ac/

the way in which university pedagogy currently tends to be characterized by academics; I then set out a more nuanced, self-critical and intellectualized version of the problem of university pedagogy; and, I use two accounts from university teachers to reveal a university teaching lifeworld that illustrates what we can realistically hope to achieve in current conditions.

Beyond a dichotomous argument about university pedagogy

It seems to me that academics are poor at engaging in debates about teaching that will earn the respect and confidence of the public and government. They are inclined to offer a dichotomous argument about the current state of affairs, and each part implies its own pedagogic practices. There are variations, but I must simplify. On the one hand, is the argument that mass higher education accompanied by a decrease of resources has led to a self-evident decline in the standard of student learning in most universities. This side of the argument either attributes all difficulties to a question of resources or calls for a return to a more selective meritocracy with no concessions made for students who appear not to cope with university-level education. Either way, there is no need to examine pedagogic practices because they are not the problem. An example is Frank Furedi's jeremiad *Where Have All the Intellectuals Gone?* (2004) in which he attributes the 'feeble presence of intellectuals' to lack of resistance to a 'culture of flattery' by which the public are treated (as fools) to 'dumbed-down' knowledge: 'Instead of affirming their authority, the cultural elites appear more interested in appearing relevant, accessible and in touch with popular opinion' (p. 6). He demonizes the 'politics of inclusion' and accuses 'advocates of widening participation [of not believing] that the democratization of cultural life can be reconciled with standards of excellence' (p. 19). Pedagogic practices founded on this belief will incorporate high expectations but are unlikely to include pedagogic content knowledge or an understanding of why students might find academic learning difficult.

The other side of the argument is that in a mass higher education with 'diverse' students we must accept that the same achievements cannot be expected of students at different types of universities: those at elite universities start and end better educated. This belief tends to lead to teaching that makes subjects less difficult and more banal, it also provides an excuse to separate teaching and research. I suspect that many of the 'hints and tips' approaches to university pedagogy are informed by these kinds of beliefs.

There is truth in both arguments, but the alternative view, which I am peddling here, is that we are forced to accept that the system is stratified and diverse and that some students are better prepared for university education than others, but at the same time there remains a core of functions (to which we should cling) that defines all universities and colours the experiences of those teaching and learning in them. Despite assertions we do not know much about the relative quality of learning in different universities (even if 'grade inflation' across the board is incontrovertible). Recently, some colleagues and I undertook a small-scale research project to investigate how the subject of English is produced through teaching in two quite different institutional settings (Jones *et al.* 2005). We had expected to find different constructions of 'English', but, in terms of the paradigms of the subject, both teachers encouraged inter-textuality; emphasized the historical specificity of the novels; and, connected literature to wider social and cultural meanings. If anything, student engagement was more pronounced and the quality of discussion better in the classroom of twenty students in an inner city university than in the seminar of seven in the research-led university that comes considerably higher up league tables on most counts.

Academics do resist technical-rational constructions of teaching (and research) and often express their resistance in an interesting, eloquent and erudite manner and genuinely seek public debate.[1] As teachers, they are distressed to see their students alienated and producing mediocre work. But they do not often turn their gaze on their own pedagogic practices, nor explore thoroughly how to draw out the potential of their students. As disappointed teachers they tend to fall back on narratives of decline which are often partial and which are not self-reflective. Academics-as-intellectuals need to turn critical eyes towards the possibilities of university pedagogy whether or not the political circumstances are auspicious.

A marvellous example of such self-reflection is Gerald Graff's[2] *Clueless in Academe: How Schooling Obscures the Life of the Mind.* The introduction is entitled 'In the dark all eggheads are gray' and starts:

> This book is an attempt by an academic to look at academia from the perspective of those who don't get it. Its subject is cluelessness, the bafflement, usually accompanied by shame and resentment, felt by students, the general public, and even many academics in the face of the impenetrability of the academic world. ... As I see it, my academic intellectual culture is not at all irrelevant to my students' needs and interests, but we do a very good job of making it appear as if it is. (2003, p. 1)

His argument, echoing Alvin Gouldner whose work I introduced in the last chapter, is that the main goal of university teachers is to induct students into the 'culture of ideas and arguments' so that they can partake in 'intellectual conversations' which endow them with the capacity to become 'public actors'. The reason that this goal is often unachieved is university teachers' 'incuriosity' about student 'cluelessness'. Graff has a gloss on the dichotomous argument that I set out earlier:

> ... for some progressive educators, to speak of cluelessness at all is inherently snobbish, elitist, and undemocratic, as if acknowledging students' deficiencies necessarily denigrates their abilities. For some traditionalists, on the other hand, who see cluelessness as a distasteful symptom of cultural vulgarity and a dumbed down popular culture, the clueless, like the poor, will always be with us, and there is nothing much anybody can do about it except teach to the best students and let the rest fend for themselves. (*Ibid.* p. 5)

Graff firmly believes that, despite the inherent difficulty of intellectual work, everyone 'is cut out for the life of the mind' and his book is a scholarly analysis of what goes wrong as well as a highly practical exploration of how to demonstrate the value of intellectualism to students.

The type of work on university pedagogy that Graff offers intellectualizes teaching by taking the debate and argument beyond oversimplified analyses and by deepening understanding of where problems might lie and what to do about them. But most university teachers are not also professors of education (as Graff is) so I now move to more mundane examples of day-to-day efforts to improve student learning because I want to demonstrate that something within reach could count as 'critical pedagogy' in the sense of developing minds capable of coming to agreements about problems in the world.

What kind of 'critical' university pedagogy can we realistically aim for?

Throughout this book I have tried to stay close to everyday practices while dealing with abstract theory about society and education; to this end I reproduce below accounts[3] by two university lecturers at the beginning of their careers about how they conceptualize teaching and learning and how they act to assist their students. I am in possession of these accounts as the director of an accredited course about teaching which the two undertook as novice teachers. The course requires a portfolio which sets out the how and why of the individual's teaching: the accounts below are extracted from portfolios and they both focus on the issue of motivating students to engage in academic work. The accounts act as backdrop and frame of reference for the rest of the book because they express an intellectualized approach to the 'actualities of teaching', representing university pedagogy that is recognizable and attainable, though not without challenges. At the same time, they describe pedagogic approaches which could be invoked to serve the purposes of critical theory.

Karen, Lecturer in Politics and International Relations

'I arrived in the UK higher education sector with experiences of educational systems elsewhere; in my case I had previously taught at universities in the United States and Canada. Upon my arrival, I was struck by the lack of student enthusiasm and engagement. Through my previous teaching experiences, I had developed an approach to teaching that I found very rewarding, which focused on producing highly motivated students. I sought to motivate students very highly on the assumption that when they were motivated they engaged with material seriously and learned from that engagement in ways that reinforced the pleasure and value of intellectual work. In what follows, I explore some of the principles that have guided my efforts to motivate students and some of the challenges faced by attempting to implement them in the context of the UK higher education system. From my perspective, figuring out how to motivate my students more highly is absolutely crucial, as without their serious engagement, not only does the quality of my experience of teaching decline, so does the quality of the teaching itself. My overall approach to teaching has been characterised by an effort to motivate through inspiring both curiosity in the student and ownership over his or her academic work. This manifests in three principles that largely guide my teaching.

1. Raise the bar

I explicitly set out high expectations of the students, both in terms of a serious workload and challenging material. I am also very careful to be clear about these expectations, and as certain as I can be that the students understand them. In general terms, what I mean by "raising the bar" is that I try to communicate to them that learning is serious and difficult business, but it is also very important business. It should be taken seriously; I expect them to do so, and this will require hard work, but their efforts will be taken seriously. For example, I encourage them to use their written work to explore concepts or problems that they find genuinely challenging, and to use their written work as an opportunity to further their thinking in relation to this challenge, rather than to demonstrate competence or mastery of it. I emphasize that their written work should document a process, a conversation between them and texts, authors or research material in which they challenge their own thinking. If their thinking hasn't changed as a result of their writing, I suggest to them they haven't engaged seriously enough with the material they are writing about. In practice I encourage this level of engagement by assigning specific pieces of reading and some written response to it as a minimum precondition for class attendance, and ensuring that seminar discussion or lectures directly engage this reading and build on it so that students benefit from their preparation.

2. Shift the responsibility

I think it is very important to ensure that students understand what they are meant to be learning and *why*, that they understand the full range of relevance of the skills and material they are engaging. But I also try to be very clear that this is an opportunity for *them*; it is not primarily about me setting a hoop for them to jump through, or about me communicating things to them and measuring how well they reproduce them. It is an opportunity for them to develop skills that will be useful to them, that will enable them to engage in the world more effectively in relation to things they care about. They need to feel that there is a reason to do this work that is far more important than what mark or degree classification they will receive. They need to own it. Furthermore, it is up to them. It is their responsibility, and they who will benefit. It is always surprising to me how much students respond to this approach. Even in universities, there remains a strong residual feeling amongst many students that education is a hoop to jump through or a set of (rather obscure) expectations set by others that they must – through guile, effort or talent – meet, rather than an opportunity for them to pursue ideas that are of interest to them and develop skills that will be of use to them. Thus I try to be clear with them what I see my role as (a facilitator, not a gatekeeper), emphasising especially that the more control they take over what they learn, the more they will benefit from the class. In the end, though, the responsibility rests with them.

3. Ensure they get feedback on and recognition of the work they do
This aspect is crucial because the skills I seek to develop in my teaching require dialogue and feedback. It doesn't have to be much feedback, especially if it is high-quality feedback. However they need to have a sense that someone is listening carefully to their ideas and arguments and they need to have encouragement. This feedback doesn't necessarily have to be from me; often I structure classes so that students read and respond to each others' writing (although this requires some training to enable them to provide each other with effective feedback). The *kind* of feedback matters, however. I find that critical engagement is better than a pat on the head in this regard. Rather than primarily evaluating the quality of their work, my feedback to students tends to focus very precisely on their analysis and argumentation, asking them questions to encourage them to clarify their ideas or respond to different possible arguments. Whenever possible I schedule formative assessment which enables me to give them substantive written feedback without actually assigning a mark to the paper, thus directing student attention away from the tendency to evaluate their work based on the mark and towards a critical conversation with their intended audience. Often they respond with dismay when they see a returned essay covered with my writing, fearing they have failed in some way, but when they actually read the feedback they see precisely what has broken down in their writing and how they can improve it. Perhaps most importantly, they are inspired to write more carefully the next time because they have a sense that someone has actually read their writing with care, so their own attention to detail will be rewarded. They have been taken seriously, and as a consequence they take themselves and their work more seriously.

As I reflect on the courses I have designed and taught, these are the three principles – in combination – that have proved to be most consistently effective for me in motivating students. There is much more I could say about how I implement them, and a whole range of other factors that also determine their effectiveness: they have to be tailored to different levels, different material, and different teaching constraints, and in the end much of their success rests on a high level of commitment from me as a teacher.

This latter point – the level of commitment required – emerged as especially relevant upon my arrival in the UK, where I encountered not only a much increased workload (particularly in the area of administration), but also the challenge of learning to function in a new and very different academic system. One of the first things that struck me about this system is how constraining it is in a variety of ways that mitigate against the kinds of practices I had used in the past to motivate students. Fewer contact hours than I was used to, rigorous controls on course design, anonymous marking, marking by people not teaching on the course, the power of the external examiner, and the structure of the degree classification scheme all seemed to constrain possibilities for innovation. The style of teaching I described above depended on developing a personal relationship with students through their writing (even in rather large classes), being very responsive to their interests and tailoring my responses to their work in ways that encouraged them to take risks and achieve successes. Adapting course material or assessment procedures "on the fly", providing personalised responses to written work, or having adequate time with students, either inside the classroom or out, all – for different reasons – seemed impossible. The single most stubborn of constraints was workload. The demands of being a junior lecturer (on a temporary contract) didn't seem compatible with devoting more than minimal attention to students. I found this very discouraging.

Over the past two years, however, as I have gained increasing control over course design and a better understanding of the flexibility of some of the teaching regulations, I have managed to implement these principles more effectively, with positive results. The benefits of having highly motivated students – as expressed both in the quality of written work and of engagement in class discussions – are enormous. Perhaps most centrally from my perspective, when they have been encouraged to engage in this manner, students leave my classes with more control over their own learning process, and better equipped to learn in any kind of context. In the best case scenario, they also leave with enthusiasm for the subject matter, confidence in their abilities to engage with it, and a sense of achievement in their own work. These are powerful motivators for good teaching.'

Leo, Lecturer in History

'In my experience, the following scenario is a familiar one to many lecturers: The students arrive for a seminar, having, the week before, been invited to "do some reading" from a list of between four and twenty books. Many have not done any reading, and if they have, they perhaps have not thought about the issues it raises for the course they are studying. Having dealt with the pleasantries, the lecturer nervously asks an opening question – "So, what strikes you as important about the position of doctors in the early nineteenth century?" An awkward silence ensues. Heads are bowed all round. Eventually, the lecturer gives in, and holds a mini-lecture answering each of his/her own questions in turn. Students are demotivated. Attendance becomes erratic. The quality of written work is mediocre and unintellectual.

And yet, when it is suggested that compulsory reading, apportioned on a named basis to individual students, might conquer this ignorant silence, and furthermore, that the completion of a piece of weekly written work might a) guarantee that the reading is actually done, b) improve learners' writing skills through practice, c) improve their analytical skills through enforcing periods of reflection, and d) enthuse and empower them by exposing them to the pleasures of acquiring and analysing knowledge, several objections have, in my experience, been made. Chief amongst them is that "they are adults", and should therefore, by nature of their "adulthood", evidence features *a* to *d* as a matter of course. Second tends to come "lecturer workload" – a theme to which I will return later.

This idea of "adulthood" was something which I felt needed to be questioned – and from two standpoints. Firstly, in the case of younger learners (who represent about 85% or more of the university I teach in), it seemed to be based on the idea that some time in August of a person's eighteenth year, a variety of quite remarkable and sophisticated changes took place which enabled people, unassisted, to make a success of the world and achieve personal fulfilment. Both from my own observations and my readings of developmental psychology, this sort of revolution struck me as unlikely. Secondly, it seems to misrepresent adulthood as most of us experience it. If we miss deadlines, do not complete work, do not attend meetings, then we are disciplined. If we are given a task without training, guidance or clear definition of the goals, we find those tasks difficult, and may well neglect them. So from both sides – an understanding of what it means to be a young person faced with challenging tasks, and of what it actually means to be an adult in the world, it seemed that learners were caught between a rock and a hard place. So, I resolved to do several *very adult* things (but things which can easily be branded "childish" or "school-masterish") in my teaching practice, and it is to these which I would now like to turn.

At the heart of the practical measures I introduced at every level was a weekly piece of written work. It was to be c. 300 words in length, and was to be a personal reaction to a specific piece of reading which a learner would agree to do. It was not oriented towards a specific assessment goal, such as the completion of an essay, but rather, towards addressing the intellectual issues at the heart of the following week's seminar. This was to reinforce the "humane" idea which drives history as a discipline, that it is the acquisition and manipulation of knowledge which is key, not its use-value. This piece of work would constitute an "entrance ticket" to the seminar. I introduced this strategy through a discussion (admittedly, very guided by me) about what students felt was an appropriate quantity of work, measure of its completion, and sanction against non-completion. My contribution was to have it marked and in pigeonholes on the day of submission. This strategy has borne many fruits.

First of these is that seminars tend to be approached with enthusiasm. By relating what students have said in small group work to the personal responses in their weekly submissions, it seems that they regard seminars as an opportunity to test their own interpretations and opinions *with their friends*, and in the case of brighter or more confident students, occasionally with me. Listening to them suggests that less able students are at least concept checking for themselves. Secondly, the students know a great deal more about the issues under discussion. Therefore, direct questioning from me is less intimidating, and more productive in terms of gaining insight and "joining the dots" which I hope they will join. Thirdly, their writing improves immeasurably. By focusing on single issues (say, the inability to distinguish between a full stop and a comma, or writing fragmentary sentences), students gradually progress in both grammar and quality of expression. Fourthly, enforcing periods of reflection in which learners are invited to evaluate what they feel to be the most interesting, controversial, significant, challenging or difficult *ideas* presented in the reading in the light of the themes and issues thrown up by the course, their critical capacities are enhanced at the same time as their attention to the learning outcomes of the course is re-focused. Fifthly, seminars are fun – they reflect more closely the model of the seminar which most of us have in our minds, the seminars which inspired us to pursue the specialisms we did. The classroom time becomes about exploring knowledge, rather than acquiring it. Lastly, the prompt feedback seems to create an indefinable "buzz" about the whole process, in which learner engagement with the material is radically transformed, and students eagerly collected their work, and had often discussed it with other students before submission.

Of course, there are downsides to this system. From the learners' perspective, it requires a quantity and quality of input which they may not yet have experienced at university, or which other lecturers may not expect. In order to overcome that, I discuss with them the types of outcomes which this learning process achieves; namely, students get better marks not just in my course, but in fact in all of their courses, and that seminars are more interesting. While some learners express shock initially, none have said it was problematic *after* having experienced it. Furthermore, it redistributes work away from the crunches of essay and exam, and spreads it through the term. Secondly, there is a major issue of workload for the lecturer. Weekly marking for groups does take up time – typically about 3–4 minutes a student. However, just as for learners, this approach has not led to an *overall* increase in work, but rather a redistribution of it. Term papers are so much better than previously that much marking time is saved there. Seminar attendance is better, so bureaucratic "chasing" time is reduced. Classes are therefore easier to plan, and they are more enjoyable for me. This student *and* lecturer workload has been recognised in the History School at X by formalising the system. Students submit a portfolio of weekly work for 20% of their course mark, although the marks are for improvement over time, not absolute measures as would be typical for terminal assessment.

Lastly, it requires a lot of personal commitment from the lecturer, as well as the confidence to deal with things when they go wrong – when work is not done for example (although in my and my colleagues' experience, this has not been a problem). This human dimension of personnel management is actually something which we, even though we are adults, are *not* trained to do – and look what an awkward job we sometimes make of it, and how we shy away from it. There is no easy solution to this – but if the "ticket" system is fully understood and discussed with students, then the system produces, through establishing a consensus on sanctions, a fairly "automatic" set of procedures. The net result of this strategy seems to have been more vigorous and participative seminars, more intellectual and literate students, and a shift in the pattern of work and marking which have enhanced the learners' experience of teaching and, crucially, my own.'

Between them the accounts of teaching above illustrate almost all of what I want to say about a university pedagogy which is likely to engage students' intellects and build their capacity to act in the world. They are what I think of as intellectual and professional accounts of teaching. Like Felicity Rosslyn, whose account of a seminar is in Chapter 5, they draw on their own experiences although they appear more in control of the pedagogic encounter than she does. They do not refer to any theoretical resources directly (though both as I indicated have completed an accredited course), nevertheless they have principles which guide them and which can be mapped on to the kinds of theories outlined in the last chapter. Karen and Leo believe in their students' potential; they have high expectations and are not content with glib analyses of their students' difficulties with learning. They tell of the demands and hardships of teaching and of what it requires: an understanding of how students learn; taking the students' part; the creation of environments in which learning is made possible; attention to detail; and, commitment and persistence. They accept the effort, discomfort and 'emotional labour' that teaching entails (Hochschild, 1983).[4] Yet they insist on the joys of teaching and that the effort is worthwhile; they also touch on how contextual factors (national or institutional) enable or constrain their pedagogic efforts. They deal with similar themes and issues but they are developing individual approaches, the sense of different disciplines is strong and their voices are individual and authentic. Karen and Leo are not proselytizing educationalists, they are young lecturers at the coalface generating their own critical rationale for how they set about teaching. The sources for both of them are their own experience, discussions with others and educational literature. I have chosen two accounts but I could have produced many more from conversations and from teaching portfolios. Despite the colonization of the lifeworlds of such academic teachers, they offer us strong grounds for hope. Their accounts contain ideas about how to scaffold students' search for ideas, ideals and values with which to reinvent their social worlds. I believe that many university teachers, like Karen and Leo, take on the responsibility for developing in students attributes that are close to communicative reason but do not make a large or loud enough claim for doing so.

Yet, it is important to be clear that well-meaning attempts at practical improvement can miss the mark because they fail to shake off a purely rational-technical approach to teaching. By way of illustration, there follows an extract from Henry Giroux's *Public Spaces, Private Lives: Beyond the Culture of Cynicism* in which he analyses an account of attempting to improve teaching by Elaine Showalter, Professor of English at Princeton University and Feminist critic:

> [Showalter] recognises the importance of sound pedagogical practice, particularly the responsibility of faculty in preparing their graduate students to teach undergraduate courses. [She] rejects the popular attitude among her professional colleagues that 'any interest in pedagogy [be seen] as the last refuge of a scoundrel.' ... Born out of a general impatience with the lack of will and effort in addressing the problem of pedagogy, Showalter brought together in 1998 a number of graduate students in a course on teaching to take up the problem. ... Conducting an intensive search on the Internet, Showalter surprised herself and her students by how many books she was able to find on teaching. For Showalter, texts on university education fall into four general categories: personal memoirs, spiritual and ethical reflections, practical guidebooks, and reports on education research. Unfortunately, Showalter's search left her and her students unaware of a long tradition of critical theoretical work on pedagogy, schooling and society.[5] The result is that both she and her graduate students came away with a conception of teaching as simply a matter of methods, exclusively and reductively concerned with practical and technical issues. Hence, their enthusiasm for books that 'provide lots of pointers on subjects as varied as choosing textbooks and getting feedback from students and colleagues' or books that 'help instructors make the most effective use of the lecture/discussion mode' ... In the end, Showalter recommends a number of books, such as Wilbert J. McKeachie's *McKeachie's Teaching Tips* and Joseph Lowman's *Mastering the Techniques of Teaching*, because they 'offer practical concrete advice about learning to ask students good questions and encouraging them to participate'.
>
> ... In her zest for 'concreteness' [Showalter] abstracts pedagogical practices from the ethico-political visions that inform them and has little to say about how pedagogy relates the self to public life, social responsibility, or the demands of critical citizenship. Showalter has no pedagogic language for dealing with student voices and experiences, nor with the social, racial, and class inequalities that animate them. ... Even basic pedagogic issues regarding how teacher authority can manifest itself without being inimical to the practice of freedom are ignored in Showalter's discourse. By defining pedagogy as an a priori discourse that simply needs to be uncovered and deployed, Showalter has nothing to say about pedagogy as the outcome of specific struggles between diverse groups to name history, experience, knowledge, and the meaning of everyday life in one's own terms. Unfortunately, Showalter offers up a depoliticized pedagogy of 'tips' [that does not address] the role pedagogy might play in educating students to take risks, engage in learning how to exercise power, and extend boundaries of economic and social justice. (2001, pp. 93–4)

The selection of this extract does not mean that I underestimate the importance of skill, technique and behaviour in teaching – I am sure that Showalter's book is useful – but they are by no means enough. For me the key phrase here is 'pedagogy as the outcome of specific struggles between diverse groups to name history, experience, and the meaning of everyday life in one's own terms'. This conflict is played out between students and university teachers: Graff (2003) expresses this struggle as a 'fundamental conflict ... between Intellectualspeak and Studentspeak' (p. 13). As an illustration of the conflict, in the following extract, Ben Knights decodes the messages of disparagement that university teachers send to students about the versions of English that they have been taught at school:

> [The] social construction of subject discipline simultaneously calls into being a model of what it is to be a student of that subject. Reduced to the abstract, the process is one where a small group with access to a body of knowledge or a set of discursive practices performs its relations with a larger group of initiates. In each case – whether the goal is the emergence of the initiate reader as agent of culture, or the person willing to embrace fearlessly their own heterogeneity as a subject – the epistemological practice prescribes an ontology. The implied student is to *become* what he or she does. In each case there is an open or covert accusation that existing disciplinary practice is characterized by masquerade, impersonation, and inauthenticity. Up til now, the charge runs, learners have been interpellated into false consciousness. They have been betrayed by slothful and self-interested teachers. It is a charge which in turn rests on a kind of disciplinary funda-mentalism, an assumption that it would be possible to return to basics simulta-neously epistemological and ontological. Like many other sects (and as equally vulnerable to the paradox of conformist non-conformity) such educational cru-sades promote forms of asceticism where the initiate aspires to cast off the bag-gage of a former, deplored, identity. To have seen through and discarded previous educational identities becomes the badge of the successful student. (2005, p. 38)

This is a very intellectual account of what is happening between university teachers and students. It is controversial, though unfortunately my broad-brush approach does not allow for in-depth exploration. I use the Knights passage here because it reveals the complexities of academic teaching, raising numerous questions: for example, What does it mean to dismantle an academic identity? Can we completely escape coercing students? How can originality and authenticity be encouraged at the same time as insisting on the conventions of the discipline? What if we made this process of enculturalization explicit to students? Could it be done differently?

Before continuing, I want to propose two ideas about university pedagogy that are interrelated through the notion of 'intellectual': first, that to develop minds or communicative reason can also be thought of as educating to become an intellectual – a person who deals in ideas, questions, argument and critique; secondly, educating students as intellectuals calls out for an intellectualized pedagogy.

The integration of the 'remarkable bundle of functions'

Habermas's phrase for the intellectual work in universities is 'scientific and scholarly learning processes', Graff's phrase is 'skills of explanation, clarification and problem-solving' (2003, p. 10). Whatever the phrase, intellectual processes are the defining feature of all the functions of the university. There are moves to separate teaching and research: universities resist but governments believe that it is inefficient to support all activities in all universities. Habermas acknowledges that the learning processes of research can be split off and 'oriented to the environments of the economy and administrative planning through the production by the individual disciplines of technically usable information' (1989, p. 105). Nevertheless, he is optimistic that universities cannot leave 'the horizon of the lifeworld completely behind' (*ibid.* p. 107) because the other functions of teaching, professional preparation and public enlightenment compel universities to deal with elements of the lifeworld – culture, identity-formation, intersubjectivity – through deliberation about social, moral and ethical issues. Furthermore, he questions whether the intellectual processes of research can remain healthy without being bound up with the other educative functions:

> The universities are still rooted in the lifeworld through [a remarkable bundling of functions]. The traditional bundling of different functions under the roof of one institution, and the awareness that in that institution the process of acquiring scientific knowledge is intertwined not only with technical development and preparation for the academic professions, but also with general education, the transmission of culture, and the enlightenment of the public political sphere might be of vital importance for research itself. Empirically, it seems an open question whether the impetus behind the scientific and scholarly learning processes became socialized exclusively for the function of research. Scientific and scholarly productivity might be dependent upon university forms of organization, dependent, that is, on the internally differentiated complex that includes the training of future scientists and scholars, preparation for the academic professions, and participation in processes of general education, cultural self-understanding, and the formation of public opinion. (*Ibid.* p. 107)

Habermas is proposing here that research will be degraded if it ceases to be embroiled in the other business of universities for it will become completely technical if it is not connected to the lifeworld. Despite similar misgivings about the 'instrumentalization of knowledge', Gerald Delanty echoes Habermas's optimism about the role that universities can still play in society:

> The university is the institution in society most capable of linking the requirements of industry, technology and market forces with the demands of citizenship. Given the enormous dependence of these forces on university based experts, the university is in fact in a position of strength, not of weakness. ... It is now in a position to serve social goals more fully than previously. (2001, p. 113)

As I pointed out in Chapter 5 Delanty identifies the same functions for universities as Habermas. He does more by explicitly connecting them to types of knowledge, role and citizenship. I have produced the table below to summarize his position.

Function	Knowledge	Role	Citizenship
Research	Accumulation of information	expert	technological
Education	Human experience/ formation of personality/*Bilding*	teacher	cultural
Professional education	Accreditation and vocational training	professional trainer	technological
Intellectual inquiry and critique	Public issues/ intellectualization of society	intellectual	cultural

For me Delanty clarifies the link – that Habermas also insists on – between science and scholarship, on the one hand, and democracy, on the other, by tying the functions of the university to forms of citizenship; a rounded citizen is both culturally and technologically competent. The configuration of the work of universities represented in the table could provide the basis for debates about academic functions and processes.

Throughout the higher education system, the lifeworld of academics is agitated; previously taken-for-granted ways of working are being disturbed, even in ancient, powerful, rich, elite universities where tradition and resistance are strong. It is argued that universities are experiencing an identity crisis which is influencing how they are seen by government and by the public. Certainly, as discussed in Chapter 4, the experiences of the audit culture which affects both teaching and research have discouraged sincere, true and just utterances; and many academics either support or are acquiescent to the fragmentation of academic work, in particular the separation of teaching and research. But the situation could be taken as an opportunity to reconstruct the academic role, drawing on old ideas, but articulating them differently for the new conditions in which we find ourselves. The basis for earning a new respect from students, the public and, possibly, government agencies could lie in making a strong argument for what Habermas (1989) calls the 'remarkable bundle of functions' that universities undertake on behalf of society. Academics could rethink an identity linking the four functions through 'learning processes'. Delanty (2001) refers to 'the intellectualization of society': commitment to public enlightenment – whether through research, professional training, the general education of students or social commentary – could restore a critical and social role to universities. This is of particular importance in a society characterized by reflexivity, new forms of knowledge and global problems. University students are the future public and future citizens and universities play an important moral role in ensuring that they bring to bear critical and analytic minds on the grave problems of contemporary society. Unfortunately though there are many signs that Gerald Delanty is correct in thinking that in the current conditions, the roles of professional research and professional trainer will 'overshadow' the roles of teacher and public intellectual (2001, p. 87). One route to restoring teaching to its position among the functions of the university could be to exploit the notion of 'intellectual' and to explain how it adheres to teaching. Academics such as Karen and Leo would be well placed to make the case.

Teachers, students and intellectuals

It is commonplace to think of academics as intellectuals in their role as researchers and, increasingly, as contributors to public knowledge through the media, but rare in their role as teachers. The notion of 'intellectual' is a rich resource that can be drawn on to delineate a lifeworld that is both attractive to academics and serves the purposes of critical pedagogy by incorporating intellectual goals for students. There is a large literature on the role of the intellectual in society, and many scholars from a variety of perspectives have discussed the role of the intellectual in the transformation of society.[6] Many constructions of the role resonate for those who have aspirations in keeping with critical theory: the intellectual as social interpreter and critic, and as reformer or rebel.

I pick up Alvin Gouldner's (1979) work again because it is particularly relevant to my argument. He highlights the pervasiveness of intellectualization in society, showing how academics and their students are drawn together by means of the culture of critical discourse which produces and reproduces intellectuals. A 'New Class composed of intellectuals and technical intelligentsia'[7] (p. 1) has arisen through decisive historical episodes which include: secularization; the emergence of diverse vernacular languages; the cessation of feudal relations; the predominance of market forces; and, the gradual giving way of extended families to nuclear families. For Gouldner, the key task of formal education in the modern era is to induct young people into the culture of critical discourse. For my purposes such rational discourse is the key to communicative reason which I defined in the last chapter as the human capacity to be analytic, critical and imaginative, on the one hand; and, on the other, to put these attributes to the service of public good. Rational, critical discourse is the discourse for moving beyond taken-for-granted quotidian modes of thinking and talking and coming to agreements about universal matters.

In theory, therefore, all students could become intellectuals and the ability to engage in rational discourse should bestow equality: 'teachers' ... role invites them to ... train students to believe that the value of their discourse does not depend upon their differing class origins, that it is not the speaker but the speech that is to be attended to' (p. 43). Yet, even if the focus is the academy alone, it is rare to find a community of intellectuals composed of students and their teachers.[8] Gouldner's explanation is that:

> The New Class is elitist and self-seeking and uses its special knowledge to advance its own interests and power, and to control its own work situation. [It is] morally ambivalent, embodying the collective interest but partially and transiently, while simultaneously cultivating its own advantage. (pp. 7–8.)

He is especially scathing about universities believing that they have allowed the colonization of rational discourse:

> The university's central problem is its failure as a community in which rational discourse about social worlds is possible. This was partly because rational discourse as such ceased to be its dominant value and was superseded by a quest for knowledge products and information products that could be sold for funding, prestige and power – rewards bestowed by the state and the larger society that is bent upon subverting rational discourse about itself. (quoted in Delanty, 2001, p. 82)

At the same time, Gouldner, like Habermas, is sensitive to ambivalence. On the one hand:

> There is no doubt that faculties [reproduce the status quo]. Academicization often withdraws concern for the major crises of society, sublimating it into obsessive puzzle-solving, into 'technical' interests. Obsequious professors ... teach the advanced course in social cowardice, and specialists transmit narrow skills required by bureaucrats. (1979, p. 45)

PEDAGOGY AND THE UNIVERSITY

On the other hand, he reminds us of a time during the 1970s when the US government curbed universities, observing that: 'While [the university] is designed to teach what is adaptive for the society's master institutions, it is also hospitable to a culture of critical discourse' (p. 45). Universities are 'committed to the cultivation of alternatives, to possibilities ... to what *might* be and not only to what *is*' (p. 32) and this commitment means that, at least some of the time, self-interest can exist alongside the desire to make sacrifices for the collectivity. So they are both emancipatory *and* elitist, both reproducing *and* subverting the larger society. We need to work with the contradictions.

Gouldner concludes that those who are capable of 'systematization, themetization, explication, rationalization, and formalization' (p. 32) might be 'the best card that history has presently given us to play' (p. 7). But to play this card we must view students as potential intellectuals – whatever their destinies – and understand their difficulties with intellectual work. Gerald Graff takes a broad view of what constitutes 'intellectuals' observing that they 'come in many different types' (p. 2) but they have in common critical capacity and social engagement:

> What these different types have in common, from the research professor to the newspaper editorist to the mythical educated lay person on the street, is a commitment to articulating ideas in public. Whatever the differences between their specialized jargons, they have learned to play the following game: listen closely to others, summarize them in a recognizable way, and make your own relevant argument. This argument literacy, the ability to listen, summarize, and respond, is rightly viewed as central to being educated. (2003, pp. 2–3)

Whether university teacher or student, I want to highlight intellectuals' endeavour to be reflexive, communicative, critical, political and transforming; such an endeavour is entirely consistent with the cognitive shift that Delanty describes as: 'A movement towards social reflexivity and discursivity which comes with the opening up of new public spheres and the empowering of social actors by knowledge' (p. 21). Viewing society as in need of intellectual activity on the part of its citizens shifts the role of universities: for Habermas, the university is the key institution in restoring confidence in the power of reason and for Delanty it is strongly positioned to 'democratize knowledge'. All those who comment on the role of intellectuals remind us that one of their functions is to contribute to self-understanding of society: academics-as-intellectuals accept a role in transforming society in their own right, but they could also do so more modestly and indirectly by teaching students who have been introduced to critique, whose minds are developed and who believe that *they* have a role in transforming society. It will be remembered that Karen is quite explicit about wanting her students to 'engage in the world more effectively in relation to things they care about.'

Academic teachers as professionals

My aim in this chapter is to construct a version of university pedagogy that might be convincing to the public and to government. In the last section, I argued that society's need for intellectual citizens can be met only by academic teachers employed in universities. There is a problem that 'intellectual' is a concept often met with suspicion in anglophone cultures. Frank Furedi (2004) captures the hostility in his discussion of anti-intellectualism and the effect that it has or 'banalizing' cultural life. I am with him about the need to champion intellectuals defined according 'to the manner in which they act, the way they see themselves, and the values that they uphold' (p. 31). But I part company with his view that the problem for society is that being an intellectual is no longer regarded as special; on the contrary, I think, like Stefan Collini, that being an intellectual should be seen as ordinary.[9]

The question here is pragmatic, what negotiations with government agencies might lead to an acceptance of intellectualized, critical pedagogy? This section takes the notion of academic teachers as professionals to explore whether it opens up such possibilities.[10] The term 'intellectual' poses problems beyond its dubious reception in the world outside universities. Many influential intellectuals are not academics, they are writers and social commentators who can think, speak and act completely independently of governments and institutions (unless they live in countries in which freedom of speech is restricted on pain of retribution). Conversely, it is argued that academics should not be described as intellectuals if they are not socially engaged. Furthermore, however attractive the idea of the 'intellectual' is to academics, the discourse of 'professionalism' is what is peddled by government agencies in relation to teaching. Should the term be rejected or can it be worked with to argue for particular conditions which support pedagogy that genuinely develops communicative reason?

The idea of being a 'professional' is regarded with some antagonism by academics. Indeed, there is a strong line of argument that the professionalization of research and teaching in academic posts is the cause of the decline of the intellectual. Edward Said (1994b) thinks of 'profession' as depoliticized in contrast to being an 'intellectual':

> By professionalism I mean thinking of your work as an intellectual as something you do for a living, between the hours of nine and five with one eye on the clock, and another cocked at what is considered to be proper, professional behaviour –

not rocking the boat, nor straying outside the accepted paradigms or limits, making yourself marketable and above all presentable, hence uncontroversial and unpolitical and 'objective'. (p. 55)

The acceptance of the notion of 'professionalism' depends on social definitions. David Mills (2005) argues that in higher education it is valued differently in the UK and USA: British academics are suspicious of a government-imposed form of 'expert professionalism' which is focused on skill and standards and stripped of moral and creative aspects; while in the USA 'social trustee professionalism' is defined as moral vocation.

Yet, there is no escaping that in most universities academics are state-funded and that the state expects something in return; at the same time, there is still an acceptance that without academic freedom the very idea of being an academic, who is motivated by the autonomy to ask questions and push boundaries, would be attenuated beyond recognition. But there are constant struggles over the extent and nature of this freedom: in the current climate it needs to be justified. Academics as intellectuals should have a critical relation with the status quo, but at the same time must survive within in it. They must manage the frequently difficult tension between being 'insiders' and 'outsiders',[11] and, in Gouldner's (1979) words, they are impelled to, at least 'a partial rejection of the prevailing system of cultural values' (p. 32). In this respect, the ideology of professionalism could be used as a weapon in a struggle against academics becoming state functionaries whose freedom to think, speak and act as they think right is compromised.

A short history might highlight the possibilities. The rise of professionalism was a response to the increasingly complex social and economic needs of modern society which called for specialized expertise; professionals are integral to the modern welfare state. There is a literature which expounds an ideal type of professional occupation: autonomy and prestige granted by the state in return for expertise in areas central to the needs of the social system; and in return for devotion to public service (Larson, 1977). Professions become communities expressing common (or vested) interests, identity and commitments.[12] But, in practice, professional work is complex and mediated; constructions of professionalism are historically and socially situated; claims to moral and technical superiority are contested; and, gains in privilege and autonomy negotiated with the state can always be withdrawn, so need to be defended. Moreover, it is argued that currently the future of professions is uncertain, that there is a 'crisis of trust',[13] and so there is an urgent need to renegotiate with the state and with the public the nature and significance of professional work. From this perspective, 'professionalism' was never neutral and apolitical and can be understood as a discourse, as part of an ongoing politics of knowledge, power and social organization.

The concept of professionalism, in all its historical and social complexities, offers a range of identities. The one I am offering here for university teachers is founded on the need for solidarity, rationality and reflection in a modern society which faces serious political and social problems. In order to find solutions states already forge relationships with professional academics. Certainly, there are important questions for education to address. First for critical theory – as well as for states because they can see the social cost of injustice – is the question of a role in bringing about social justice. Other questions are contingent: for example, how to develop a theoretically based pedagogy; how to address questions about the dichotomy between academic and vocational, theory and practice; and, how to take up issues of entitlement and diversity. A 'new' professional university teacher, which is how I see Karen and Leo, would be able to tackle these issues; and, they would seek to earn the trust of the public by being explicit about what they do.

By and large academics – as researchers, trainers, teachers and commentators – are perceived as professional specialists. What needs to be fought for is an extension of the notion of professional specialist to incorporate the intellectual's role of contributing to critical self-understanding of society. But this needs to be earned: as Delanty puts it, 'The jargon and career-riddled nature of academics is antithetical to public enlightenment' (2001, p. 85). We know that in academics' lifeworld narrowness, conformity and mediocrity exist alongside utopian ambitions. We know, too, that teaching which makes students feel and appear stupid is carried on alongside teaching that engages their minds and lifts their spirits. Perhaps in these contradictory circumstances it is not realistic to seek the status of intellectuals who are at liberty to do whatever it is they want. Though humble, perhaps a more productive way forward is to embrace the notion of 'professional', but to eschew managerial and technical versions for a construction that includes acting expertly, critically, morally and responsibly in respect of *all* the functions of the university. Such a stance could lead to involvement in shaping the future. Paul Standish (2002) discusses Derrida's idea that 'the idea of profession requires something tantamount to a pledge, to the freely accepted responsibility to profess truth' (p. 15). He continues:

> The academic work of professing must then be something more than the ... statement of how things are ... the work of profession involves always some attempt to see it *as if*. ... Openness to the impossible possible, something beyond the range of predetermined categories or a purely autonomous control (effective performance) is essential to the exercise and growth of the imagination that this professing requires. (p. 16) (emphasis in the text)

What is suggested here is a homology between profession and academic professing that legitimizes the work of shaping social and cultural futures.

Conclusion

This chapter has attempted to demonstrate that simple models will not achieve critical university pedagogy that mobilizes communicative reason. It needs teachers who are intellectuals, who prepare their students as intellectuals and who intellectualize teaching and learning. There are grounds for hope: examples from everyday practice and from scholarly literature about teaching show us university teachers who go about this business on a daily basis. But, as well as action on the ground, we need to explain our work and to agitate for debates about university work. These days it is often remarked that teaching takes second place to research, and there are elaborate schemes devised to reward teaching similarly to research to signal that teaching is valued. But, however skilled, creative, inspiring and responsible an individual teacher, individual performance is not enough for genuine pedagogic improvements in universities. What is essential is that relevant actors come to agreements about what counts as good pedagogy, for what purposes and what is to be done to make it happen. Genuine progress will be made by a concerted effort to defend the integrity of universities in terms of all their functions (research, general education, professional preparation and public enlightenment): the special scientific and scholarly learning processes into which we want to induct students characterize universities and rely on the unity of functions.

I have argued here that a feasible and politically acceptable critical pedagogy might be fostered by drawing on the resources of both 'public intellectual' and 'professional' with specialized knowledge of teaching. As Leach and Moon (1999) put it, an intellectualized university pedagogy 'should provide the cornerstone to legitimating teaching as a professional activity' (p. 275). This means asking difficult questions about the educational enterprise and drawing in a scholarly fashion on a range of resources (such as those introduced in the last chapter). The claim for pedagogic professionalism is not for university teachers to be regarded as a particularly privileged group, but rather as one that has the attributes and qualifications to be trusted to direct its own educative efforts. It might not work. But in the next chapter I discuss what institutions themselves could do to nurture the academic capacities, identities and dispositions necessary for a critical pedagogy which prepares students as citizens who are capable of intellectual independence and judgement.

Notes

1 See, for example the stimulating Volume 47, Nos 1 and 2 (2005) of *Cultural Quarterly*, which is devoted to higher education.

2 Professor of English and Education at the University of Illinois at Chicago.

3 In the interest of space, I have made précis of longer accounts and I have omitted footnotes which in the original versions referred to educational literature that supported the authors' claims. I have changed the names of the lecturers for anonymity.

4 See Chapter 6.

5 Although Giroux does not say so, I believe that one of the problems for university pedagogy, at least in the UK, is that it does not draw on the much longer tradition of school education research which is based on the foundation subjects of history, psychology, philosophy and sociology; nor on adult education research, which often draws on a critical tradition.

6 They include: Benda (1959), Bauman (1987), Collini (1991), Debray (1981), Eyerman (1994), Gramsci (1971), Jacoby (1987), Mannheim (1966), Said (1994b) and Shils (1972).

7 He distinguishes between the two, but the distinction does not concern me here.

8 Rare but not non-existent; I am thinking of postgraduate research students and their supervisors in some sites and, perhaps, some disciplines in some Oxbridge colleges. These derive from my experience, and I am sure that are more across the world.

9 Quoted in Furedi (2004), p. 9.

10 The business of 'professionalizing' teaching is an issue in the UK where compulsory training of new university teachers has become commonplace in institutions.

11 For a discussion, see Jennings, J. and Kemp-Welch, A. (1997) *Intellectuals in Politics: From the Dreyfus Affair to Salman Rushdie*, London: Routledge.

12 Gouldner (1979) draws attention to how Talcott Parsons' traditional 'flattering conception [of professions which stresses their] dedicated moral character ... glosses their own self-seeking character as a status group with vested interests' (p. 37), but the issue here is how this 'flattering conception' can be used to make a case for a particular construction of academic-as-intellectual.

13 ONora O'Neill spoke about the crisis and 'distorting forms of accountability' in the BBC Reith Lectures in 2002.

8

Creating the environment for critical pedagogy

It can be argued that the greater threat to the University's inability still to articulate some vision of the good society comes from 'inside', from the decay of notions of academic authority (through which a culture, and codes, of rationality are expressed) and of scientific and professional expertise (which imply social and ethical responsibilities as well as power and privilege) rather than from the 'outside', from the intrusion of alien, instrumental and anti-intellectual values. (Peter Scott, 'The transformation of the idea of a university[1])

Introduction

Throughout this book I have defined critical pedagogy for universities as teaching and learning focused on developing students' intellectual and moral attributes (communicative reason) so that they are disposed to think creatively and act responsibly with others to ameliorate the problems of contemporary society. In general, Habermas's critical theory emphasizes the potential of rational argument for resisting the distortions of money and power and promoting communicative reason in citizens. Keeping in mind, then, both the *telos* and the means of critical pedagogy, this chapter's question is: How can we secure for academic teachers like Karen and Leo an occupational culture and mentality which promotes collective deliberation in open discussion about what is worth teaching, why it is worth teaching and how it should be taught? In terms of Habermas's critical theory this can be thought of as how to mobilize the resources of teachers' lifeworlds towards ideal speech conditions in which truth, truthfulness and justice are collectively pursued (Abbas and McLean, 2003). Although I deal briefly with the broader policy context, I have chosen to explore this question from the point of view of insiders who are the academic teachers and their managers working in institutions.

Since this chapter concerns options and constraints, a summary might be helpful of where I think we are in terms of grounds for hope for a pedagogy which will fulfil the promises of modernity and educate citizens and professionals capable of tackling the huge social, political and economic problems of the world; and also of where we are in terms of the considerable obstacles that stand in the way of what Habermas calls 'promissory notes'. As I set out earlier in the book, old and sound ideas still constitute the lifeworld of many academics: these are the critical and emancipatory power of knowledge, inquiry and reason; the autonomous pursuit of knowledge; the connection between science and progress; the usefulness of knowledge for society; and, the contribution to equality, citizenship and democracy. There is also strong adherence to the unity of a 'bundle of functions' that includes research, teaching, professional training and public enlightenment. University teaching can transform the lives and minds of students who become 'intellectualized' like their teachers.

Threats to the lifeworld sketched above come from the fragmentation and stratification of the system; from quasi-market imperatives and a shortage of resources; and, from an untrusting audit culture and unnecessary standardization. Academics are often resistant, and they can become recalcitrant and some of them explain their distress in scholarly publications. But they are also deferent, compliant and collusive; become cynical as a response to a sense of alienation from their culture and identity; display self-interested behaviour at the expense of others (I shall make more of this later); regard teaching as a self-evident, technical-practical activity; and, engage in research at the expense of teaching.

There will always be such contradictions, but, nevertheless, we can ask what kind of institutional environment can be created that will encourage promissory notes and hold up colonizing tendencies; and, as a subsidiary question, we can ask what would characterize an environment in which teaching is reinvested with moral purpose and not seen as a technical matter. Habermas (1989) proposes for universities a form of self-conscious idealism that unifies around the reproduction of culture, identity-formation and services to society: 'the integrative normative force of an ideal center anchored in a corporative self-understanding' (p. 106). Habermas's point is that an 'ideal center' based on ideas about learning processes exists in the minds and hearts of academics and this is what we should build upon: why jump too quickly to deciding what is possible and what impossible to change for the better?

Drawing on previous chapters about the communicatively structured nature of university pedagogy, an environment conducive to critical pedagogy would allow university students and their teachers to work in a climate of trust; to be authentic; and, to focus on intellectual growth and transformation. Such an environment would be characterized by rational argumentation about pedagogy; and, most importantly, by a sense of community in which knowledge is produced and reproduced with students. It would also protect academic freedom, but, nevertheless, demand that academic teachers explain themselves to students, colleagues, the public and government.

Making arguments, giving explanations and deciding the practical matters that university teaching demands requires time for individuals to think. Moreover, the version of critical pedagogy I am promoting here requires *collective*, critical self-reflection, for the power of reflecting together is the key to resisting technical-rational constructions of pedagogy: 'Our only hope for the rationalization of the power structure lies in conditions that favor political power for thought developing through dialogue' (Habermas, 1971, p. 61). For thinking about the possibilities for action that arise from 'thinking together'[2] I find Alberto Melucci's (1995) concept of 'collective identity'[3] helpful because he defines it as a process of constructing an action system in which collective identity is understood as the 'formation of a "we"' which incorporates three aspects: self-reflection that produces meanings that actors as a collective recognize; a sense of belonging and 'causality' that endows actors with the ability to 'attribute the effects of their actions to themselves'; and, a sense of permanence that 'enables actors to establish a relationship between past and future and to tie action to its effects' (pp. 43, 46, 47).

This chapter is motivated by the goal of an academic teacher identity the crux of which is collective reflection and action. The chapter is in two parts: the first examines the institutional context in terms of policy, management and the issue of the unequal treatment of teachers; and, the second part explores the institutional environment in terms of programmes of support for teaching and for pedagogical research.

Policy contexts

It is possible to think that we can work towards pedagogy for communicative reason, for it chimes with the aspirations of many university teachers and students to enjoy the life of the mind and to live in a just and peaceful world. It cannot be denied that 'an age of diminishing possibilities'[4] is reflected in national and local educational policies which ignore the lifeworld of culture, society and identity and delegitimize social, cultural and ethical considerations. Policies do not seek to encourage autonomous, socially reflective, critical, creative thinking in academic teachers or their students. Even so, despite severe constraints, there are options which academics as human agents can take up and, we can be optimistic because, according to Habermas, groups become more reflective when the lifeworld is threatened.

Neither state nor local policy is implemented in an algorithmic fashion without hitches; it is always mediated, interpreted and reworked (Bowe *et al.* 1992). We know from our own experiences and from other accounts and studies that institutions and academic teachers – individually and collectively – have a range of ways of dealing and coping with the policy environment in which they find themselves: some creative, some accommodating, and some resistant and distancing. Academic teachers have suffered from an erosion of autonomy, status and conditions; yet their experiences and responses are ambivalent. For example, in *Academic Identities and Policy Changes in Higher Education* (2000) which reports academics' responses to policy changes in the UK during the 1980s and 1990s, Mary Henkel notes that 'Young academics were ambitious, determined and focused' (p. 265), but I have found a wide variation of response in young university teachers, some have embraced the new forms of accountability as a sign that teaching matters; some are anxious about their future and comply; and others in old-fashioned manner construct their hoped-for life's work researching and teaching as a vocation. Academics' attachment to their disciplines inflects responses to policy: interviews with new university teachers of anthropology find them 'pragmatic, reconciling the short-term horizons and language-games of their own institution's policies and expectations with the *longue durée* of disciplinary discourse' (Mills, 2004, p. 23). Mills and Harris (2004) conclude that disciplinary identity and the enactments of disciplines in departments 'serve[s] to act as a conceptual buffer to the everyday vicissitudes of "audit culture" [so that academic teachers can] find ways of living with the incommensurability of disciplinary traditions and institutional demands' (p. 9). Henkel (2000) concludes her study with two possibilities:

> The outcome of the combination of loss, ambiguity, reappraisal and 're-professionalisation' of academic identity is uncertain. They might result in a renewal of higher education, in which academics succeed in adapting their frameworks of knowledge and values to meet new demands. They might be part of a restructuring of higher education and a re-ordering of relationships between academics and other interest groups in society in which collaboration, negotiation and justification are more central and autonomy no longer taken for granted. (p. 234)

How can we understand and make use of a policy situation that is ambiguous? Bowe and Ball (1992) suggest a heuristic representation of the policy process in which they identify the contexts of 'influence', 'policy text production' and 'practice'. In each of these contexts policy is contested. The 'context of influence' in which policy discourses are constructed is where 'interested parties struggle to influence the definition and social purposes of education, what it means to be educated' (p. 19), these days it is a context 'often related to the articulation of narrow interests and dogmatic ideologies' (*ibid.* p. 20). However, texts are needed to *represent* policy; and in the 'context of policy text production' narrow, dogmatic interests are expressed as claims to 'popular (and populist) common-sense and political reason' (*ibid.*). In the last two decades policy text production has become prolific: it comes in written and verbal texts from government, government agencies and local officials. While such agents might like to control the interpretation of their texts, it is never possible. Policy texts change, evolve or disappear as projects proceed. Policy texts always allow interpretations for they are 'fraught with the possibility of misunderstanding, texts are generalized, written in relation to idealizations of the real world, and can never be exhaustive, they cannot cover all eventualities' (*ibid.* p. 21). We can see the interpretation process in consultations of varying degrees of authenticity set in train by authorities. Such consultations represent a struggle to grasp control of the arena of practice which is the focus of the text.

Responses to the textual interpretations of policies take place in the 'context of practice' where texts are again reinterpreted or recreated:

> Practitioners do not confront policy texts as naive readers, they come with histories, with experience, with values and purposes of their own, they have vested interests in the meaning of policy. Policies will be interpreted differently as the histories, experiences, values, purposes and interests which make up any arena differ. The simple point is that policy writers cannot control the meanings of their texts. Parts of texts will be rejected, selected out, ignored, deliberately misunderstood, responses may be frivolous etc. (*Ibid.* p. 22)

From the perspective of my experience, I should like to express this process of policy interpretation a little differently. Common to accounts of teachers' adaptation to change is that they are doing more than finding gaps and spaces; they are actively attempting to create professional identities. Teachers attempt to create the lifeworld they would like to inhabit: this includes forging a personal, professional identity (what Habermas calls personality), but also contributing to a culture and forms of interpersonal relations. In work such as teaching that is dependent on communication there appears to be a drive to harmonize work and lifeworld. From this point of view, if university teachers regard policy texts as incursions which impose an alien identity or culture, or put obstacles in the way of intersubjectivity, they will treat them to forms of defiance, resistance or strategic compliance.

The process of responding to policy can be unconscious, recalling

Habermas's 'pre-reflective form of taken-for-granted background assumptions' (in Outhwaite, 1996, p. 168[5]) or can be entered into with awareness. The possibility of self-consciously recreating education policy constitutes an option 'to achieve a new definition of the situation which all participants can share' (Habermas in Outhwaite, 1996, p. 120[6]). Communicative action for critical pedagogy in universities will require coming to agreements. The most productive university environment might be one in which the tension is exploited between academics-as-professionals negotiating with government agencies and policy-makers locally and nationally; and academics-as-intellectuals whose task is 'still to expose false claims to knowledge and advance true ones [and ask] one question too many for comfort in the search for truth'[7] (Jennings and Kemp-Welch, 1997, p. 299). In such an environment, academics-as-teachers would seize the discourse and attempt sincere, true and just utterances about pedagogy. They would forge a language that expresses the often-disappointing realities of teaching at the same time as expressing possibilities and joys. The new discourse(s) would allow principled positions to be taken on pedagogic issues (while keeping questions open). Academics are well placed to recreate policy texts: they are, by profession, used to thinking, arguing and writing.

But I must not lapse into unrealizable utopianism. At a local level, the vulnerable, casualized academic teachers who make up a large proportion of the university teaching force (discussed in more detail later in the chapter) must be highly courageous to mount defences of ethical and socially conscious pedagogy. More broadly, Michael Apple (1998) has analysed the extensiveness of conservative trends in society which pose enormous obstacles for 'creating the conditions ... to defend and build progressive policies' (p. 199). Nevertheless, we should keep in mind that some national policy contexts pose less obstacles than others: for example, Karen, the young lecturer whose teaching work I introduced in the last chapter, returned to a Canadian university because the system as a whole allows more flexible institutional environments in which teachers are given less teaching and limited administrative responsibility'.[8] Her view is corroborated by another young lecturer who describes teaching in Canada as 'unimaginably better' than in England because the students are more enthusiastic and the bureaucratic requirements minimal. He believes that the students are less strategic than in England because the system does not encourage 'quick fix' attitudes.[9] Other examples of differences that impact on the teaching climate are Scotland (unlike England) enshrining in law academic freedom for all universities;[10] and Alan Ryan, Warden of New College, Oxford where the vote in Congregation of academics can over rule the vice-chancellor, tells us that, by contrast, elite US universities have 'a bruising style of management where rank-and-file faculty have a lot of freedom to manage their individual academic lives but a wholly inadequate say in the direction of the university as a whole'.[11]

Such differences suggest – to return to Michael Apple's analysis – that locally and regionally what he calls a 'decentred unity' is possible.[12] Local movements often do not have resources but:

> ... show us in the most eloquent and lived ways that educational policies and practices do not go in any one unidimensional direction. Even more importantly, these multiple examples demonstrate that the successes of conservative policies are never guaranteed. This is crucial in a time when it is easy to lose sight of what is necessary for an education worthy of its name. (1998, p. 199)

We can expect battles. Cary Nelson[13] believes that (at least in universities in the USA) a stage has been reached in which the 'traditional modes of argument' no longer work for negotiating because managers and politicians are indifferent to them. Academics, he argues, should turn to the 'old tradition of civil disobedience' though he does not hold out much hope for he also believes that 'Faculty are mostly spineless'. Nelson elaborates his arguments in *Office Hours: Activism and Change in the Academy* (2004) in which, with Stephen Watt, he claims that there is 'but one way to resist all the forces at work to disempower and degrade the professoriate and instrumentalize education – collective action' (p. 2). In their view, academics themselves are 'substantially to blame for higher education's difficulties [for] our present situation represents ... a failure to negotiate collective forms of identity, a failure of collective institutional self-analysis, and a failure of collective action' (p. 10).

The call to universities to become organizations 'grounded in solidarity, common purpose and shared understandings' (*ibid.*) might seem abstract, but there are many issues concerning teaching that academics could demand should be subjected to reasoned argument and ethical consideration. I shall deal with two in this chapter: the plight of vulnerable teachers and forms of control of and support for teaching. But first, I turn to the problem of university management because it seems to me that central to realizing a pedagogy that approximates to 'critical' is to attempt to come to agreements with managers.

Transformative management for critical pedagogy

In earlier chapters, I discussed the misery of academic teachers coping with audit cultures in techno-bureaucratic universities. Even if managers are not wholly sympathetic, they might respond to evidence that a sense of pressure and isolation is inhibiting young academics' capacity to focus on teaching and improve it (Knight and Trowler, 2000). My purpose in this section is to suggest that those who manage teachers in universities could decide to think about how to ameliorate problems discussed in Chapter 4 which are associated with the audit culture and which have a detrimental effect on work.

Of course, universities, especially if they are conceived of as collegiate, are complex organizations requiring systems and procedures that ensure that functions are carried out and which enable goals to be met. However, Martin Parker's *Against Management* (2002) attacks management as: 'a generalized technology of control of everything – horses, humans and hospitals ... as the universal solution, not a personal assessment of a local problem' (p. 11). Parker sees management practices as colonization of organizations and private life and insists that there are ways other than 'management' to 'do organization'.[14] He wants to persuade his readers to stop perceiving management as the commonsense, inevitable and natural form of ordering matters for society, organizations and the economy, for to do so is to believe a 'very large story' which equates social progress with separating management from 'the everyday skills through which life [is] lived' (p. 5). Management, claims Parker, makes 'control' and 'ordering' synonymous and is cruel and unjust 'in the name of a neutral and efficient technology of organizing' (p. 15).[15]

Parker would like to 'fan the flames of discontent' (p. 9) – which he sees in, for example, hostility to bureaucractic rationalization in popular culture and in anti-capitalist movements – to a legitimation crisis for management. He wants people to consider non-managerial ways of organizing work that centre on such alternative concepts as 'co-ordination, co-operation, barter, participation, collectivity, democracy, community, citizenship' (p. 11). Taking a broad view he asks whether managers themselves might be re-educated to think differently about organization but concludes that this is highly unlikely for they have too much invested in their management work to rebel: 'identities, qualifications, salaries and status' (p. 189). Is this the case for managers in universities? For some, perhaps, but the academy is replete with well-articulated discontent about management; furthermore, in most universities (though not all) managers – vice-chancellors, deans, heads of departments and so on – have been or are themselves academics, some taking on managerial roles for short periods only. So, in Parker's words, there is often not the 'permanent association of particular persons to particular roles'[16] (p. 206); it should be easier for university managers to be seen as 'co-ordinators' rather than managers and not as a 'separate group' from academics.

In a chapter in a collection edited by Melanie Walker and Jon Nixon (2004) entitled 'Sitting uneasily at the table' Judyth Sachs (2004) describes how as Chair of the Academic Board at the University of Sydney and as a professor of education, who strives to espouse the principles of deliberative democracy, she negotiates the tension 'to maintain my independence and not be captured by managerialist agenda that are shaping contemporary university policies or to be seduced by the influence and access to information that this position affords' (p. 101). Although maintaining the balance between, on the one hand, the dictates of management and government and, on the other, academic independence is risky and difficult, Sachs reports that the work of the Board has been received as 'collegial' by academic colleagues. That a good number of academic managers are, like Sachs, 'betwixt and between' (p. 112) probably already keeps in check the worst excesses of the techno-bureaucratic university,[17] nevertheless, the task of avoiding reproducing established norms and bolstering dominant interests is a difficult one, especially for managers.

In another chapter in Walker and Nixon's book, Colin Bundy (2004), Director and Principal of the School of Oriental and Asian Studies in London and Deputy Vice-Chancellor of the University of London, provides a rare account of university management that is both critical and *for* management. I set out his case here as a possible alternative future for university managers that accords with critical pedagogy as I configure it. For Bundy, teaching is a 'moral vocation [and] universities can and must link education and democracy' (p. 174). His diagnosis of the current state of affairs is that academics and managers do not share such a vision of the role of universities and that institutional management is seen as constraining research and teaching and the connection between them.

Bundy's analysis begins with 'unlovely' fictional vice-chancellors[18] who between them illustrate 'a shift from a self-governing profession to a self-consciously managerial authority' (p. 162) in the context of expansion, resource cuts, the rise of auditing, deterioration of academic status and conditions of employment, changes in teaching practices, and 'drastically narrowed expectations of higher education' (p. 164). Bundy's critical history charts the rise of management specialists and practices but does not envisage their retreat because universities have become so large and complex; because there are constant crises caused by reduced resources; and, because the blend of regulation and deregulation enforced by the state has changed the relationship between state and universities. Acknowledging that 'proponents and critics [of university management] occupy little common ground' (p. 170), he proposes 'to contest the excesses of managerialism, conserve the success of management, and reconstruct the purpose, worth and value of the university' (p. 170) by exploring 'what space exists for academics and administrators to refashion forms of governance that support rather than inhibit ... research and teaching' (p. 171). The space can only be found, Bundy asserts, by critiquing the '(mis)fit between managerialism and academy'; by working with contradictions; and, by engaging in a process of 'rearticulation' (*ibid.*). He is at pains to make the point that if management can impose an alien discourse, which antagonizes academics, it can also encourage a return to a more authentic discourse; and, if management can close down creativity and critique, it can also open it up. Finally, the rapprochement between academics and managers is not about internal functioning only. It is also necessary for the higher education system as a whole to regain ground with the broader society. He believes that managers and academics together should eschew 'cynical service to the prior claims of market know-how' (p. 174) and reclaim universities' 'critical, reflexive, and independent function' (*ibid.*).

At the 'meso' level of the institution, it is difficult to imagine that anyone would make objections to Bundy's goals to 'find ways of bridging the divide between academics and administrators, of coupling effective and decisive management with the disciplinary expertise, professional pride and intellectual passion of academics [to create] a shared organizational space and structure' (p. 173). But what kind of concrete changes might be expected to emerge from the approach that he suggests? The examples that are embedded in his chapter are: taking seriously rhetorical commitments that suggest progressive ends (for example, 'partnership' and 'relevance'); devolving decision-making; and, putting an understanding of the actualities of academics' everyday lives at the heart of management practices. All these issues are important; however, universities cannot claim moral high ground if they do not acknowledge and tackle their own injustices. There are injustices concerning students that I raised in Chapters 5 and 6; there are also injustices perpetrated on teachers and I discuss these in the next section of this chapter.

Managers are usually regarded as responsible for making unreasonable demands on time. Transformative managers would be alert to unequal and unreasonable workload allocation. We saw in Chapter 4 that time spent on managerially determined objectives and on demonstrating good performance causes stress, while in contrast, time spent on one's own genuine professional concerns is rewarding. At the same time, one of the most important issues is the amount of time spent on teaching: Karen left England for a 'reasonable teaching load'. If we accept that university teaching is not mechanical and that it requires scholarship and research then it requires time. As Nelson and Watt (2004) put it: 'the system as a whole requires a significant amount of leisure to function' (p. 3) for learning processes take time.

From the perspective of critical theory, managers should re-conceive their role as one of 'stimulating self-reflection and overcoming the blockages of established institutions and modes of thought' (Alvesson and Skoldberg, 2000). It is clear that, while there might be no single way to improve organizational practices, those like Bundy who are interested in

management for transformational purposes imply the need for communicative reason – dialogue, critique, communication, enquiry, justification,
sincerity and truthfulness – which requires an environment approximating
to ideal speech conditions in which actors can partake in discussion without
fear of consequences. It is with this in mind that I turn to look at the plight
of what I have called 'vulnerable teachers'.

Vulnerable university teachers

In *Office Hours* (2004) Cary Nelson and Stephen Watt tell a story of the
discipline of English that I think can be applied to other disciplines. It is 'of
astonishing intellectual advancement and ambition . . . founded on a basis of
cheap instruction provided by slaves deceived into thinking they are serving
a high cause' (p. 24). Their trenchant exposé of 'the diaspora of teachers' is
motivated by their commitment to universities modelling 'responsible and
politically engaged citizenship' (p. 7). They argue that unless the issue of the
flexible labour teaching force in universities is addressed universities can
never be sites of progressive opposition. In this version of what is happening, managers are the enemy with whom activist academics must fight:
'nothing is more addictive to managers than hiring at a clerk's rate someone
to do all the teaching'.[19] They argue that increasing reliance on casualized
labour is a part of the university environment that is having a drastic effect:
'It diminishes our ability to do creative work and undermines our capacity
to serve our students, while simultaneously undercutting our independence, our dignity, and our potential to have any critical impact' (p. 7).

My definition of a 'vulnerable university teacher' encompasses a categorization and a description. In terms of a category the vulnerable can be
part-time teachers, those on fixed-term contracts, PhD students who teach,
those compelled to sign 'teaching-only' contracts, those threatened by
compulsory redundancy or denied tenure for ever, novice, black and
women teachers and any university teacher who is allocated too much or
soul-destroying teaching.[20] The description of vulnerable teachers is that
they do not have the same rights and privileges as others. Although not all
individuals who fall into the broad categorization above are treated badly,
many are. There is, for example, ample evidence that black and women
academics are more likely to have short-term contracts and less likely to be
promoted than white men. Vulnerable teachers are under assault – they are
underpaid; they do not have access to office space and other material; they
are not included in decision-making processes; their insecurity is exploited
and advancement is made difficult. I limit the discussion here to what is
referred to as the casualization of teaching.

Over the last two decades a trend is reported towards the casualization of academic work manifested in the growth of fixed-term contract and casual work. The scale is difficult to establish. In the USA the trend is unabated and the enormous difficulty in securing a tenured track started earlier than in the UK (Nelson and Watt, 2004) where the Higher Education Statistics Agency (HESA) calculated that the proportion of academic staff with temporary contracts was approximately 45% in the academic year 1997–98 which appears to have dropped to 40% during 2002–3,[21] perhaps because there has been a partially successful union campaign to press universities to curtail the time an individual is tied to fixed-term contracts. According to the same statistics, just under one-third of all full-time appointments are temporary. However, Husbands (1998a) and Husbands and Davies (2000) argue that this is an underestimate because data is severely limited and non-standard. Many part-time categories do not appear in HESA statistics and some universities do not compile full data: for example, it has been estimated that the number of PhD students who teach in British universities' anthropology departments almost equals the number of full-time staff (Gibb, 2004). Although an apprenticeship model of the PhD is adhered to, very small numbers are destined to secure full-time academic posts. There is also a question of shame. Universities are reluctant to admit to the use of a large 'peripheral' workforce because it may be seen as an admission of the 'semi-professionalization' of teaching at a time when students and their parents are scrutinizing league tables.[22] Although it is argued that the expansion of higher education has presented employment opportunities in universities for women, they are more likely to be in temporary, part-time posts.[23]

I want to emphasize the human cost found in the stories of debt, loss and struggle of many who aspire to be university teachers. The effects can be terrible of being insecure, of being anxious and fearful, of doing what other people want, and of hoping against hope for too long. I cannot do better than reproduce the quotation that Nelson and Watt (2004) select from a book called *Ghosts in the Classroom: Stories of Adjunct Faculty:*

'I am an adjunct ... I bought the bag of lies we call the American Dream. I was intoxicated on the Nitrous Oxide idealism forced upon me in graduate school. I believed caring, working hard, doing a good job mattered and would add up to something concrete. Instead, I find myself on a wheel that turns but goes nowhere. I don't expect this situation to change. I know I have joined the huge group of teachers who become permanent adjuncts, who do a good job only to get one more chance to do it again ... I have watched my self-esteem drop, drop, drop from doing work that is, theoretically, enhancing the self-esteem of my students. I have seen tired eyes, the worn clothes, the ancient eyes of long-term adjuncts. ... I have known adjunct teachers who hand out As and Bs like vitamins and help students cheat on their exams so they'll get good course evaluations. I've watched people fall into obsessive relationships with their idealism and their pedagogy, because it's the one defence against despair ... I am a dreamer. I am an idealist. I am a victim. I am a whore. I am a whore. I am an adjunct.' (quoted on p. 28)

Elaine Showalter (2005) claims that 'academic life has so much pain, so many lives wasted or destroyed'.[24] Surely this is true, I am convinced by my own research studies[25] and by my own experiences and others. But why is this so? Perhaps it is because the attachment to discipline and scholarship and the accompanying intellectual labour is so often intimately connected with identity formation. There is little doubt that academic work elicits strong identification, as Henkel (2000) puts it: 'ideals and values and the inheritance of language and myth in which they are expressed constitute significance and motivation in academic working lives' (p. 22).

Those who aspire to an academic life are often pursuing matters strongly felt by their Damasio's autobiographical self.[26] Identification with being a researcher or with a discipline or topic is often strong at the beginning of a PhD and the intensity of the process – the obsession and passion it requires – could mean that incorporation into autobiographical self with a particular anticipated future is swift. When Nelson and Watt (2004) describe their generation of PhD students in the 1970s as the 'lost generation' still haunted by their inability to secure tenure, they refer in part to loss of a defining identity which ties professional interests to personal passions. It is because academic work is so tied up with the lifeworld – what matters viscerally to human beings – that it elicits strong emotions: Lee and Boud (2003) examine emotion and identity in relation to academics writing for publication and note that fear and desire are generated because the work is bound up with fundamental senses of self and self-worth. It can be argued that the more strongly identified with a professional identity an individual is, the more that identity will become part of a core identity with emotion attached to it and to the threat of its loss.

But there is even more to it. Arlie Russell Hochschild's work, *The Managed Heart: Commercialization of Human Feeling* (1983), which was introduced in Chapter 6 is again illuminating. In the context of the workplace it highlights how the individual is under the sway of the power of bureaucracy and the interests it serves. The concept of the 'sale of personality' reveals that survival for individual workers depends on actively managing feelings and on understanding and following the social rules of the workplace. Hochschild makes us aware of the effort it takes to pay the 'emotional dues' that institutions demand even if they are benign (p. 219). However, if individual workers must 'sell' their emotion, deceive or try to change their feelings the cost is estrangement from their own emotions and a loss of a 'sense of wholeness' (p. 184). Would it be far-fetched to suggest that the adjunct teacher quoted above describes emotional abuse? Constant anxiety,

Hochschild (1983) suggests, is the realization of danger that: '... impinges on our sense of self that is there to be endangered, a self we expect to persist in a relatively continuous way' (p. 221). So it is their very selves, the core of their being, that vulnerable teachers may fear for and desire to preserve.

What can we expect to be the effects on teaching of a flexible teaching labour force that is not well treated in the ways I outlined above? It is, of course, under documented,[27] but we know both that such teachers are committed and teach well,[28] but also that they 'burn out'. Here are some hourly-paid lecturers interviewed for a national educational newspaper – all were frightened of being named:[29]

> 'I am sure that having so much teaching done by hourly-paid lecturers who feel marginal to the university is damaging. I find myself having to reassure students that their studies will be fine even if I am not there. The truth is that they may not be.'

> 'Student feedback forms often praise individual lecturers but are critical of university management. Students can see we are insecure and worried about who will teach them in the future.'

At the London School of Economics (LSE) Husbands (1998b) found decreasing student satisfaction with part-time teachers teaching over a three-year period and suggests that the reason is: '... a psychological response of lower commitment, lesser morale, greater alienation and a reluctance to overexert when both long-term and short-term rewards for doing so are niggardly' (p. 140).

The consequences are more subtle than lack of student satisfaction. The experience and role of vulnerable teachers has impacts not only on the quality of teaching, but also on the future development of disciplines and on the professional status of academics. Teaching is core academic work: it centrally concerns the reproduction of the discipline – its meaning, practices and principles. If what we currently understand as 'disciplines' and 'inter-disciplines' have developed out of the practices and writings of academics of the past, then 'disciplines' and 'interdisciplines' of the future will also depend on the current workforce. Furthermore, bolstering injustice jeopardizes the capacity of disciplines to renew themselves from the standpoint of ideas about the university that might want to claim that they embody Enlightenment values.

Nelson and Watt (2004) launch a searing attack on academics.[30] They accuse them of hiding 'self-promoting agendas and aggrandizing self-interests' (p. 33) behind claims to universal truth and social concern. They draw attention to widening salary gaps and the rise of contingent academic labour and ask: 'Is not the indifference of the lucky, the wealthy, the comfortable, the empowered, fast becoming an intolerable scandal, at least for an industry that seeks to be admired and supported for commitments of a higher order?' (p. 32). Their diagnosis is that because scholarship, research and teaching have come to be about self-promotion, universities as communities have become unreflective and socially blind: 'When an unreflective community investment in research meets [a] careerist model of disciplinarity, the result is a faculty member who sees self-advancement and careerism as transcendental virtues' (p. 34). I do not think we can deny this, we have all seen it and in smaller or larger ways most of us are complicit, which makes moral cowards of us.[31] Keeping quiet about institutional exploitation and feathering our own nests undermines the legitimacy and authority of academics as public intellectuals.

For all this we must not underestimate the importance of local gains that are being made.[32] The message of Nelson and Watt's book resonates with critical theory: academics themselves must confront what is happening and 'seek a more ethical academic workplace [by balancing] individual ambition with community responsibility and collective action' (pp. 25–6). They make the large claim that if academics are willing to critique their own identity formation they can 'show others how to address the inequities of the global economy' (p. 26). More modestly, academics might take a moral and practical interest in vulnerable teachers as a significant part of their *habitus* who are, at the moment, not well managed, are marginalized and treated unfairly. Such university teachers are also part of the academy of the future whose shape is still uncertain and may still be influenced. Much is at stake, for example the silencing of authentic and critical discourse about teaching and unacceptable treatment of a vulnerable occupational group. In institutional environments conducive to critical pedagogy, academics and managers would pull together to model Enlightenment values.

This brings me to the end of the first part of the chapter which might be summarized by the suggestion that, in Nelson and Watts' words, 'institutional devotion to profit at all costs' (2004, p. 38) is at the expense of traditional ideas about the university that could be revived, especially the idea of collegiality directed towards creating an environment where intellectual activity can take place.

Education for critical pedagogy: the next generation

The second part of the chapter shifts the focus to the more specific topic of what kind of education, training and support for teaching critical pedagogy would require. To keep the topic focused, I will concentrate the discussion on the identity formation of a new generation of university teachers. In general, critical theory can help an analysis of what might support the formation of an academic identity (which integrates teaching, scholarship and research) which would help to create university environments in which Enlightenment ideals can be pursued.

To frame the discussion, I hazard the following broad configuration of what kind of academic would push forward the social, critical and moral aims of universities: they would be committed to and derive satisfaction from both producing and reproducing their disciplines, for disciplines are ways of understanding and acting in the world that will safeguard and promote justice in many forms; and, they would be skilled and competent teachers who can convincingly defend their educational practices and who are oriented towards teaching as a social act rather than towards teaching as a technical problem. The question addressed here is what type of institutionally based education, training and support might help to produce such an academic identity?

By way of preamble, it is important to address the antagonism that academics feel towards education and training for teaching. It is difficult to ascertain the extent of hostility – there are certainly new academics who have found courses useful, but not all of them[33] and many established academics are not convinced of their value:[34] for example, Frank Furedi, Professor of Sociology, sees these courses as a form of indoctrination[35] and is clearly horrified by the 'philistine ... crusade to turn academics into trained teachers'.[36] I think that, at least in part, the ambivalence arises from ill-conceived courses that do not intellectualize teaching.

By way of illustration I reproduce below Deborah Cameron's (2003) caustic judgement on those, like me, employed to support teaching in universities and who peddle, as she puts it, 'the powerful new ideology of "teaching and learning"' (p. 138). The basis of her antipathy is an encounter with what is often called 'educational development' in her first post during the 1980s:

> [I] was required to attend a three-day training course on how to teach under-graduates. It was run by a man I will call Barry Owen, whose title was 'Co-ordinator for Educational Technology'. On day one he videotaped and critiqued us giving mini-lectures. On day two he introduced us to some research on what constituted 'effective communication in a classroom context' and showed a film made (by the look of it in 1970) for the Royal Navy on the use of visual aids. (We complained because it was offensively sexist; it was also antediluvian in other, less ideological ways. The technologies examined included the epidioscope, an ancient machine that none of us had ever heard of, but not the overhead projector, which was actually in our classrooms.) On day three, Dr Owen explained the principles of designing multiple choice tests and student evaluation questionnaires [...] and then took us to the pub down the road to help us bond with one another.
>
> We did bond, though not around the professional concerns Dr Owen fondly hoped we would want to discuss. We bonded around our astonishment that the

likes of Dr Owen should be given house room in an academic institution. Though all of us were anxious about our new teaching responsibilities and very much aware of how unprepared we were, we were unanimous in regarding the 'training' we had just received as a monumental insult to our intelligence. Dr Owen was pleasant and well meaning, but he did not command our respect. The body of research literature he drew on struck all of us, from the chemist to the poet, as pseudo-science, providing neither real evidence supporting the use of particular teaching methods nor practical tips on what to do in a classroom. Above all, it was patent that Dr Owen was not what he was supposed to be helping us to become – a good teacher. His expositions were confusing and dull; his responses to questions and comments suggested he himself was not very bright. He did not know how to use his OHP, flipchart and coloured pens (… today it would be PowerPoint), but his presentation skills could not compensate for the vacuity of content.

In time I discovered that every university has its Barry Owen; his title varied from place to place ('Coordinator for Educational Technology', 'Head of Educational Development', 'Staff Development Officer'), but he was invariably held in contempt by his academic colleagues. Not infrequently, he had moved sideways into the field from an academic department where his mediocrity as a psychologist or a geographer had been legendary. His job was seen as a sinecure for academic failures. Although this was partly intellectual snobbery about education as a field of expertise, that wasn't all there was to it. A lot of people who oversaw educational development in universities then were, like Barry Owen, visibly inferior teachers and scholars, and the standard of training they offered was often so poor that even academics who supported the principle declined to endure the practice more than once. (p. 138)

It is possible that matters are a little improved since 'then', but what remains is a constant struggle against technical-rational constructions of teaching that educational development is prone to. Cameron continues:

We should not be telling our students things, we should be 'managing their learning' and enabling them to develop 'transferable skills'. This is a matter of technique and procedure: who the teacher is, what s/he knows and what s/he cares about are or should be unimportant. (p. 139)

Cameron finds it 'astonishing that there hasn't been more collective resistance to this view of what teaching is' (p. 140). I think that the reason is partly because academics' teaching tends to be instinctive, they do not have an educational language with which to defend their practices and this, ironically, is something that courses could provide. David Mills (2004) thinks that a 'trading zone' should be set up between education and discipline experts. But this requires mutual trust and respect. Although there will always be exceptional individuals, I do not believe that people who take on this role should come from personnel training backgrounds, they should be academic educationalists or discipline experts (or both) and respected teachers and researchers (unlike Dr Owen). Academic educationalists responsible for such courses should themselves be on the right side of the barricades – resisting the technical rational constructions of teaching which antagonize academic teachers and engaging with socio-economic and political matters that are essential for a university pedagogy for social transformation.

To convey what an alternative to Dr Owen's offering might look like, I take as an example (but not an exemplar) a programme[37] which carried accreditation – I shall refer to it simply as *certificated programme* – which I led for several years and regarded as 'critical' but which also gained the acceptance of university managers.[38] The programme was underpinned by theories about the nature and acquisition of professional knowledge and competence: good teaching demands a reflective, self-critical, research-informed approach and new teachers need a great deal of assisted practice to build confidence and skill. The rigour of the programme resided in engaging the new academic teachers in reflective practice, professional conversations and applying pedagogic theory to student learning and teaching as it is experienced. These three practices refer to the three contexts in which pedagogic knowledge is generated – reflections on one's own practice, discussions with others and public pedagogic theories. I will deal with each in turn.

Reflective practice

Being self-reflective is a central tenet of critical theory: Freire's (1996) definition of praxis is: 'reflection and action on the world in order to transform it' (p. 28). But exhortation to be reflective is often viewed with suspicion by academics when it is a component of programmes for teaching. I want, therefore, to emphasize my distance from reflexivity as a form of self-regulation complicit in social and political structures. This form can be seen when reflective practice is presented as a slogan signalling espousal of 'good practice', while serving to inculcate the teacher into prescribed and technical versions of what it is to teach well from which there is no dissenting: values are invisible and the teachers are drastically separated from the knowledge generated from their own experiences.

Habermas's fluid use of the term 'reflection' is helpful. Outhwaite (1996) explains that in different pieces of writing Habermas uses the term to refer '*both* to a subject's reflection on what makes it possible for him or her to perform certain actions *and* to a more critical insight into the distortions built into those and other processes' (p. 116) (my emphasis). From the point of view of developing capacity for critical pedagogy the two are fused: that is, self-reflection to improve day-to-day classroom practice is bound up with self-reflection aimed at understanding the influence of power in classrooms, institutions and in the world. Both forms of reflection are necessary to achieve pedagogic autonomy and enlightenment.

So for *certificated programme* while I avoided the self-referential version by which agents subject themselves to surveillance and which does not incorporate the influences of the socio-political context, at the heart of the programme was the notion of reflective practice. The work of Donald Schon (1983, 1987) provides a conceptual framework for considering the relationship between professional competence and reflection on action. Briefly, a distinction is made between 'theories-in-use', which are used when action is being taken and contain assumptions about the professional situation, and 'espoused theories' which are used to describe and justify behaviour, and which may or may not be theoretically informed. Problems in professional practice can arise when practitioners are unable to make explicit and interrogate the relationship between their theories-in-use and their espoused theories. An example from higher education is the espoused theory which insists that teaching is designed to make students critical and questioning, while the theory-in-use encourages students to repeat the lecturer's pronouncements. In order to improve practice, teachers examine their theories-in-use – what they are actually doing – in the light of well-informed espoused theories – what they think they are or should be doing, given the socio-political contexts – and, if possible, adapt their practice in the light of what they learn.

Professional conversations

The term 'professional conversations' was used in *certificated programme* to legitimize intersubjectivity as a form of learning about pedagogy. New teachers are often fearful which leads them to fall back on familiar, but inadequate, theories-in-use. Open discussion among colleagues creates a climate in which anxiety about teaching is acknowledged and can be converted to continual problem-solving. Just as important, from the perspective of critical theory, was giving credence to the notion of reflection-on-action as a *collective* enterprise. So *certificated programme* was designed to create opportunities for fruitful conversations about teaching within and across disciplines: when participants met in sessions and out of sessions (for example, when observing each other's teaching[39]), with mentors and with other academic colleagues who looked at their written accounts about their growing understanding of teaching and student learning. An important aim was to minimize the defensiveness of worried new teachers which prevents them from examining their practice and thinking about alternative action;

the most important aim, though, was to emphasize the nature of pedagogy as a communicatively structured area of activity about which agreements are made.

Talking across disciplines can be particularly fruitful. Stephen Rowland's (1996) instances from interviews with academics shed light on how discipline-specific research might influence perceptions of pedagogy:

> A medic described how the insights gained from his research in community care, with its concern for the social context, was often applied to his teaching. A mathematician explained how the aesthetic experience of research at the frontiers of mathematics, and its concern to simplify mathematical structures – a fundamental issue in mathematics – had a direct bearing upon helping first year undergraduates appreciate the subject. A literary critic claimed that insights from critical studies related to one author – the subject of his own research – could often be applied in teaching undergraduates studying different authors. (p. 14)

Participants in university programmes similar to *certificated programme* often observe how illuminating is the cross-fertilization of such ideas about what it is to learn a discipline. In such programmes it is possible to bridge the differences between disciplinary cultures by exposing the paradigms that affect thinking about teaching and exploring common ground.

The allocation of a teaching mentor in the participant's department was considered an integral part of the programme. In a general way, in order to flourish, new academics need to be looked after by more senior colleagues in their departments, Nelson and Watt (2004) put it succinctly: 'We all know that early luck and good mentoring play important roles in successful careers' (p. 18). There is a literature which suggests that good mentoring is compassionate, humane, allows informal, honest and open discussion[40] and supports all aspects of academic work.[41] In connection with the earlier part of the chapter, it is clear that it would be difficult to arrange for mentoring with such features in circumstances in which equity is not regarded as an important issue. In *certificated programme*, the most successful mentoring took place in departments in which novice lecturers, part-time teachers and PhD students felt themselves to be well treated and in which, in turn, established academics were respectful and, for example, treated PhD students as members of department.

Pedagogic theories

I spent some time in Chapter 6 arguing that we should synthesize theoretical resources to construct principles of pedagogic practice that emphasize human capacity for second-order learning and the moral nature of education. There is a justifiable view which contends that university teachers do not need theory to teach well; partly because it is correctly observed that teachers can teach well without being aware of public pedagogic theory or research; and, also because it is held that it is experience not theory that will reveal what it is to teach well. This is Deborah Cameron again:

> As a head of department I spend a lot of time looking at student evaluation forms and reports of meetings where students' views were solicited. It is striking to me that the comments students make are almost always about two things. One is the course content (whether it was interesting, boring, easy or difficult) and the other is their relationship with the teacher (whether they like the teacher, had individual contact with the teacher, felt the teacher knew them and engaged with them on a personal level). (2003, p. 140)

It is true that at some level what it is to teach well can be reduced to some fairly self-evident principles (in Cameron's case they appear to be to make the subject matter interesting and challenging, and be concerned about students' academic progress): but such principles are often difficult to pursue in practice and it is not always obvious why this is so. Academics adopt theory in their own disciplines yet often reject it in relation to teaching and student learning, but I do not believe that we can both reject technical-rational constructions of university pedagogy and, at the same time, deny that its complexities demand theories. From the perspective I am espousing, the problem with many efforts to improve university teaching is that they are built on a shallow intellectual base.

Of course, theory in a programme for professional practice *must* have purchase on practice and this is a challenge. Jerome Bruner (1999) wrote of the need for teachers to move beyond 'folk pedagogies' pointing out that: 'Thoughtful folk have been forever troubled by the enigma of applying theoretical knowledge to practical problems ... The challenge is always to *situate* our knowledge in the living context that poses the "presenting problem"' (p. 4). There are several good reasons, which I list below, for the incorporation of theory and research evidence into all efforts to improve teaching:

- All discursive practices associated with university teaching and learning are founded on implicit or explicit theories, and Donald Schon's (1987) work suggests that improving teaching, especially collectively, is more likely when teachers can articulate what personally held theories are leaning them towards particular strategies in pedagogic encounters. Theoretical ideas about teaching and learning sustain reflection and professional conversations by providing a framework for teachers who are attempting to explain what is happening in a teaching/learning interaction. Prosser and Trigwell (1999) couch their advice for the improvement of university pedagogy in terms of expanding awareness expressed in the following principles, teachers need to become aware of the way they conceive of learning and teaching within the subjects they are teaching; to examine carefully the context in which they are teaching in order to become aware of how that context relates to or affects the way they teach; to be aware of and seek to understand the way their students perceive the learning and teaching situation; and, to be continually revising, adjusting and developing their teaching in the light of this developing awareness (p. 173).

- Critical frameworks can restrain academic teachers from reinforcing each other's ill-founded views about and undesirable attitudes to teaching.
- Theory can suggest principles which act as 'high ground' for dealing with different modes of teaching (tutorials, seminars, lecturing, research supervision, course design), students at different points in their studies and in different institutional settings.
- The substance offered by theory can keep professional interest alive beyond that offered by achieving technical competence.
- Mounting a defence against colonization needs a language beyond 'folk pedagogies'. Pedagogic theories and knowledge about research can provide this. Expert knowledge is associated with 'professionalism' and can legitimate defence of and argument for particular pedagogic practices and principles.

None of this should imply that what is being discussed here is a simple matter of the application of theory to practice: as Schon (1987) claims, the heart of the problem with technical rationality is the assumption that practice is grounded in knowledge derived from scientific research, so that professional competence is seen as the skilful application of theoretical knowledge to the instrumental problems of practice. This leads to attempts to work out standardized and technical versions of good practice that will never lead to genuinely high quality professional work: 'Inherent in the practice of professionals we recognize as unusually competent, is a core of artistry. ... Artistry is a kind of intelligence, a kind of knowing through different crucial aspects from our standard model of professional knowledge' (p. 13). Alongside developing competence is the business of developing a critical rationale for pedagogic practice. Theories are resources to be examined critically and made use of whether phenomenography, communities of practice, pedagogic content knowledge, academic literacies, or a synthesis of theories. It should be recognized that the processes of professional development are slow and, to repeat the point, three sources of knowledge are involved: one's own experience of all kinds of variations (for example of methods, modes, student groups, institutions and so on); discussions with others; and, ideas about pedagogy based on research and theory. I believe that universities' introduction to educational literature should include an exploration of conflicts about pedagogy, and only institutional conditions that allow openness and authenticity will guard against any version of pedagogic theory becoming a thoughtless orthodoxy.

The effects of *certificated programme*

What then can be claimed for the effects of a programme which emphasizes critical reflection and collective enquiry? I analysed many teaching portfolios[42] and found that, when encouraged to do so, novice teachers openly admit mistakes and difficulties and make positive use of them; they think of explanations for difficulties and mistakes and frame them as problems open for alternative solutions; and, they struggle to make their espoused or ideal theories about teaching congruent with their theories-in-use or working practices ('I hope that I will not become a cynical hack who no longer strives for the holy grail' [McLean and Blackwell 1997, p. 91]). What they write resonates with Rowland's view that: 'the constant of teaching is not the student, or the technique, but the nature of professional judgements we have to make' (1993, p. 6); and with Ramsden's (2003) assertion that improving teaching involves a process of conceptual change analogous to the process of student learning.

Here I will emphasize the effects of the opportunities for collective thinking and talking about teaching that such programmes can offer. Participants were encouraged to think in terms of the context in which they teach because, as far as the improvement of teaching is concerned, the department is the critical unit: individual competence and intentions are always modified by the working environment. So mentoring was conceived as a two-way process between established and new academic teachers which not only supported the new teacher, but also aimed to influence departmental thinking about teaching: when new academic teachers with new ways of thinking about teaching meet in systematic ways with established staff to discuss teaching there is the *potential* of collective, collegial improvement. The following quotations from mentors demonstrate that change did occur through this process:

> 'Amongst X's particular strengths is a capacity to learn from her interrogations of procedures: she grows continually from constant evaluation ... her willingness to listen and to experiment has resulted in solid advice to the department generally in helping to rethink its practices ... much of what she has learned will be fed

into our own procedures as we try to respond pro-actively to the current changing demands of higher education.' (Mclean and Blackwell, 1997, p. 94)

'He ... has proposed a course on literature from the 1950s to the present. This course is admirably unified and it has already won the support of several colleagues. He has also made valuable suggestions for the tightening of the Level 2 course Novels into Film. ... I expect him to take on an increasingly important role in developing courses and encouraging us to think seriously and freshly about our teaching practices. (*Ibid.*)

And simply: 'X.is an inspiration to the ... Department' (*ibid.*).

Certificated programme also drew senior academic staff (deans, heads of departments and professors) into the process of teacher education by establishing that they had a responsibility to assess teaching portfolios. These assessors explicitly approved the exploratory, self-correcting approach which was described by candidates in their portfolios: for example, 'what particularly impresses is the willingness to change and adapt'; 'a commendably self-critical attitude'; 'It was enjoyable for me to read how she coped with the never-ending tasks of trying to satisfy herself of the manner and content of what she taught' (McLean and Blackwell, 1997, pp. 94–5). Some assessors were chastened: 'It made me feel amatuerish'; 'It's frightening really, when I think what I was doing when I arrived'; and 'Is this a covert way of getting us to change?' (*ibid.*)

Of course university teachers should be skilful and competent but more than that is needed: to do justice to teaching, it needs to be intellectualized, furthermore there is some evidence that the students of teachers who think that teaching their subject is transformative are more likely to take a 'deep' approach (Trigwell *et al.* 1999). To achieve anything, I believe that attempts to improve teaching must be congruent with the lifeworld of academics. It is not so difficult. Attempts that foreground reflective practice, critical inquiry, problem-solving communication and the use of evidence are consonant with how academics set about their business. Perhaps, in general, managers, educationalists and academic teachers could act collectively to overthrow the 'new' alien, colonizing discourse borrowed from business management and forge another discourse with which teachers will identify because it deals with the actualities of teaching and with goals for students that express a renewal of the critical and transformative role of the university.

Pedagogic research and critical pedagogy

It is not controversial to assert that discussions and decisions about teaching and learning should be informed by research and evidence[43] but, on the whole, university education research, evaluation and development are fragmented. In this section I want to demonstrate that critical pedagogy demands a unity between pedagogic research and the practices of teaching.

A framework for thinking about pedagogic investigation in relation to improving teaching is provided by Paul Ashwin and Keith Trigwell (2004) and distinguishes three levels: 'Level 1' is 'reflective practice' or 'the scholarship of teaching' already discussed in relation to programmes of education for teaching; 'Level 2' comprises investigations which, more formally, inform groups' policies and practices (course teams, academic units, institutions); and, 'Level 3' is published research with national or international audiences, but which can also influence policy and practice. The table below shows the relations between the purpose, process and outcomes in the levels of investigation:

Level	Purpose of investigation	Evidence gathering methods and conclusions will be	Investigation results in
1	To inform oneself	Verified by self	Personal knowledge
2	To inform a group within a shared context	Verified by those within the same context	Local knowledge
3	To inform a wider audience	Verified by those outside that context	Public knowledge

A key feature of this framework is that it integrates research and development, it also coincides with the three contexts in which knowledge about teaching is generated (reflection on one's own practice, discussions with others and public knowledge). It allows a broad, inclusive definition of 'pedagogic research'. This is crucial. I have made a great deal of the use of theory and research about pedagogy, but it remains that teachers make their own theories. As Carr and Kemmis (1986) put it: 'theories may be provocative, interesting, plausible or arresting but they only become compelling when they are authentically understood and critically evaluated [by the teacher]' (p. 199).[44] The three levels of the framework allow all university teachers to be engaged in pedagogic research and my argument is that a critical university pedagogy needs all levels – individual and collective investigation, as well as research that will be published undertaken by qualified researchers from a wide range of disciplinary perspectives. And no level of investigation should be subject to the imperatives of a techno-bureaucratic system.

Whatever the level, interest in investigation will arise out of everyday pedagogic problems that are informed by critical interests. Examples of suitable questions for investigations with critical intent are: How can we engage the minds of students in ways which encourage a sense of responsibility for society? How can we assist all students to grapple with difficult subjects? What pedagogical practices express justice? How does unfair treatment of teachers impact on pedagogic practices? How is 'quality' constituted in different universities? and so on. The purpose is not to discover definitive answers to such questions but to address them in a principled manner. It is possible to find principles for the research process (at all three levels) in Habermas's theory of communicative action and in his ideas about a 'critical social science', defined as being geared towards human, social and political concerns. In *Becoming Critical* Wilfred Carr and Stephen Kemmis (1986), draw on Habermas's work to make a strong case for educational research allied to critical theory. They emphasize that for Habermas the process of critical social science is 'a form of disciplined self-reflection aimed at enlightenment and improvement of the social and material conditions under which the practice takes place' (1986, p. 145).

Carr and Kemmis (*ibid.*) discuss the relationship of critical social science to the tradition of action research, which supplies a useful paradigm for the second level of investigation undertaken collectively to inform local practices.[45] Although, it is often domesticated, action research has a long and radical history. Its origins are attributed to Kurt Lewin who, in the 1930s, experimented with improving productivity in factories through democratic participation (Adelman, 1993). Typically, it requires that teachers become researchers into their own practices and circumstances. It is similar to Freire's process of conscientization: 'the process in which people, not as recipients, but as knowing subjects, achieve a deepening awareness of both the sociohistorical reality which shapes their lives and of their capacity to transform that reality'.[46] In the radical tradition, action research aims for transformation and is always participative and collaborative. Carr and Kemmis (1986) describe action researchers as undertaking 'a deliberate process [of emancipation] from the often unseen constraints of assumptions, habit, precedent, coercion and ideology' (p. 192). The phrase 'unseen constraints' recalls Habermas's 'unreflected lifeworld' emphasizing the need to bring hidden matters to consciousness so that they can be scrutinized.

The principles of action research are harmonious with Habermas's theory of communicative action because 'it gives credence to the development of powers of reflective thought, discussion, decision and action by ordinary people participating in collective research on "private trouble" that they have in common' (Adelman, 1993, p. 8). Action research – which frequently features as a part of programmes for university teaching – can be seen to prefigure the possibility of a self-critical community. All forms of reflection and action research have the potential to mobilize the capacity for self-critical reflection, social action and the development of expert knowledge in relation to pedagogy.

I think that the third level of published work on critical pedagogy poses more problems. Social scientists, Habermas argues, need to *'come to terms'* (1972, p. 312, Habermas's emphasis) with the three interests that constitute knowledge: toward technical control, toward mutual understanding in the conduct of life and toward emancipation from seemingly natural constraints. A challenge for educational research with critical intentions is to combine all three because teachers and students relate simultaneously to objective, subjective and social worlds. Habermas makes it clear that rejecting 'scientism' for investigating social areas of life is not straightforward – for example, we often need quantitative data to perceive trends and make fair and sensible decisions. The kinds of questions that arise from an interest in critical pedagogy demand both rigorously collected data and sophisticated analysis grounded in an understanding of sociology, economics, history and philosophy. Habermas asks:

> ... how can the promise of ... providing practical orientation about what is right and just in a given situation be redeemed without relinquishing, on the one hand, the rigor of scientific knowledge ... and on the other, ... the promise of social philosophy to furnish an analysis of the interrelationships of social life?

To produce sound ideas about pedagogy for a risky world we need to fuse hard evidence with ethical speculation.

A further problem for career researchers in critical pedagogy such as me is the press to publish with the attendant danger that one is read only by other researchers in the same field. Critical social science should be participatory and offer purchase on practice or seek to have some social consequences. Habermas puts it like this: 'Critique understands that its claim to validity can be verified only in the successful process of enlightenment, and that means in the practical discourse of those concerned.'[47] In practice there are fruitful connections between the three levels of investigation: it is not unusual for a piece of published research to have its genesis in reflection on practice, or for educationalists to collaborate with those teaching in other disciplines.[48] So perhaps there is a future in educationalists and university teachers from other disciplines entering the 'trading zone' David Mills (2004) suggests and developing together forms of 'social organization in which the power of their educational arguments can be discursively tested and examined in practice' (Carr and Kemmis, p. 207). It is important to grasp that there is a synergy between the 'processes of learning' for practical pedagogic purposes and for pedagogic research purposes: interpretative understandings of theory and practice will both guide practice and generate theory. At whatever the level of investigation, for critical pedagogy the aims are to use Habermas's words, 'true statements ... authentic insights ... and prudent decisions'.[49]

Conclusion

The right conditions for a critical university pedagogy approximates to what Habermas calls 'ideal speech conditions' in which teachers and students can explore questions about teaching and learning and come to agreements about practices free of domination and coercion. This state of affairs might be unrealizable, but, if it is not an ideal to strive towards in universities, where else can we expect to find such an attempt? I believe that those academic teachers and managers who themselves believe that universities have a role in the transformation of society can move in the direction suggested by critical theory, even if they are going against the grain. Moreover, there is a consonance between conditions that will improve teaching and learning and conditions for critical pedagogy. There is also unity of method between how to improve teaching and how to investigate it. Decisions about the improvement of teaching and learning made at institutional levels should focus on the quality of the environment for teaching and learning as a whole; and, crucially, encourage a critical interest in knowledge of what helps and inhibits good teaching and student learning.

Notes

1 Inglis, F. (2004) (ed.) *Education and The Good Society*, p. 89.
2 The phrase that Bill Readings used in *The University in Ruins*.
3 He uses it as a tool to think about social movements, but I think it can be usefully applied to academics searching for common cause.
4 Quoted by Giroux (1995) p. 243.
5 From *The Theory of Communicative Action*, Vol. 1 (1984).
6 From *Communication and the Evolution of Society* (1979).
7 These words can be found in the final paragraph of J. Jennings and A. Kemp-Welch's book, *Intellectuals in Politics: From the Dreyfus Affair to Salman Rushdie*, which comes to the conclusion that intellectuals must adhere to the Enlightenment quest of the pursuit of truth.
8 Personal communication, 9 January 2005.
9 Personal communication 20 September 2005.
10 Olga Wojtas, 'Scots are free not to toe the line', *The Times Higher*, 29 April 2005, p. 9.
11 Alan Ryan, Warden of New College, Oxford, 'In American public universities, if you want to have a good philosophy department, you need politicians to feel good about your football team'. *The Times Higher*, 25 March 2005, p. 15.
12 Cites the National Coalition of Educational Activists and Rethinking Schools.
13 I heard what follows when Cary Nelson gave the Centre for Anthropology,

Sociology and Politics (C-SAP) Annual Lecture on 7 June 2005 at the Barber Institute of Fine Arts at Birmingham University, UK.

14 Parker suggests that 'organization is a general description for what human beings do. Organizing involves making patterns that endure in some way. When we organize something we give it a shape, a direction, a meaning' (n7, p. 214).

15 In August 2005, television showed dead bodies floating in the flood waters in New Orleans while individuals from different relief and security agencies looked on idly, telling interviewers that it was not their responsibility to recover the bodies. Is this a management madness that colonizes the ordinary, decent human impulse to do something with dead people?

16 Though, my perception is that 'career' managers are more prevalent in the less prestigious universities and that this is the trend.

17 In fact, in the industrialized world there are many different forms of university governance. In the UK the 'new' universities tend to be highly managed, whereas at the University of Oxford 'Congregation' every member of the university can debate and vote (nevertheless, a contentious governance review is in process).

18 The Principal of the 1950s 'second-rate' university of Kingsley Amis' *Lucky Jim*; the 1980s Vice-Chancellor in Frank Parkin's *The Mind and Body Shop*; and, Sir Stanley OxBorrow, Vice-Chancellor of East Midlands University in Ann Oakley's *Overheads*.

19 Cary Nelson, Centre for Anthropology, Sociology and Politics (C-SAP) Annual Lecture on 7 June 2005 at the Barber Institute of Fine Arts at Birmingham University, UK.

20 Nelson and Watt (2004) illustrate this: '... there are some tenure-track jobs out there very possibly not worth having. A teacher of composition may easily grade 120 papers a week. ... It's like taking home a badly written 600-page novel that repeats itself every five pages. Over the course of a thirty-year career you may grade 120,000 or more composition papers' (p. 21).

21 Before 2002–3 HESA did not record numbers of teaching – only staff directly, so comparisons are difficult to make.

22 See Husbands (1989 a and b) and 'Onward march of the no-research regiment', *The Times Higher*, 24 June 2005, pp. 8–9.

23 Some references can be found from authors concerned about the gendered aspect of the trend. Brooks (1997) finds that in both New Zealand and the United Kingdom 'the only grade of post where academic women outnumber academic men is the very lowest grade – the part-time lecturer' (p. 25); and Weiner (1996) comments that, although career opportunities for female academics have opened up, they are more likely to be on lower grades, on short-term and part-time contracts, and more slowly promoted than their male counterparts.

24 'Campus follies', the *Guardian Review*, 10 September 2005, pp. 4–6.

25 See Abbas and Mclean (2001), a report of an investigation of part-time teachers of sociology in nearly fifty UK universities; and, a longitudinal study of PhD teachers in one university (unpublished paper 'Emotion, identity and the experience of being an aspiring academic').

26 See for example, Colin Evans' *Language People* (1988) and *English People* (1993); and Tony Becher and Paul Trowler's *Academic Tribes and Territories* (2001).

27 Perhaps the ambivalent attitude of full-time academics who seek remission from teaching to do research has had something to do with this.

28 I have much personal evidence gleaned from many years of leading a course for PhD students who teach.

29 All quoted in 'Onward march of the no-research regiment', *The Times Higher*, 24 June 2005, pp. 8–9.

30 See, in particular, the chapter by Helson and Watt 'Anonymity, celebrity and professional identity' in *Office Hours: Activism and Change in the Academy*, pp. 27–39.

31 Nelson and Watt record instances and name people who have not supported vulnerable teachers in their own interests and who have celebrated the 'new feminism while destroying women's lives' (p. 24); I could do the same (for a more measured account see Abbas and McLean, 2001).

32 Nelson and Watt's *Office Hours* records example of successful direct action on US campuses; and in the UK unions have negotiated better conditions for hourly-paid teachers and those on fixed-term contracts.

33 Lipsett, A., 'Lecturers bored by lessons in teaching', *The Times Higher*, 22 June 2005, p. 1, also Mills (2004).

34 The problem is probably most acute in the UK where many universities have made such programmes compulsory for new staff on probation.

35 Furedi, F. (2005), 'For accreditation read indoctrination', *The Times Higher*, 6 May 2005, p. 54.

36 Furedi, F. 'Have a bit of faith in the soul of learning', *The Times Higher*, 5 November 2004, p. 54.

37 The term 'programme' is used in preference to 'course' to convey aspects of support embedded in what was offered, such as mentoring.

38 More detail about the programme can be found in McLean and Blackwell (1997), Bullard and McLean (2000) and McLean and Bullard (2000).

39 The approach taken to observation of teaching is all important: prescribed behaviours are not helpful and 'the prime determinant of the value of the information is the teacher' (Taylor 1994). See also Blackwell and McLean (1996c) for approaches to peer observation of teaching.

40 Blackwell and McLean (1996a, 1996b).

41 Mills (2004).

42 See McLean and Blackwell (1997).

43 Governments are keen on educational research that claims to have identified 'what works' in classrooms. Perhaps more sensitive would be studies, which, like Pierre Bourdieu's *Homo Academicus* (1988), critique universities as sites of the reproduction of inequalities.

44 More than once a university teacher has described to me a shift from conceptualizing teaching as transmission of knowledge to making student learning possible as 'the penny dropping'.

45 An example from higher education is Melanie Walker's *Reconstructing Professionalism in University Teaching* (2001).

46 Freire quoted in Carr and Kemmis, pp. 157–8.

47 From *Theory and Practice* (1974) quoted in Carr and Kemmis (1986), p. 158.
48 I have done this on a number of occasions; see as examples MacMillan and McLean (2005) and Jones *et al.* (2005).
49 From *Theory and Practice* (1974) quoted in Carr and Kemmis (1986), p. 145.

9

University pedagogy for justice, communication and reason

But if we reflect on an increased sensitivity to the environment, to sexual difference, to gender, to people different from ourselves in a whole variety of ways, we can see small hard-won, fragile, but undeniable causes of pride. If we are careful, and mature, and imaginative, and fair, and nice, and lucky, the moral mirror in which we gaze at ourselves may not show us saints. But it need not show us monsters, either. (Simon Blackburn, 2001, *Being Good*, p. 135)

'If you ask me,' observed the Bursar, 'we discuss everything a great deal too much in this university. We argue about this and that and why and wherefore, instead of getting the thing done.'

'But oughtn't we to ask what things we want done,' objected the Dean. ...
Before ten minutes had passed, somebody had introduced the word 'values'. An hour later they were still at it. (Dorothy L. Sayers, 1987, *Gaudy Night*, p. 37, first written and set in 1935)

Introduction

Rather than finishing by re-capping all the arguments of the book, I want to highlight what for me are the most important elements and muse on a few further points that I have not had space to expand. I have been especially keen to persuade readers that some form of critical university pedagogy is a realistic proposition. But the first condition is not to succumb to pessimism:

Processes of differentiation that have accelerated over the last two decades do not *have to* be described in terms of systems theory, and they do not *have to* lead to the conclusion that universities have now left the horizon of the lifeworld. (Habermas, 1989, p. 107)

Being optimistic assumes that there is good in people and following from this assumption, I have tried to argue why adherence to the horizon of the lifeworld matters and how critical pedagogy can assist in the project. I have elaborated the term critical pedagogy as the book has progressed to denote a range of ideas about the purposes and the processes of university education. Foremost among these ideas is that university education should concern itself with problems in society, particularly with problems associated with inequalities, so I will say more about this later. I have tried to convey that my version of critical pedagogy is not incommensurate with current circumstances; much of the work I have implied for university teachers is work of rearticulation and reclamation rather than innovation. In terms of ambitions for university education even small advances and humble goals are worthwhile as long as they have some connection to more ambitious social goals; that is, education can make a difference and I will say more about this too. In terms of the business of teaching students on a day-to-day basis, I hope that I have made it clear that I see critical university pedagogy and good university pedagogy as homologous. The processes of critical pedagogy that I have been promoting converge on Habermas's notion of communicative reason: people's capacity for arguing with others in an effort to solve social problems. Belief that students can become citizens displaying a capacity for communicative reason is the irreducible part of my argument. Since human problems do not now appear to arise from technological and scientific barriers but from problems of what Alain Touraine (2000) calls 'living together', it is possible that great advances could come from learning to argue about values with each other – and the university is a good place to learn to do this. The rest of this chapter will discuss these points in more detail.

By way of conclusion

The question introduced in Chapter 1 around which this book has been based was 'How can university teachers practise pedagogy which is attentive to how their students might as citizens of the future influence politics, culture and society in the direction of justice and reason?' I have attempted an answer by building a version of university pedagogy that is based on critical theory and also on the idea that universities link education and democracy for there is an 'historical link between the freedom of science and learning and the other basic freedoms of an open society [and] the promise of cultural democracy remains one of the most important legitimations of the university' (Delanty, 2001, pp. 63–4). My account of what it is that university students should learn and how we might teach them incorporates a number of features:

- It prioritizes social goals for university education, in particular the notion of urgent moral–political liabilities in contemporary society.
- It writes culture, morality, power and purpose into theories about university student learning.
- It insists on the centrality of questions of justice for university pedagogy;
- It proposes that all humans have the capacity for analytic and critical thinking that can be nurtured by university educational processes.
- It attempts to demonstrate how quotidian teaching practices can enliven (or obscure) the life of the mind.
- It connects interests in the reformulation of the purpose of the university and the role of academics with teacher and institutional action that develops student capacity to learn.

I have been at some pains to show how general pedagogic principles might be formulated which do justice to student capacities and which will equip them to act for good in society; at the same time, I have wanted to stress that prescriptions about how to teach well counter these goals. Bill Readings puts the case in an extreme form when he asserts 'We must seek to do justice to teaching rather than to know what it is. A belief that we know what teaching is or should be is actually a major impediment to just teaching' (1996, p. 154). A major question, which Readings' formulation begs, is what will energize and motivate university teachers to do justice to teaching? David Acheson (2005) is a mathematics tutor at Oxford who has won a 'National Teaching Fellowship Award'. Nearing the end of a long and distinguished teaching career he asks what makes one lecturer better than another. He rejects the following characteristics: has attended a course on communication skills; is younger and therefore more enthusiastic; and is an active researcher (although he does think that being an active researcher *does* help teaching greatly). He suggests instead that the crucial difference is that some lecturers 'really *want*' (p. 15) to be good. He recalls his teaching ventures and claims that if they were successful it is because 'I really *wanted to do it*' (p. 15, his emphasis). His point is this kind of motivation can only arise in a climate of trust (p. 15).

Pedagogy is a moral–practical activity, nevertheless, in contradiction to Readings, I believe that we *can* come to know what teaching is or should be, but only provisionally and only through coming to agreements with our students, our colleagues (inside and outside our institutions) and the public. *Pace* Readings, what should be promoted is thought about university teaching and student learning which allows pedagogic questions to be held open.

Thought, of course, can go anywhere and I have chosen to base mine on Habermas who (with other social theorists) points out that cultural and technological changes in modern society retrieve the human potential for communicative reason. In relation to the goals of universities this means to educate students to be critically reflective about society and to feel solidarity; and, to operate with ease and skill in the objective, subjective and intersubjective worlds. Such attributes might render them future citizens capable of communicative action – which means working with others to address the urgent moral–political liabilities of our time. The public sphere of university education itself is one such liability for, even in rich countries, individuals are denied equal access on the basis of social origins. Basil Bernstein explained the effects on individuals and on democracy:

> Biases in the form, content, access and opportunities for education have consequences not only for the economy; these biases can reach down to drain the very springs of affirmation, motivation and imagination. In this way such biases can become, and often are, an economic and cultural threat to democracy. Education can have a crucial role in creating tomorrow's optimism in the context of today's pessimism. But if it is to do this then we must have an analysis of the social biases in education. These biases lie deep within the structure of the educational system's processes of transmission and acquisition and their social assumptions. (1996, p. xix)

Globally, problems that arise from inequalities between humans are alarmingly severe. In the world at large the poor are becoming poorer. The latest United Nations' (UN) Human Development Report (2005) contains shocking statistics and claims that inequality between and within countries is the main barrier to human development.[1] This is the UN definition of human development:

> The basic purpose of development is to enlarge people's choices. In principle, these choices can be infinite and can change over time. People often value achievements that do not show up at all, or not immediately, in income or growth figures: greater access to knowledge, better nutrition and health services, more secure livelihoods, security against crime and physical violence, satisfying leisure hours, political and cultural freedoms and sense of participation in community activities. The objective of development is to create an enabling environment for people to enjoy long, healthy and creative lives.[2]

We are very far away from this vision: the physical and psychological effects of inequality are devastating the human lifeworld: Michael Marmot's *Status Syndrome* (2004) leaves us in no doubt that above a basic level of need, human flourishing depends less on national wealth than on equality and social inclusion. Similarly, Richard Wilkinson's *The Impact of Inequality: How to Make Sick Societies Healthier* (2005) demonstrates that the wider the gap between social classes the more dysfunctional the society: that is, poorer countries with fairer wealth distribution are healthier and happier than richer more unequal countries.

To take a further example of a moral–political urgency, few would now refute that the environment is a liability of our age and, in theory, nations have the capacity to cooperate to sustain the earth.[3] In *Citizenship and the Environment* (2003), Andrew Dobson argues that a new form of citizenship which he calls 'ecological' embodies commitment to justice and compassion and is what is necessary to achieve sustainable development. In a chapter on education Dobson explores the potential of schools to develop ecological citizens. He proposes a curriculum that focuses on the normative aspects of sustainability, on the responsibilities of citizenship, and on the question 'what kind of society do we want to live in and pass on to our future generation?' He concludes that the conditions exist for teaching for ecological citizenship in the mainstream curriculum in England, though we cannot know yet whether or not it will succeed. We can combine the idea of an ecological citizen with Delanty's idea of a culturally and technologically adept and responsible citizen who negotiates a cosmopolitan world and extrapolate the possibility of university education for new forms of citizenship committed to addressing social problems.

Solutions to poverty, inequality and the environment are in the hands of future generations. Our students are the future public and citizens, and we need them to be open to hearing the truth about the world and acting on it, even if it appears to involve self-sacrifice. Education has always contributed to individual prosperity and economic growth, but global moral–political liabilities call out for rich countries to reassert the importance of individual and social transformation as educational goals.

Whether we like it or not, new modes of knowledge are changing what we do and how we see ourselves and what we are capable of. All the same, while theories and histories of cognitive and cultural shifts can allow us to imagine societal transformations, there are no guarantees that conditions for social renewal can be secured. For example, despite the achievements of mass education, which in theory gives people access to Gouldner's (1979) culture of critical discourse, there is still in rich developed countries an uncomfortable amount of magical or 'pre-reflective' thinking.[4] And more mundanely Bryan Turner suggests quite concrete conditions that universities require to be able to play a role in social matters:

Of course whether social theory can make a contribution to the public domain through moral and social analysis will depend ultimately on a number of material social factors such as the continuity of the university, the possibility of the intellectual as a social role, the nature of publishing, and the role of the state in supporting academic activity. (1996, p. 17)

There *are* contemporary examples across the world of adult education community projects based on critical pedagogy (Mayo, 1999), and although it could be argued that to incorporate critical pedagogic principles in mainstream education poses quite a different challenge, I have wanted to show that good university teaching (of which there are many renditions all over the world) is often not far away from critical pedagogy. What, though, can be done to make the odds shorter of forging university education for communicative reason? I think that a judicious mix of dissent or defensiveness at national levels and determined creation at the level of institutions would, at least, improve matters in the direction of developing communicative reason. In broad terms, a starting point is Habermas's dictate that universities should 'embody an exemplary form of life, in which its members share intersubjectively' (1989, p. 101). The exemplary form of life he refers to is the core work of producing and reproducing human culture, society and identity (the human lifeworld) through research, teaching, professional preparation and public enlightenment. The unity of the functions is essential:

> Once the unifying bond of its corporative consciousness disintegrates, the university too ceases to form a whole. The functions the university fulfils for society must preserve an inner connection (via a web of intentions), as it were, with the goals, motivations, and actions of the members cooperating in its division of labour. (*Ibid.*)

Recently, English universities have provided an example of partial success in protecting the unity of functions. A government White Paper *The Future of Higher Education* (DfES, 2003) argued that there is no demonstrable connection between research productivity and teaching quality (despite a long-standing, substantial and inconclusive literature on the research-teaching nexus [McLean and Barker, 2004]). *The Future of Higher Education* asserted that research funding should be concentrated in research-intensive universities while other universities should be encouraged to focus on 'other parts of their mission' (paragraph 2.6). The hostile response to the attempt to separate research and teaching has been recorded by a parliamentary select committee whose report[5] strongly criticizes the government for 'play[ing] down the connection between good teaching and high quality research' (paragraph 52). Although the government is set on diversification, the resistance to it has led the Higher Education Funding Council for England (HEFCE) to 'climb down on research concentration'.[6] This adjustment only means that a few more departments will be awarded the highest star status so that the number of 'elite' departments is larger.[7] There has, though, been a more subtle positive effect: many universities that *were* previously close to 'teaching-only' are bolstering research in a variety of ways, even if they will not be able to compete for large amounts of government funding. It is as if there is a collective will to ensure that, as the select committee commenting on *The Future of Higher Education* puts it 'teaching should take place in a research-active environment' (paragraph 52).[8] Such tussles characterize the reception of policies, and perhaps constant struggle and resistance of this kind is preferable to revolt; Alain Touraine (2000) claims that the student movement of the 1960s failed because it was too oppositional.

Policy-makers need addressing on a broad range of issues that concern what universities do (I have confined myself to issues of pedagogy[9]). At present, though, critiques of policy developments tend to be confined to academic circles rather than being taken seriously at the level of policy and practice.[10] In Chapter 7 I suggested that a new form of professionalism, which incorporates ideas about public intellectuals, would be a useful guise in which to gain the attention of governments and the public. An essential component of the type of new professionalism to which I refer is continuous critical public debate about purpose and practice emanating from universities which model social responsibility. The question is whether there is a will. In Chapter 3 I discussed the perception of a number of commentators that universities have lost direction and that their legitimacy is being challenged. This state of affairs, I argued, opens up the possibility of reformulating the ideas of the university accumulated from the Enlightenment that academics hold dear and are relevant today. Certainly some of these ideas will need to be explored in a different light than in previous eras: the autonomous pursuit of truth can never be interpreted as it was before postmodern critiques; and, the connection of science and progress has been thrown into doubt by global problems that emanate from unequal progress and from the damaging effects of some science. Nevertheless, surely universities can still think of themselves as useful to society and as making a contribution to equality, citizenship and democracy. Above all it should be possible to reinstate the critical and emancipatory power of reason, even if our understanding of reason must also be subjected to critique. Although the concept of communicative reason includes creativity, imagination and commitment and, above all, the capacity to have true, sincere and just exchanges with others, I refer here also to arguments that tacit knowledge and what is sometimes called 'emotional intelligence' are important capacities for living together in a complex society (Wheeler, 2005).

In several places I have pushed the idea that responsibility for reformulating the idea of the university lies with academics themselves. In *Office Hours* (2004) Nelson and Watts identify a dual crisis 'in the status of the professoriate and the fundamental goals of education' (p. 1), and are mordantly pessimistic about the response of academics:

... many faculty opt for denial or fall prey to delusion. Accustomed to a lifetime of privilege, faculty at prestige institutions continue to dig for fool's gold in their imaginations and predict the return of the good times. At disadvantaged schools, co-opted faculty may resort to the alternative lure of alienated sacrifice in which to ground their self-esteem. [W]ell-endowed and high prestige universities will be able to sustain the status quo if they choose, and some private liberal arts colleges will continue to deliver education that is both intimate and challenging. (Ibid. pp. 1–2)

Yet, there is a choice. Universities are well placed if, as Delanty claims, society needs a 'zone of engagement between power and knowledge, politics and culture' (2001, p. 73). Even so, communications about education with authority will never be smooth:

The purpose of education, finally, is to create in a person the ability to look at the world for himself [sic], to make his own decisions, to say to himself this is black or this is white, to decide for himself whether there is a God in heaven or not. To ask questions of the universe, and then learn to live with those questions, is the way he achieves his own identity. But no society is really anxious to have that kind of person around. What societies really, ideally, want is citizenry which will simply obey the rules of society. If a society succeeds in this, that society is about to perish. The obligation of anyone who thinks of himself as responsible is to examine society and try to change it and to fight it – at no matter what risk. This is the only hope society has. This is the way societies change. (from an essay by James Baldwin called 'A talk to teachers' quoted in Tierney, 1989, p. 80)

Baldwin speaks of the all-important individual experience of education; but for my argument, it is most important to take a long historical view of education and the accumulated effects of its experience on many individuals and on society as a whole. In 'Can education change society?' (2005) Brian Simon tells us that historically there have been shifts in interpretations of the relation between education and society. He rejects the 'frigid or pallid fatalism' (p. 142) of the interpretation that sees education as merely reflecting society and carrying no force for social change. He cites the social movements for self-education of workers during the nineteenth and early twentieth centuries to show the sometimes extraordinary power of education:

It would be rash to deny that this experience had no effect in bringing about social change, because these were mass popular activities which brought thousands, and, in the case of the Chartist movement in Britain, hundreds of thousand of people into new forms of social and political activity and were themselves educative and profoundly so.... From all this there developed a self-conscious and deliberate movement for political and social change; in particular for the extension of the franchise; for full and genuine citizenship; for the right to leisure

– the ten hour and later the eight hour bill; for the right to education. The measures that resulted, though never gained in their pure form as originally demanded, certainly effected social change – and on a massive scale; nor was there anything inevitable about it. Further, those measures that were achieved, once gained, acted as springboards for further demands, for new perspectives. (pp. 143–4)

And lest it be thought that this power can emerge from voluntary movements only, he records how the systematization of education in England from the mid-Victorian period was intended to mirror the social hierarchy, but that:

Once the whole population was brought into the system of schooling – and this was not really so long ago – new contradictions, new perspectives, inevitably arose. Among those relegated to the lowest rung in the elementary schools, new aspirations developed. [I]t was a mere thirty years after the establishment of universal elementary education that a political and social crisis arose closely related to the upward thrust of a system which had been intended (and, indeed, carefully designed) to preserve the social structure inviolate.' (pp. 146–7)

Since then a tiered secondary school system has given way to what was originally a grassroots movement for comprehensive education and now 90% of all pupils are educated in comprehensive schools. Indeed, it is a system that is criticized for not living up to early promise, but as Simon points out, it is still a relatively new system and it embodies values and objectives that are a challenge to some entrenched interests. The process was never going to be easy; nevertheless, it is a system which has survived the onslaught of the Conservative 1980s even if in a changed form.

All the above about schooling is to illustrate how history can reveal the way that education as social control is never wholly successful because it rouses people to wrestle for its transformatory potential. In a parallel way to secondary schooling in the early part of the twentieth century, global mass higher education is in its infancy, and moral panic about, for example, a drop in standards attributed to admitting students who do not have the requisite ability could well appear foolish a hundred years from now. Our view, even now, will depend on whether we believe in the educability of our students to reason and communicate at the levels demanded by universities. Universities could make a contribution to individual development and to human development, but that achievement will depend on the students' experience of education and their understanding of its purposes.

From Jürgen Habermas's perspective hope for the future resides in reflection, critique and reason. And the justification of a university education is being reasonable: 'only from the university can the wider society learn how to conduct its own debates, practical and theoretical, in a rationally defensible way' (Alistair MacIntyre quoted in Standish, 2002, p. 11). The wider society will increasingly be made up of graduates: if they can conduct themselves rationally, morally and responsibly in relation to moral–political liabilities, society might benefit. In *Towards a Rational Society* (1971) Habermas reminds us that, if students experience their universities as agents of change they will be more likely to form identities which will predispose them to being actors in the world. The aim of communicative reason is not ridiculously utopian (even if in practice it is difficult to achieve); taking Habermas's argument about universal capacity, to aim for communicative reason is to build on what we are and what we do – perhaps what Simon Blackburn refers to as the 'good' in us:

> Human beings are ethical animals. I do not mean that we naturally behave well, nor that we are endlessly telling each other what to do. But we grade and evaluate, and compare and admire, and claim and justify. We do not just 'prefer' this or that, in isolation. We prefer that our preferences are shared; we turn them into demands on each other. Events endlessly adjust our sense of responsibility, our guilt and shame and our sense of our own worth and that of others. We hope for lives whose story leaves us looking admirable. (2001, pp. 4–5)

Just as Blackburn's version of goodness is about how we try to live with others, so the modern rationality that Habermas draws us towards *must* involve communication and coming to agreements with others. Gerald Delanty is unequivocal: 'Contemporary society is integrated not by national culture, nor is it integrated by the functional prerequisities of the occupational system, be those of money or power; it is *integrated by communication*' (2001, p. 6) [my emphasis]). In the following quotation Habermas explains how fulfilling the potential of language and acting according to communicative reason can help us be less self-interested and shape futures with each other:

> A subjectivity that is characterized by communicative reason resists the denaturing of the self for the sake of self-preservation. . . . It refers . . . to a symbolically structured lifeworld that is constituted in the interpretative accomplishments of its members and only reproduced through communication. This communicative reason does not simply encounter ready-made subjects and systems; rather, it takes part in structuring what is to be preserved. The utopian perspective of reconciliation and freedom is ingrained in the conditions for the communicative sociation of individuals; it is built into the linguistic mechanism of the reproduction of the species. (1974, p. 398)

For all this, I have repeatedly said that heroic ideas about the place of the university are out of place. It will not be helpful to claim too much. The ideas of the commentators I have drawn on are quite modest: of particular significance are the ideas that the university is one place among many where thinking can take place, questions are kept open and people speak freely and the place, therefore, where a new generation become skilled in critical discourse. There is no doubt that working in universities is tricky in the current climate. Yet, history shows us that the products of universities are contradictory, which is cause for some optimism:

> We must distinguish between the functions universities publicly promise to perform – the social goods they are chartered to produce – and certain of their actual consequences which, while commonly unintended, are no less real: the production of dissent, deviance, and the cultivation of an authority-subverting culture of critical discourse. (Gouldner, 1979, p. 45)

To be practical, though, individuals will gain little, but collective action and solidarity at the level of institutions might create the conditions for a more critical form of pedagogy to segue from current practices. Just as it is for the world we find ourselves in, the future for universities is not predictable for there are many possible futures, so we have to accept provisionality at the same time as trying to construct ideas about and shape an unknown future. Nonetheless, critical pedagogy encourages us to keep the goals of justice, communication and reason at the front of our minds; it reminds us that we must learn to live well with each other; and, it foregrounds the texture and detail of everyday university life.

Notes

1 For example the following were reported in the *Guardian*, Thursday 8 September 2005, p. 17: the world's richest 500 people own more wealth than the poorest 416 million; for every $1 rich countries spend on aid, they allocate another $10 to military spending; a Zambian has less chance of reaching 30 than someone born in England in 1840; and, Europeans spend more on perfume each year than the $7 billion neded to provide 2.6 billion people with access to clean water.
2 http://hdr.undp.org/hd/
3 In *Collapse: How Societies Choose to Fail or Survive* (2005), Jared Diamond uses as case studies ancient societies faced with eco-disasters of one kind or another. His message is that we can learn and make choices for survival.
4 As Francis Wheen so convincingly demonstrates in *How Mumbo-Jumbo Conquered the World* (2004) – see Chapter 5.
5 Select Committee on Education and Skills, Fifth Paper, July 2003 (www.publications.parliament.uk/cgi-bin/ukparl).
6 Goddard, A. (2003), Rethink doubles 6* winners', *The Times Higher*, 15 August 2005.

7 In effect, as the article points out, the proposals 'shift funding from Oxford and Cambridge to Southampton and Bristol' (p. 1).

8 See Note 2.

9 In this respect the focus on pedagogy has been an obstacle. I have not had space to discuss at any length all aspects of this unity: for example, the role of disciplines and interdisciplines which are produced through academic research or the preservation of the teaching research nexus or, indeed, matters concerning curriculum.

10 Although a possibly positive sign in the UK is that pedagogic research and practice appear to be drawing closer. A number of universities – mainly those known as 'teaching-led' – are making professorial appointments to carry out pedagogic research and to embed a research-informed approach to teaching in institutions.

References

Abbas, A. and McLean, M. (2001), 'Becoming sociologists: professional identity for part-time teachers of university sociology', *British Journal of Sociology of Education*, 22 (3), pp. 339–52.

——(2003), 'Communicative competence and the improvement of university teaching: insights from the field', *British Journal of Sociology of Education*, 24 (1), pp. 69–82.

Acheson, D. (2005), 'What I really, really want . . .', *Oxford Magazine*, Second Week, Michaelmas Term, 2005, p. 15.

Adelman, C. (1993), 'Kurt Lewin and the origins of action research', *Educational Action Research*, 1 (1), pp. 7–24.

Ainley, P. (1994), *Degrees of Difference: Higher Education in the 1990s*. London: Lawrence Wishart.

Alvesson, M. and Skoldberg, K. (2000), *Reflexive Methodology: New Vistas for Qualitative Research*. London: Sage.

Amis, K. (1976), *Lucky Jim*. London: Penguin.

Apple, M. W. (1988), 'Work, class and teaching', in J. Ozga (ed.), *Schoolwork: Approaches to the Labour Process of Teaching*. Milton Keynes: Open University Press, pp. 99–118.

——(1993), *Official Knowledge: Democratic Education in a Conservative Age*. New York: Routledge.

——(1995), *Education and Power*. New York: Routledge.

——(1998), 'Education and the new hegemonic blocs: doing policy the "right" way', *International Studies in Sociology of Education*, 8 (2), pp. 181–202.

——(2000), 'Between neoliberalism and neoconservatism: education and conservatism in a global context', in N.C. Burbules and C.A. Torres (eds), *Globalization and Education*. London: Routledge.

——(2004), *Ideology and Curriculum*, third edition. New York: RoutledgeFalmer.

Archer, L., Hutchings, M. and Ross, A. (2003), *Higher Education and Social Class: Issues of Exclusion and Inclusion*. London: RoutledgeFalmer.

Ashwin, P. and McLean, M. (2005), 'Towards a reconciliation of phenomenographic and critical pedagogy perspectives in higher education through a focus on academic engagement', in C. Rust (ed.), *12th International Improving Student Learning Symposium, Diversity and Inclusivity*, Oxford: The Oxford Centre for Staff and Learning Development, pp. 377–89.

Ashwin, P. and Trigwell, K. (2004), 'Investigating staff and educational development', in D. Baume and P. Kahn (eds), *Enhancing Staff and Educational Development*. London: RoutledgeFalmer pp. 117–31.

Ashworth, P., Clegg, S. and Nixon, J. (2004), The redistribution of excellence: reclaiming widening participation for a just society, paper presented at the *12th Improving Student Learning Symposium, Inclusivity and Difference*, Birmingham, 6–8 September, 2004.

——(1978), *Organizational Learning*. Reading: Addison-Wesley.

Avis, J., Bloomer, M., Esland, G., Gleeson, D. and Hodkinson, P. (eds) (1996), *Knowledge and Nationhood: Education, Politics and Work*. London: Cassell.

Ball, S. J. (1993), 'Culture, cost and control: self-management and entrepreneurial schooling in England and Wales', in J. Smyth (ed.), *A Socially Critical View of the Self-Managing School*. London: The Falmer Press, pp. 63–82.

Ball, S. J., Davies, J., David, M. and Reay, D. (2002), ' "Classification" and "Judgement": social class and the "cognitive structures" of choice of higher education', *British Journal of Sociology of Education*, 33 (1), pp. 51–72.

Ballinger, G. (2003), 'Bridging the gap between A-level and degree: some observations on managing the transitional stage in the study of English', *Arts and Humanities in Higher Education*, 2 (1), pp. 99–109.

Barnett, R. (1990), *The Idea of Higher Education*. Buckingham: Society for Research into Higher Education and Open University Press.

——(1994), *The Limits of Competence: Knowledge, Higher Education and Society*. Buckingham: Society for Research into Higher Education and Open University Press.

——(1996), 'Being and becoming a student', *International Journal of Lifelong Education*, 15 (2), pp. 72–84.

——(1997), *Higher Education: A Critical Business*. Buckingham: Society for Research into Higher Education and Open University Press.

——(2000), *Realizing the University in an Age of Supercomplexity*. Buckingham: Society for Research into Higher Education and Open University Press.

——(2003), *Beyond All Reason: Living with Ideology in the University*. Buckingham: Society for Research into Higher Education and Open University Press.

Barroso, J. (2003), 'New perspectives for learning briefing paper 63', Regulations and inequalities in European Systems, www.pjb.co.uk/npl/bp63.htm.

Barrow, R. (1999), 'The higher nonsense: some persistent errors in educational thinking', *Journal of Curriculum Studies*, 31 (2), pp. 131–42.

Bauman, Z. (1987), *Legislators and Interpreters: On Modernity, Post-Modernity and Intellectuals*. Oxford: Polity Press.

Becher, T. and Trowler, P. R. (2001), *Academic Tribes and Territories: Intellectual Enquiry and the Culture of Disciplines*, second edition. Buckingham: Society for Research into Higher Education and Open University Press.

Beck, U. (1992), *Risk Society: Towards a New Modernity*. London: Sage.

——(2000) *What is Globalisation?* Cambridge: Polity Press.

Benda, J. (1959), *The Betrayal of Intellectuals*. Boston: The Beacon Press.

Bernstein, B. (1971), 'On the classification and framing of educational knowledge', in M. F. D. Young (ed.), *Knowledge and Control*. London: Cassell and Collier Macmillan Publishers Ltd.

——(1973), *Class, Codes and Control: Applied Studies Towards a Sociology of Language*, Vol. 2, Ch. 10. London: Routledge & Kegan Paul.

——(1996), *Pedagogy, Symbolic Control and Identity: Theory, Research and Identity*, revised edition. Maryland: Rowman & Littlefield Publishers, Inc.

Bernstein, R. J. (1985), *Habermas and Modernity*. Cambridge: Polity Press.

Blackburn, S. (2001), *Being Good: A Short Introduction to Ethics*. Oxford: Oxford University Press.

Blackmore, J. (2004), 'Quality assurance rather than quality improvement', *British Journal of Sociology of Education*, 25 (3), pp. 383–94.

Blackwell, R. and McLean, M. (1996a), 'Mentoring new university teachers', *The International Journal of Academic Development*, 1 (2), pp. 80–5.

——(1996b), 'Formal pupil or informal peer', *Facets of Mentoring in Higher Education*, Vol. 1 SEDA Paper 94, pp. 23–32.

——(1996c), 'Peer observation of teaching and staff development', *Higher Education Quarterly*, 50: 2, pp. 157–172.

Biggs, R. (2003), *Teaching for Quality at University*, second edition. Buckingham: Society for Research in Higher Education and Open University Press.

Bourdieu, P. (1988), *Homo Academicus*. London: Polity Press.

Bourdieu, P. and Passeron, J.-C. (2000), *Reproduction in Education, Society and Culture*, second edition. London: Sage.

Bowe, R. and Ball, S. J. with Gold, A. (1992), *Reforming Education and Changing Schools: Case Studies in Policy Sociology*. London: Routledge.

Bowles, S. and Gintis, H. (1976), *Schooling in Capitalist America: Educational Reform and The Contradictions of Economic Life*. New York: Basic Books.

Brecher, B. (2005), 'Complicity and modularisation: how universities were made safe for the market', *Critical Quarterly*, 47 (1–2), pp. 72–82.

Brookfield, S. (1990), *The Skilful Teacher*. San Francisco: Jossey-Bass.

Brooks, A. (1997), *Academic Women*. Buckingham: Society for Research into Higher Education and Open University Press.

Bruner, J. S. (1974), *The Relevance of Education*. Harmondsworth: Penguin Books.

——(1999), 'Folk pedagogies', in J. Leach and B. Moon (eds), *Learners and Pedagogy*. London: Paul Chapman Publishing, pp. 4–20.

Bullard. J. E. and McLean, M. (2000), 'Jumping through hoops?: Philosophy and practice expressed in geographers' teaching portfolios', *Journal of Geography in Higher Education*, 24 (1), pp. 37–52.

Bundy, C. (2004), 'Under new management? A critical history of managerialism in British universities' in M. Walker, and J. Nixon, (eds), *Reclaiming Universities from a Runaway World*. Maidenhead: The Society for Research into Higher Education and Open University Press, pp. 160–77.

Cameron, D. (2000), *Good to Talk? Living and Working in a Communication Culture*. London: Sage.

——(2003), 'Doing exactly what it says on the tin: some thoughts on the future of higher education', *Changing English*, 10 (2), pp. 133–41.

Carr, E. H. (1990), *What is History?* Harmondsworth: Penguin.

Carr, W. and Kemmis, S. (1986), *Becoming Critical: Education, Knowledge and Action Research*. Geelong, Australia: Deakin University Press.

Casey, C. (1995), *Work, Self and Society after Industrialisation*. London: Routledge.

Castells, M. (1997), *The Information Age, Economy, Society and Culture, Volume II, The Power of Identity*. Oxford: Blackwell.

Castells, M., Flecha, M., Freire, P., Giroux, H.A., Macedo, D. and Willis, P. (1999), *Critical Education in the New Information Age*. Oxford: Rowman and Littlefield Publishers, Inc.

Child, D. (1981), *Psychology and the Teacher*. London: Holt, Rinehart and Winston.

Clarke, J. and Newman, J. (1997), *The Managerial State*. London: Sage.

Collini, S. (1991), *Public Moralists: Political Thought and Intellectual Life in Britain, 1850–1930*. Oxford: Clarendon Press.

Cooper, A. (2000), 'The state of mind we're in', *Soundings*, 15, pp. 118–38.

Costello, C.Y. (2001), 'Schooled by the classroom: the (re) production of social stratification in professional school settings', in E. Margolis (ed), *The Hidden Curriculum in Higher Education*. New York: Routledge.

Craib, I. (1998), *Experiencing Identity*. London: Sage.

Critchley, S. (2001), *Continental Philosophy: A Very Short Introduction*. Oxford: Oxford University Press.

Dale, R. (1989), *The State and Education Policy*. Milton Keynes: Open University Press.

Damasio, A. (1999), *The Feeling of What Happens: Body, Emotion and the Making Of Consciousness*. London: Vintage.

Dant, T. (2003), *Critical Social Theory*. London: Sage.

Dearing, R. (1997), *Higher Education in the Learning Society: The Report of the National Committee of Inquiry into Higher Education* (The Dearing Report). London: The Stationery Office.

Debray, R. (1981), *Teachers, Writers, Celebrities: The Intellectuals of Modern France*. New York: Basic Books.

de Groot, G. J. (ed.) (1998), *Student Protest: The Sixties and After*. London: Longman.

Delanty, G. (2001), *Challenging Knowledge: The University in the Knowledge Society*. Buckingham: Society for Research into Higher Education and Open University Press.

Dewey, J. (1916), *Democracy and Education*. New York: The Free Press.

DfES (2003), *The Future of Higher Education*. London: Department for Education and Skills.

Diamond, J. (2005), *Collapse: How Societies Choose to Fail or Survive*. London: Allan Lane.

Dobson, A. (2003), *Citizenship and the Environment*. Oxford: Oxford University Press.

Donaldson, M. (1978), *Children's Minds*. Glasgow: Fontana/Collins.

Eagleton, T. (2001), 'For the hell of it', review of N. Bobbio (2000) In Praise of Meekness: Essays in Ethics and Politics, *London Review of Books*, 23 (4), pp. 30–1.

Ecclestone, K. (2004), 'From Friere to fear: the rise in therapeutic pedagogy in post-16 education', in J. Satterthwaite, E. Atkinson and W. Martin (eds), *The Disciplining of Education: New Languages of Power and Resistance*. Stoke-on-Trent: Trentham Books.

Evans, C. (1988), *Language People: The Experience of Teaching and Learning Modern Languages in British Universities*. Milton Keynes: Open University Press.

——(1993), *English People: The Experience of Teaching and Learning English in British Universities*. Milton Keynes: Open University Press.

Eyerman, R. (1994), *Between Culture and Politics: Intellectuals in Modern Society*. Cambridge: Polity Press.

Fineman, S. (ed.) (2000), *Emotion in Organisations*. London: Sage.

Freire, P. (1972a), *Pedagogy of the Oppressed*. London: Penguin Education.

——(1972b), *Cultural Action for Freedom*. London: Penguin Education.

——(1973), *Education: The Practice of Freedom*. London: Writers and Readers Publishing Cooperative.

——(1978), *Pedagogy in Progress: The Letters to Guinea-Bissau*. London: Writers and Readers Publishing Cooperative.

——(1996), *Pedagogy of the Oppressed*. London: Penguin.

——(1998), *Pedagogy of Freedom: Ethics, Democracy, and Civic Courage*. Oxford: Rowman and Littlefield Publishers, Inc.

Furedi, F. (2004), *Where Have All the Intellectuals Gone: Confronting 21st Century Philistinism*, London: Continuum.

Gibb, R. (2004), 'Seminar culture(s), rites of passage and the unmentionable in contemporary British social anthropology', in D. Mills and M. Harris (eds), *Teaching Rites and Wrongs: Universities and the Making of Anthropologists*. Birmingham: Sociology, Anthropology, Politics (C-SAP) The Higher Education Academy. pp. 40–74.

Gibbons, M., Limoges, C., Nowotny, H. *et al.* (1994), *The New Production of Knowledge*. London: Sage.

Giddens, A. (1985), 'Reason without revolution?', in Bernstein, R.J. (ed.), *Habermas and Modernity*. Cambridge: Polity Press, pp. 95–125.

Giddens, A. (2001), 'Dimensions of globalisation', in S. Seidman and J. C. Alexander (eds), *The New Social Theory Reader*. London: Routledge.

Giddens, A. and Pierson, C. (1998), *Conversations with Anthony Giddens: Making Sense of Modernity*. Cambridge: Polity Press.

Giroux, H. A. (1981), *Ideology, Culture and the Process of Schooling*, London: Falmer Press.

——(1983), *Theory and Resistance in Education*. London: Heinemann.

——(1988), *Teachers As Intellectuals: Towards a Critical Pedagogy of Learning*. Granby: Bergin and Garvey.

——(1989), *Schooling for Democracy: Critical Pedagogy in the Modern Age*. London: Routledge.

——(1992), *Border Crossings: Cultural Workers and the Politics of Education*. London: Routledge.

——(1995), 'Beyond the ivory tower', in M. Berube and C, Nelson (eds), *Higher Education Under Fire: Politics, Economics and the Crisis of the Humanities*. New York: Routledge, pp. 238–58.

——(2001), *Public Spaces, Private Lives: Beyond the Culture of Cynicism*. London: Rowman and Littlefield Publishers Inc.

——(2005), The corporate war against higher education, *louisville.edu/journal/workplace/issue5pl/giroux.html*.

REFERENCES

Gouldner, A. W. (1979), *The Future of Intellectuals and the Rise of the New Class: A Frame of Reference, Theses, Conjectures, Arguments, and an Historical Perspective on the Role of Intellectuals and Intelligentsia in the International Class Contest of the Modern Era*. New York: Seabury Press.

Graff, G. (2003), *Clueless in Academe: How Schooling Obscures the Life of the Mind*. New Haven and London: Yale University Press.

Gramsci, A. (1971), *Selections from the Prison Notebooks*. London: Lawrence and Wishart.

Habermas, J. (1971), *Towards a Rational Society: Student Protest, Science and Politics*, trans. J. J. Shapiro. Boston: Beacon Press.

——(1972), *Knowledge and Human Interests*, trans. J. J. Shapiro. London: Heinemann.

——(1974), *Theory and Practice*. London: Heinemann.

——(1979), *Communication and the Evolution of Society*. Boston: Beacon Press.

——(1984), *The Theory of Communicative Action, Volume One: Reason and the Rationalization of Society*, trans. T. McCarthy. Boston: Beacon Press.

——(1985), *The Philosophical Discourse of Modernity*, trans. F. G. Lawrence. Cambridge: Polity Press.

——(1987), *The Theory of Communicative Action, Volume Two: Lifeworld and System: A Critique of Functionalist Reason*, trans. T. McCarthy. Boston: Beacon Press.

——(1989), 'The idea of the university: learning processes', in J. Habermas, trans. S. Weber Nicholson, *The New Conservatism: Cultural Criticism and the Historians' Debate*. Cambridge: Polity Press.

——(1990), *Moral Consciousness and Communicative Action*, trans. C. Lenhardt and S. Nicholsen, Cambridge: Polity Press in association with Basil Blackwell.

——(1994), *The Past as Future*, interviews by M. Haller, trans. and ed. by M. Pensky, Cambridge: Polity Press.

——(1995a), 'The critique of reason as an unmasking of the human sciences: Michel Foucault', in M. Kelly (ed.), *Critique and Power: Recasting the Foucault/Habermas Debate*. Cambridge: MIT Press, pp. 47–77.

——(1995b), 'Some questions concerning the theory of power: Foucault again', in M. Kelly (ed), *Critique and Power: Recasting the Foucault/Habermas Debate*. Cambridge: MIT Press, pp. 79–107.

——(1997), 'Modernity: an unfinished project', in M. Passerin d'Entreves and S. Benhabib (eds), *Habermas and the Unfinished Project of Modernity: Critical Essays on The Philosophical Discourse of Modernity*. Cambridge: MIT Press.

Haggis, T. (2003), 'Constructing images of ourselves? A critical investigation into "approaches to learning" research in higher education', *British Educational Research Journal*, 29 (1), pp. 89–104.

——(2004), 'Meaning, identity and "motivation": expanding what matters in understanding learning in higher education?', *Studies in Higher Education*, 29 (3), pp. 335–52.

Hall, S. (1996), 'Introduction: who needs identity', in S. Hall and P. Du Gay (eds), *Questions of Cultural Identity*. London: Sage.

Hammersley, M. (1995), *The Politics of Social Research*. London: Sage.

Hargreaves, A. (1994), *Changing Teachers, Changing Times: Teachers' Work and Culture in the Post Modern Age*. London: Cassell.

——(2002), 'The end of quality?', *Quality in Higher Education*, 8 (1), pp. 5–22.

Hayes, D. (2003), 'New Labour, new professionalism', in J. Satterthwaite, E. Atkinson and K. Gale (eds), *Discourse, Power and Resistance: Challenging the Rhetoric of Contemporary Education*. Stoke-on Trent: Trentham Books, pp. 28–41.

Henkel, M. (2000), *Academic Identities and Policy in Higher Education*. London and Philadelphia: Jessica Kingsley Publishers.

Hochschild, A. R. (1983), *The Managed Heart: Commercialization of Human Feeling*. Berkley and Los Angeles: University of California Press.

Horkheimer, M. [1937](1972), *Critical Theory: Selected Essays*, trans. M. J. O'Connell. New York: Herder and Herder.

How, A. (2003), *Critical Theory*. New York: Palgrave Macmillan.

Hughes, A.G. (1956), *Education and the Democratic Ideal*. London: Longman, Green and Co.

Husbands, C. T. (1998a), 'Assessing the extent of use of part-time teachers in British higher education: problems and issues in enumerating a flexible labour force', *Higher Education Quarterly*, 53 (3), pp. 257–81.

——(1998b), 'Job flexibility and variations in the performance and motivations of longer-term part-time teaching auxiliaries at the London School of Economics and Political Science,' *Work, Employment and Society*, 12 (1), pp. 121–44.

Husbands, C. T. and Davies, A. (2000), 'The teaching roles, institutional locations, and terms and conditions of employment of part-time teachers in United Kingdom higher education', *Journal of Further and Higher Education* 24 (3) pp. 337–62.

Inglis, F. (2000), 'A malediction upon management', *Journal of Education Policy*, 15 (4), pp. 417–29.

Inglis, F. (ed.) (2004), *Education and the Good Society*. Basingstoke: Palgrave Macmillan.

Jacoby, R. (1987), *The Last Intellectuals; American Culture in the Age of Academe*. New York: Basic Books.

Jaspers, K. (1960), *The Idea of the University*. London: Peter Owen.

Jennings, J. and Kemp-Welch, A. (1997). *Intellectuals in Politics: From the Dreyfus Affair to Salman Rushdie*, London: Routledge.

Johnston, B. (2005), The ESRC criticality project: theory and outcomes seminar given at the Institute for the Advancement of University Learning, University of Oxford, 2 December.

Jones, C., Turner, J. and Street B.V. (1999), *Students Writing in the University*. Amsterdam/Philadelphia: John Benjamin's Publishing Company.

Jones, K. (2003), *Education in Britain: 1944 to the Present*. Cambridge: Polity Press.

Jones, K., McLean, M., Amigoni, D. and Kinsman, M. (2005), 'Investigating the production of university English in mass higher education: towards an alternative methodology', *Arts and Humanities in Higher Education*, 4 (3), pp. 245–62.

Kelly, M. (ed.) (1995), *Critique and Power: Recasting the Foucault/Habermas Debate*. Cambridge: MIT Press.

Kenman, G. and Jones, F. (2004), *Working to the Limit: Stress and Work-Life Balance in Academic and Academic-Related Employees in the UK*. Leeds: Leeds University.

Knights, B. (2005), 'Intelligence and interrogation: the identity of the English student', *Arts and Humanities in Higher Education*, 4 (1), pp. 33–52.

REFERENCES

Larson M. S. (1977), *The Rise of Professionalism: A Sociological Analysis*. London and Berkeley: University of California Press.

Larson M. S. (1990), 'In the matter of experts and professional, or how impossible it is to leave nothing unsaid', in R. Torstendahl and M. Burrage (eds), *The Formation of Professions: Knowledge, State and Strategy*. London: Sage, pp. 24–50.

Laurillard, D. (2002), *Rethinking University Education: A Conversational Framework for the Effective Use of Learning Technologies*, second edition. London: Routledge-Falmer.

Lave, J and Wenger, E. (1991), *Situated Learning: Legitimate Peripheral Participation*. Cambridge: Cambridge University Press.

Law, I., Phillips, D. and Turney, L. (2004), *Institutional Racism in Higher Education*. Stoke-on-Trent: Trentham Books.

Lawn, M. (1996), *Modern Times? Work, Professionalism and Citizenship in Teaching*. London: Falmer Press.

Lawton, D. (1977), *Education and Social Justice*. London: Sage.

Lea, M. (2004), 'Academic literacies: a pedagogy for course design', *Studies in Higher Education*, 29 (6), pp. 739–56.

Lea, M. R. and Street, B.V. (1998), 'Student writing in higher education: an academic literacies approach', *Studies in Higher Education*, 23 (2), pp. 157–72.

Leach, J. and Moon, B. (1999), *Learners and Pedagogy*. London: Paul Chapman Publishing.

Leathwood, C. and O'Connell, P. (2003), 'It's a struggle': the construction of the "new student" in higher education', *Journal of Educational Policy*, 18 (6), pp. 597–615.

Lee, A. and Boud, D. (2003), 'Writing groups, change and academic identity: research development as local practice', *Studies in Higher Education*, 28 (2), pp. 187–200.

Lemaitre, M. J. (2002), 'Quality as Politics', *Quality in Higher Education*, 8 (1), pp. 29–37.

Lindqvist, S. (undated), *A History of Bombing*. London: Granta Books.

Lowe, H. and Cook, A. (2003), 'Mind the gap: are students prepared for higher education?', *Journal of Further and Higher Education*, 27 (1), pp. 53–76.

Lucas, L. and Webster, F. (1998), 'Maintaining Standards in higher education?: a case study', in D. Jary and M. Parker (eds), *The New Higher Education: Issues and Directives for Post-Dearing University*. Stoke-on-Trent: Staffordshire University Press.

Luke, C. (1997), 'Quality assurance and women in higher education', *Higher Education*, 33, pp. 433–51.

Lyotard, J.F. (1989), *The Postmodern Condition: A Report on Knowledge*. Manchester: Manchester University Press.

MacMillan, J. and McLean, M. (2005), 'Making first-year tutorials count: operationalising the assessment-learning link', *Active Learning in Higher Education*, 6 (2) pp. 94–105.

Malcolm, J. and Zukas, M. (2001), 'Bridging pedagogic gaps: conceptual discontinuities in higher education', *Teaching in Higher Education*, 6, pp. 33–42.

Mann, S. (2001), 'Alternative perspectives on the student experience: alienation and engagement', *Studies in Higher Education*, 26 (1), pp. 7–20.

Mannheim, K. (1966), *Ideology and Utopia* eighth edition. London: Routledge and Kegan Paul.

Margolis, E. (ed.) (2001), *The Hidden Curriculum in Higher Education*. London: Routledge.

Marmot, M. (2004), *Status Syndrome*. London: Bloomsbury.

Marton, F. and Booth, S. (1997), *Learning and Awareness*. New Jersey: Lawrence Erlbaum Associates.

Marton, F., Hounsell, D. and Entwistle, N. (1997), *The Experience of Learning: Implications for Teaching and Studying in Higher Education*, second edition. Edinburgh: Scottish Academic Press.

Marton, F. and Saljo, R. (1976), 'On qualitative differences in learning: 1. Outcome and process', *British Journal of Educational Psychology*, 46, pp. 4–11.

May, T. (1997), *Social Research: Issues, Methods and Process*. Buckingham: Open University Press.

Mayo, P. (1999), *Gramsci, Freire and Adult Education: Possibilities for Transformative Action*. London and New York: Zed Books.

McLean, M. and Barker, H. (2004), 'Students making progress and the "research-teaching" nexus', *Teaching in Higher Education*, 9 (4), pp. 407–19.

McLean, M. and Blackwell, R. (1997), 'Opportunity knocks? Professionalism and excellence in university teaching', *Teachers and Teaching: Theory and Practice*, 3 (1), pp. 85–99.

McLean, M. and Bullard, M. (2000), 'Becoming a university teacher: evidence from teaching portfolios (how academics learn to teach), *Teacher Development*, 4 (1), pp. 79–101.

Melucci, A. (1995), 'The process of collective identity', in H. Johnston and B. Klandermans, (eds), *Social Movements and Culture*. London: University College London Press, pp. 41–63.

Mills, D. (2004), 'Disciplinarity and the teaching vocation', in D. Mills and M. Harris (eds), *Teaching Rites and Wrongs: Universities and the Making of Anthropologists*. Birmingham: Sociology, Anthropology, Politics (C-SAP) The Higher Education Academy.

——(2005), 'Anthropology and the educational "trading zone": disciplinarity, pedagogy and professionalism', *Arts and Humanities in Higher Education*, 4 (1), pp. 9–32.

Mills, D. and Harris, M. (eds) (2004), *Teaching Rites and Wrongs: Universities and the Making of Anthropologists*. Birmingham: Sociology, Anthropology, Politics (C-SAP) The Higher Education Academy.

Morley, L. (1999), *Organising Feminisms*. Basingstoke: Macmillan.

——(2003), *Quality and Power in Higher Education*. Buckingham: Society for Research into Higher Education and Open University Press.

Morris, P. (ed.) (1994), *The Bakhtin Reader*. New York: Hodder Arnold.

Morrow, R. A. and Torres. C. A. (2000), 'The state, globalization and education policy', in N. C. Burbules and C. A. Torres (eds), *Globalization and Education: Critical Perspectives*. London: Routledge.

Mouffe, C. (1998), 'The radical centre: a politics without adversary', *Soundings*, Issue 9, pp. 11–23.

Naidoo, R. (2003), 'Repositioning higher education as a global commodity:

opportunities and challenges for future sociology of education work', *British Journal of Sociology of Education*, 24 (2), pp. 249–59.

Nelson, C. and Watt, S. (eds) (2004), *Office Hours: Activism and Change in the Academy*. New York and London: Routledge.

Newby, G. (1997), 'Gassing and bungling: between facts and norms by Jürgen Habermas', *London Review of Books*, 19 (9), pp. 14–15.

Newman, J. H. (1960), *The Idea of a University*. San Francisco: Rinehart Press.

Nixon, J. (1995), 'Teaching as a profession of values' in J. Smyth (ed.), *Critical Discourses on Teacher Development*. London: Cassell.

Northedge, A. (2003a), 'Rethinking teaching in the context of diversity', *Teaching in Higher Education*, 8 (1), pp. 17–32.

——(2003b), 'Enabling participation in academic discourse', *Teaching in Higher Education*, 8 (2), pp. 169–80.

Oakley, A. (2000), *Overheads*. London: Flamingo.

Offe, C. (1996), *Modernity and the State, East West*. Cambridge: Polity Press.

O'Neill, O. (2002), *A Question of Trust*. Cambridge: Cambridge University Press.

Outhwaite, W. (1996), *The Habermas Reader*. Cambridge and Oxford: Polity Press in association with Basil Blackwell.

Ozga, J. (1994), 'Frameworks for policy analysis in education', in D. Kallos and S. Lindblad (eds), *New Policy Contexts for Education: Sweden and United Kingdom*. Umea, Sweden: Pedagogiska Institutionen.

Parini, J. (2005), *The Art of Teaching*. Oxford: Oxford University Press.

Parker, J. (2002), 'A new disciplinarity: communities for knowledge, learning and practice', *Teaching in Higher Education*, 7 (4), 373–86.

Parker, M. (2002), *Against Management*. Cambridge: Polity Press.

Parkin, F. (1987), *The Mind and Body Shop*. London: Atheneum.

Parsons, T. and Platt, G. (1973), *The American University*. Cambridge: Harvard University Press.

Perry, W. G. (1999), *Forms of Intellectual and Ethical Development in the College Years*. San Francisco: Jossey-Bass.

Power, M. (1994), *The Audit Explosion*. London: Demos.

Power, S., Edwards, T., Whitty, G. and Wigfall, V. (2003), *Education and the Middle Classes*. Milton Keynes: Open University Press.

Pring, R. (1976), *Knowledge and Schooling*. Somerset: Open Books.

——(2001), 'Education as a moral practice', *Journal of Moral Education*, 30 (2), pp. 101–12.

Prosser, M. and Trigwell, K. (1999), *Understanding Learning and Teaching: The Experience in Higher Education*. Buckingham: Society for Research in Higher Education and Open University Press.

Ramsden, P. (2003), *Learning to Teach in Higher Education*, second edition. London: RoutledgeFalmer.

Randle, K. and Brady, N. (1997), 'Managerialism and professionalism in the cinderella service', *Journal of Vocational Education and Training*, 49 (1), pp. 121–39.

Read, B., Archer, L. and Leathwood, C. (2003), 'Challenging cultures? Student conceptions of "belonging" and "isolation" at a post-1992 university', *Studies in Higher Education*, 28, (3), pp. 261–77.

Readings, B. (1996), *The University in Ruins*. Cambridge: Harvard University Press.

Rhoades, G. and Sporn, B. (2002), 'Quality assurance in Europe and the US: professional and political economic framing of higher education policy', *Higher Education*, 43, pp. 355–90.

Robbins, L. (1963), *Higher Education: Report of a Committee*. (Chairman: Lord Robbins) Cmnd 2154, London: HMSO.

Robinson, A. and Tormey, S. (2003), 'New Labour's neoliberal *Glichschaltung*: the case of higher education', *The Commoner*, Spring-Summer, *www.commoner.org.uk/previous_issues.htm # 7n*

Rosenthal, R. and Jacobsen, L. (1968), *Pygmalion in the Classroom: Teacher Expectation and Pupils' Intellectual Development*. New York: Holt, Rinehart and Winston.

Rossen, J. (1993), *The University of Modern Fiction: When Power is Academic*. New York: St. Martin's Press.

Rosslyn, F. (2004), 'Literature for the masses: the English Literature degree in 2004', *The Cambridge Quarterly*, 33 (1), pp. 1–10.

Rowland, S. (1993), *The Enquiring Tutor: Exploring the Process of Professional Learning*. London: Falmer Press.

——(1996), 'Relationships between teaching and research', *Teaching in Higher Education*, 1, pp. 7–20.

——(2000), *The Enquiring University Teacher*. Buckingham: Society for Research into Higher Education and Open University Press.

Rustin, M. (2004), 'Rethinking audit and inspection', *Soundings*, 26, pp. 86–107.

Sachs, J. (2004), 'Sitting uneasily at the table', in M. Walker and J. Nixon, (eds), *Reclaiming Universities from a Runaway World*. Maidenhead: Society for Research into Higher Education and Open University Press, pp. 100–13.

Said, E. (1993), 'Opponents, audiences, constituencies and community', in H. Foster (ed.), *Postmodern Culture*. London: Pluto Press.

——(1994a), *Culture and Imperialism*. London: Vintage Press.

——(1994b), *Representations of the Intellectual*. London: Vintage Press.

Sayers, D.L. (1987), *Gaudy Nights*. London: Hodder & Stoughton.

Schon, D.A. (1983), *The Reflective Practitioner*. New York: Basic Books.

——(1987), *Educating the Reflective Practitioner*. San Francisco: Jossey-Bass.

Scott, P. (2004), 'The transformation of the idea of a university', in F. Inglis (ed.), *Education and the Good Society*. Basingstoke: Palgrave Macmillan.

Sennett, R. (2000), *The Corrosion of Character: Personal Consequences of Work in the New Capitalism*. New York and London: W. W. Norton and Co. Ltd.

Sharp, R. (2003), Marxism and its engagement with management in the corporate academy: some personal reflections, paper given at *Marxism and Education: Renewing Dialogues*, Institute of Education, London, May.

Sharp, R. and Green, A. (1975), *Education and Social Control: A Study in Progressive Primary Education*. London: Routledge.

Shils, E. (1972), *The Intellectuals and the Powers and Other Essays*. Chicago: University of Chicago Press.

Simon, B. (1999), 'Why no pedagogy in England?', in J. Leach and B. Moon (eds), *Learners and Pedagogy*. London: Paul Chapman Publishing.

——(2005), 'Can education change society?', in G. McCulloch (ed.), *The RoutledgeFalmer Reader in History of Education*. London: Routledge, Taylor and Francis Group, pp. 139–50.

Smith, A. and Webster, F. (eds) (1997), *The Postmodern University? Contested Visions of Higher Education in Society*. Buckingham: Society for Research into Higher Education and Open University Press.

Smith, P. (2002), 'Regimes of emotion', *Soundings*, 20, pp. 98–101.

Snyder, B. R. (1970), *The Hidden Curriculum*. Cambridge and London: MIT Press.

Soucek, V. (1994), 'Flexible education and new standards of communicative competence', in Kenway, J. (ed.), *Economising Education: The Post-Fordist Directions*. Geelong, Australia: Deakin University.

Standish, P. (2002), 'Disciplining the profession: subjects subject to procedure', *Educational Philosophy and Theory*. 34(1), pp. 5–14.

Stewart, F. (1996), 'Globalisation and education', *International Journal of Educational Development*, 16 (4), pp. 327–33.

Strathern, M. (1997), ' "Improving ratings": audit in the British university system', *European Review*, 5, pp. 305–21.

Strathern, M. (ed.) (2000a), *Audit Cultures: Anthropological Studies in Accountability, Ethics and the Academy*. London: Routledge.

Strathern, M. (2000b), 'The tyranny of transparency', *British Educational Research Journal*, 26 (3), pp. 309–17.

Street, B. V. (1984), *Literacy in Theory and Practice*. Cambridge: Cambridge University Press.

Taylor, L. (1994), 'Reflecting on teaching: the benefits of self-evaluation', *Assessment and Evaluation in Higher Education*, 19 (2), pp. 109–22.

Therborn, G. (1996), 'Critical theory and the legacy of twentieth-century Marxism', in B. S. Turner (ed.), *The Blackwell Companion to Social Theory*. Oxford: Blackwell Publishers.

Thomas, K. (1990), *Gender and Subject in Higher Education*. Buckingham: Society for Research into Higher Education and Open University Press.

Thomson, E. P. (1963), *The Making of the English Working Class*. New York: Vintage.

Tierney, W. G. (1989), *Curricular Landscapes, Democratic Vistas: Transformative Leadership in Higher Education*. New York: Praeger.

Touraine, A. (2000), *Can We Live Together: Equality and Difference*. Cambridge: Polity Press.

Trigwell, K. and Prosser, M. (2003), 'Qualitative difference in university teaching', *Access and Inclusion*, 2, pp. 185–216.

Trigwell, K., Prosser, M. and Waterhouse, F. (1999), 'Relations between teachers' approaches to teaching and students' approaches to learning', *Higher Education*, 37, pp. 57–70.

Turner, B. (1996), *The Blackwell Companion to Social Theory*. Oxford: Blackwell Publishers.

United Nations (2005), *International Cooperation at a Crossroads: Aid, Trade and Security in an Unequal World*, Human Development Report available at www.undp.org.

Van de Werfhorst, H.G. (2002), 'A detailed examination of the role of education in intergenerational social class mobility', *Social Science Information*, 41(3) pp. 407–38.

Vidovich, L. (2004), 'Global-national-local dynamics in policy processes: a case of "quality" policy in higher education', *British Journal of Sociology of Education*, 25 (3), pp. 341–54.

Vidovich, L. and Slee, R. (2001), 'Bringing universities to account? Exploring some global and local policy tensions', *Journal of Education Policy*, 16 (5), pp. 431–53.

Vincent, D. (1981), *Bread, Knowledge and Freedom: A Study of Nineteenth-Century Working Class Autobiography*. London and New York: Methuen.

Volosinov, V.N. (1973), *Marxism and the Philosophy of Language*. Cambridge: Harvard University Press.

Walker, M. (ed.) (2001), *Reconstructing Professionalism in University Teaching: Teachers and Learners in Action*. Buckingham: Society for Research into Higher Education and Open University Press.

Walker, M. and Nixon, J. (2004), *Reclaiming Universities from a Runaway World*. Maidenhead: Society for Research into Higher Education and Open University Press.

Webb, G. (1997), 'Deconstructing deep and surface: towards a critique of phenomenography', *Higher Education*, 33, pp. 195–212.

Weiner, G. (1996), 'Which of us has a brilliant career? Notes from a higher education survivor', in R. Cuthbert (ed.), *Working in Higher Education*. Buckingham: Society for Research into Higher Education and Open University Press, pp. 58–68.

Wenger, E. (1998), *Communities of Practice: Learning, Meaning and Identity*. Cambridge: Cambridge University Press.

Wheeler, W. (2005), 'The complexity revolution', *Soundings*, 29, pp. 72–84.

Wheen, F. (2004), *How Mumbo-Jumbo Conquered the World: A Short History of Modern Delusions*. London: Fourth Estate.

Whitehead, A.N. (1967), *The Aims of Education and Other Essays*. New York: The Free Press.

Wilkinson, R.G. (2005), *The Impact of Inequality: How to Make Sick Societies Healthier*. London: Routledge.

Wittrock, M.C. (ed.) (1986), *Handbook of Research on Teaching*, third edition. New York: Macmillan.

Wolf, A. (2002), *Does Education Matter? Myths about Education and Economic Growth*. London: Penguin.

Wright Mills, C. (2000), *The Sociological Imagination* (first published 1959). Oxford: Oxford University Press.

Young, M. F. D. (2000), 'Rescuing the sociology of educational knowledge from the extremes of voice discourse: towards a new theoretical basis for the sociology of the curriculum', *British Journal of Sociology of Education*, 21 (4), pp. 523–36.

Index